Liberalization's Children

Liberalization's Children

Gender, Youth, and Consumer Citizenship in Globalizing India

RITTY A. LUKOSE

Duke University Press • Durham & London 2009

© 2009

DUKE UNIVERSITY PRESS

ALL RIGHTS RESERVED

PRINTED IN THE UNITED STATES

OF AMERICA

ON ACID-FREE PAPER ∞

DESIGNED BY KATY CLOVE

TYPESET IN QUADRAAT

BY KEYSTONE TYPESETTING, INC.

LIBRARY OF CONGRESS

CATALOGING-IN-PUBLICATION

DATA AND REPUBLICATION

ACKNOWLEDGMENTS APPEAR

ON THE LAST PRINTED

PAGES OF THIS BOOK.

For my parents—
ALEYAMMA and
PATTIYALMEPURATH LUKOSE

CONTENTS

ACKNOWLEDGMENTS

This book has been a long journey and therefore has accumulated many debts. While it is impossible to thank all those that have helped to make it possible, I will mention a few here. The research for this book has been generously supported by the Department of Anthropology, University of Pennsylvania, the American Institute of Indian Studies, the Fulbright-Hays Fellowship Program, the National Academy of Education Postdoctoral Fellowship, a grant from the University Research Foundation at the University of Pennsylvania, and The Trustee's Council of Penn Women Summer Research Award from the Alice Paul Center for Research on Women, Gender and Sexuality at the University of Pennsylvania. The writing of this book has also been supported by the Spencer Foundation. I have been greatly helped during the writing process by Kathy Chetkovich, Karen Seriguchi, Laura Helper-Ferris, and Ken Wissoker.

I am deeply indebted to N. Shasidaran and the S.N. Trust for initially facilitating this research and to all the students, teachers, and administrators who so warmly and generously gave of themselves and their time. Many of the students and my hostelmates have become good friends over the years and I wish I could thank them all individually. Given the conventions of ethnographic writing, I will refrain. Needless to say, both this book and I have been enriched and sustained by their patience, generosity, and friendship. I am grateful to Dr. K. K. Kusuman for providing an institutional context for my research. I thank Mrs. Menon, Soja Madhavan and her family (especially Siddhu and Viveka), Jayashree Prasad (and Mikki and Chinnu), and Satish G. and Sangeetha Raj for providing community and friendship. Holly Hapke and Devan Ayyankaril greatly facilitated my initial fieldwork. Devan especially was full of encouragement. Sindhu V. and Sheba R. nurtured me with their warmth and humor. If it were not for P. Kurian, I would have been without a room of my own much longer than would have been tolerable.

I am grateful to G. Arunima, Uday Kumar, and Dilip Menon for their intellectual and personal friendship over the years. In particular, I have learned so much from G. Arunima's substantive research and writing and from the ways in which she lives her mind and heart. K. Saradamoni is a shining example to me of what it means to live an engaged intellectual life. Her own work, her perspectives on contemporary Kerala society, and her spirit have sustained me and this book. I cannot begin to thank Tejaswini Niranjana for all that she has done to make this a much better book than it would have been and for her warm friendship. In addition, I am grateful to Mary John for her encouragement and enthusiasm. I have also learned much from the work of J. Devika and from our conversations. In addition, Ratheesh Radhakrishnan has been most helpful, pointing me to relevant new work, correcting some mistakes in the manuscript, and through his own developing work on gender politics in contemporary Kerala.

Arguments contained in this book have been presented at seminars, colloquia, and conferences at the University of Chicago, the University of Minnesota, Yale University, the University of Pennsylvania, Harvard University, the New School for Social Research, Washington University in St. Louis, and the Centre for the Study of Culture and Society in Bangalore, India. I appreciate the suggestions of my interlocutors and this book is much better for their engagements with my work.

I am also grateful to my teachers at the University of Pennsylvania and Chicago. Sandra Barnes, Peter Van der Veer, John Lucy, Suzanne Gaskins, Nancy Farriss, and Raymond Smith introduced me to anthropology and history and its possibilities. Jean Comaroff has always been deeply encouraging. Her intellectual acuity and breadth is something I can only hope to emulate. Bernard Cohn has since passed on, but I will always treasure the week that I spent reading to him the dissertation that started this book project. As I struggled to find a voice in the discipline of anthropology, his advice that it is all right to think of oneself as an anthropologist as long as one is embarrassed by it was both enabling and comforting. I will always carry with me his example of how to combine skepticism, critical passion, and learnedness.

I owe a very special debt to Arjun Appadurai and Carol Breckenridge. The very terms of this project have been shaped by their work and would not have been possible without it. In addition to what he has taught me in the classroom and elsewhere, the creativity and energy of Arjun's evolving work has been an important example for me. Carol provided one of the most helpful readings of a very early version. What this book has become owes much to her critical and encouraging feedback. Equally important, Carol's spirit, warmth, and continuing encouragement have sheltered me at some crucial times over the years.

The intellectual and personal friendships of Malathi De Alwis and Pradeep Jeganathan have been invaluable, together and individually. I cannot begin to enumerate the ways in which this is true. Needless to say, my thinking about anthropology, politics, and feminisms has been transformed and enriched by Malathi and, in different ways, Pradeep. I would also like to thank Vyjayanthi Rao and Nicholas De Genova for what they have contributed toward the completion of this book. Falu Bakrania and Bakirathi Mani have sustained me with their humor and friendship, displacing "India" in productive ways for me, both personally and intellectually. Amy Trubek's personal and intellectual friendship has been invaluable. Her comments on earlier versions and the example of her own work and how she goes about it have guided me through this process. I have also been supported and encouraged by many others over the years: Paulla Ebron, Miyako Inoue, Veena Das, Kamala Visweswaran, Mrinalini Sinha, Mark Liechty, Jennifer Cole, Cecilia Van Hollen, Ann Gold, David Ludden, Jean Lave, Ray McDermott, Bradley Levinson, Dorothy Holland, Doug Foley, Sophia Villenas, and Amy Stambach.

I have had a sustaining community of colleagues and students at the University of Pennsylvania who have furthered this book. While I cannot name them all, I owe a special thanks to Kathleen Hall for her personal and intellectual support. Stanton Wortham has been exemplary as a senior colleague and mentor. Vivian Gadsden has been a special source of wisdom, warmth, and encouragement. I would also like to thank Susan Furhman, Janine Remillard, Margaret Beale Spencer, Lisa Bouillon, Howard Stevenson, Kathy Schultz, Peter Kuriloff, Nancy Hornberger, and Dan Wagner. Ania Loomba and Suvir Kaul have been warm and energetic friends and colleagues. Conversations with Greg Urban, Rogers Smith, Michael della Carpini, Stanton Wortham, Sigal Ben-Porath, and Kathleen Hall enhanced my understandings of citizenship. Ann Farnsworth-Alvear has been a lightning rod of insight and energy. I have also benefited from conversations with Lisa Mitchell, Ram Rawat, Deborah Thomas, John Jackson, Asif Agha, Gautam Ghosh, and Cecilia Novero. Conversations with Anita Chikkatur, Nana Ackatia-Armah, Susan Thomas, Azra Hromadzic, Costas Nakassis, Kerry Dunn, Sonya Gwak, Jennifer Riggan, Jaskiran Dhillon, Katerina Zacharia, Rachel Throop, Rabia Kamal, and Amy Bach have helped me think through the arguments of this book.

This book would not have been possible without my family—old and new, near and far. I would particularly like to thank my uncle and aunt, P. M. and Annamma Thomas, who provided a home away from home, as did Philomena, Benedict, Rajeev, and Preethi Machado. Meena Vari was both cousin and friend during much of the research for this book.

My brother, Rajan Lukose, and my sister-in-law, Mona Shah, have been nothing short of encouraging and supportive. In particular, Rajan has kept me company with both his love and his criticisms. I dedicate this book to my parents; while they sometimes struggled to understand what I was doing in this work, they have loved and supported me in all the lofty and mundane ways that matter. Quite literally, chapters and pages of this book could not have been written without my mother flying in to help with house and home. I can only hope that they see something of themselves and the trajectories of their lives in its pages.

Nimal Eames-Scott has pushed me along when he has periodically asked me over the years, "Is it the same book that you are working on?" and I have had to say yes. My daughter Anju was born in the middle of the years it took to write this book. Along with the enormous joy and love that she has brought into my life, when she so matter-of-factly tells her teachers that her mother is writing a book and has to go to the library to work, her sense of the ordinariness and everydayness of producing this book contributed greatly to it actually getting done. Finally, David Scott and our life together have had to live through the many years it has taken to produce this book. This has been so in the most practical ways—who cooks dinner, or rather, who doesn't—and in all the ways he has sheltered me intellectually, but more importantly, emotionally. It would not have come into being without his encouragement, love, support, and patience.

Liberalization's Children—Nation, Generation, and Globalization

It was a warm and humid day as Priya and I strolled through the long, empty corridors of the college where I was conducting ethnographic research. Located in a small town in the South Indian state of Kerala, the college was closed, yet again, by student strikes protesting the economic reform policies of the Indian government that were intended to open up the Indian economy to larger global forces. Earlier that day, striking male students had marched through the same corridors, shouting "Inquilab Zindabad!" (Long Live the Revolution!), as they participated in a wider campaign with other left-affiliated political parties to protest what they called "the sale" of India to global capitalist forces and "the spread of consumerism." Later, as part of the same campaign, one of these student groups would stage another protest, attempting to disrupt a fashion show that was part of a youth festival in a nearby college, claiming that such shows were "an affront to the cultural ethos of Kerala." Priya was someone who opposed the presence of this type of student politics in her college, going so far as to express her support for legal cases that sought to ban this politics from college campuses, arguing it was an impediment to the proper and adequate education that she felt she needed for the lucrative career in Information Technology (IT) she desired.

As Priya and I approached the edge of the campus on the way back to our hostel, we came upon a garden some students had planted for a university-wide student competition. We surveyed what was left of it—trampled grass, uprooted plants, shredded bushes. The center of the garden, an expanse of grass in the shape of territorial India, had been ripped up, clumps of grass and soil strewn among the tall bushes and wild plants. It seemed clear this was also the work of the striking male students. Tired and fed up—it was the second time this had happened over the past year—Priya, who had been very involved in planting the garden, threw up her hands, turned to me, and said, "Here, there is no modernization."

Priya's investment in the garden in the shape of territorial India, and the male students' destruction of it, are apt metaphors for intense debates over the meaning of India under globalization. The nation as well-tended garden speaks to the optimistic narrative of work, growth, and progress that underlies the nationalist modernization paradigm, an important component of colonial modernity, postcolonial nationalism, and international development. For Priya, the garden represented an orderly and well-functioning college—a site for familiar understandings of national development—and the attack on it felt like evidence that the state of Kerala had not, after all, developed as far as she had hoped. Yet the belief that there is "no modernization" in Kerala is somewhat puzzling, for is this not the most progressive, developed state in India, where female students like Priya are well educated?

In fact, the idea of Kerala as laboring to modernize belongs to an almost outdated narrative of Indian nationalism. Priya also responded to a more contemporary and shifting set of conceptions about India's place in a globalizing world, particularly to images and discourses, increasingly popular since the early 1990s, that proclaim India to be an emerging global power.[1] This is "India Rising," as an essay in *Newsweek* put it (Zakaria 2006). Reform policies that opened up the Indian economy to global market forces, colloquially known as "liberalization," have significantly transformed the political, economic, and cultural landscape of India.[2] Media representations of third world poverty, an uneducated, rural, and traditional society, and an inefficient and corrupt bureaucratic state—all backward or underdeveloped in comparison to the "modern" West—jostle with images of a world-class information technology industry, a robust economy, and a media-saturated, highly educated, urban, affluent, and globally oriented consumer middle class. The political assertiveness of India as a nuclear power, its economic strength and power, and a newfound global prominence in film, literature, music, art, and fashion have created a sense both globally and within the country that India is fast approaching its moment of arrival on the world stage. Priya's investment in the garden and her frustrations with its destruction must be understood in light of such discourses that proclaim India to no longer be struggling at the bottom of the modernization ladder: when she frames the destruction as the absence of modernization in her college, she is anxiously wondering if she will be left behind in this new India.

The male students who destroyed the garden question and reject the promise of opportunities in a newly globalized India. One way of understanding their explicit politics of antiglobalization is through the framework of inclusion and exclusion. Some popular discourses hold that liberalization has produced two Indias: an urban, metropolitan middle class disengaged and disconnected from the problems and contestations of a wider Indian society through its new global orientation and consumerism and, as Priya feels so keenly, a rural, semirural and small-town India that is outside the boundaries of liberalized India. According to such formulations, those who protest globalization do so because they are being excluded from its opportunities and promises.

Based on my fieldwork on youth social and cultural life in a low-caste college in a small town in the Indian state of Kerala, this book argues that straightforward notions of inclusion and exclusion are far too simple by analyzing the workings of globalization among young people who are on the margins of its dominant articulations yet fully formed by its structures of aspiration and opportunity. Kerala sits at the crossroads of development and globalization; held up as an exemplary and relatively egalitarian model of successful modernization, it has now been transformed through an extensive and largely nonelite migration circuit of labor, money, and commodities, to the Persian Gulf and elsewhere. Mass-mediation and an expanding commodity culture have differentially incorporated young people across the boundaries of gender, caste, and class at the intersection of nation and region into the structures and aspirational logics of globalization. In turn, this has generated a wide-ranging politics of globalization in the everyday spaces of education and youth; a politics that reveals the everyday cultural mediations of globalization. It is within this *cultural* politics that I locate the explicit politics between Priya, who supports neoliberal economic reform, and her politicized male classmates, who oppose them.

Student political protests against "the spread of consumerism" and fashion shows in colleges, as part of a wider campaign against liberalization, demonstrate that new forms of consumerism in Kerala are connected and engaged with contestations about citizenship, politics, and democracy in globalizing India. Indeed, practices of consumption and their perceived impact are highly salient and contested sites for debates over the meanings and impact of globalization. In this way, globalization is a framework for understanding these young people's lives, contextualizing their social and cultural practices, their hopes, frustrations, and aspirations. Young people—men and women, pro- and anti-liberalization—are caught up both by powerful market forces that fashion them as consumers and by state-centric discourses and institutions such as education and politics that fashion them as citizens. How do students, as both citizens and consumers, navigate the increasingly mass-mediated cultural and social worlds of youth in globalizing India? To answer these questions, let us further define how globalization marks these students as distinctive: in their generational and geographical positioning, their identities as consumer citizens, and as gendered youth.

The Zippies of "India Rising"

While Priya and her classmates vigorously debate liberalization, the discourse of "India Rising" celebrates the role of their generation as a key instantiation of globalized India. Media discussions of liberalization often highlight statistics showing that 54 percent of Indians are below the age of twenty-five, making India one of the youngest nations in the world.[3] In Kerala, people between the ages of fifteen and twenty-five are said to make up 45 percent of the total population.[4] These youth form a potent new market for fashioning India's newly globalized middle class. One major publication has labeled them "zippies":

. . . a young city or suburban resident, between 15 and 25 years of age, with a zip in the stride. Belongs to Generation Z. Can be male or female, studying or working. Oozes attitude, ambition and aspiration. Cool, confident and creative. Seeks challenges, loves risks and shuns fear. Succeeds Generation X and Generation Y, but carries the social, political, economic, cultural or ideological baggage of neither. Personal and professional life marked by vim, vigour and vitality (origin: Indian).[5]

This definition does not name specific commodities but draws attention to an embodied demeanor, an attitude, and a set of values. Its reference to the "baggage" of previous generations names a shift in generational sensibilities, attitudes, and values, in which "zippies" are an almost evolutionary alternative to their more backward predecessors.

The media has drawn an even sharper contrast between generational sensibilities in characterizing "zippies" as "liberalization's children." Again embodying India's newly found confidence and ambition on the global stage, they are urban, hip, and cool.[6] The term is a play on "midnight's children"—the generation named after the Salman Rushdie novel which focused on those born during the first hour of the year 1947, when India gained its independence from British colonial rule.[7] The term intertwines the lives of those born in the immediate aftermath of independence with the life of the nation, a nation shaped by the socialist-inspired understanding of national development represented by Jawaharlal Nehru, India's first prime minister. In contrast to liberalization's children, midnight's children seem mired in the ideological baggage of Nehruvian nationalist development, with its focus on the rural poor and service to the nation; as lacking in ambition; and being risk averse, "uncool," and fearful.

This narrative directly links the values and attitudes of this new generation to the economic liberalization of the economy and the cultural impact of globalization. It juxtaposes midnight's and liberalization's children in order to dramatize the idea that the liberalization of the Indian economy and its cultural and political effects through the spread of consumerism were a primary cause for the eclipsing of the Nehruvian vision of the Indian nation. In a special section on India's newly globalized youth in the magazine *Business Week*, a table titled "How India's New Generation is Different" elaborates a set of generational contrasts.[8] The "older generation" has idealized "Gandhian poverty" and socialism, grew up in the midst of famine, had only one state-run television channel, was technophobic, was thrifty, grew up within a stable single-party system led by upper castes, favored civil service careers, and had low levels of literacy. In contrast, the "new generation" admires capitalism and wants to get rich, grew up in the era of food surpluses, can watch fifty television channels, is technology savvy, consume guiltlessly, grew up with shaky coalition governments and assertive lower-caste political parties, favors jobs in the private, corporate sector, and has higher literacy rates. This construction of the lifestyle and generational sensibilities of globalized Indian youth encompasses ideology (capitalism versus socialism), the state of agriculture (from famine to surplus), the spread of mass media, technology, and consumption, the breakdown of the post-independence hegemony of the dominant nationalist political party, the Indian National Congress, and the rising political assertion of lower-caste political parties, shifting career choices, and rising literacy rates—all harbingers of India as a modernized, global power rather than a poor third-world country. The article's mention of "more voice for lower castes," rising literacy rates, and food surpluses, amid the more conventional indices of globalization such as media, technology, and consumption, is noteworthy and suggests that journalists see globalization "trickling down" to impact the masses. In short, youth and generation are a key site for popular cultural reconfigurations of the Indian nation in the age of liberalization.

Yet these celebrations of globalizing India, heralding a newly consumerist, globally oriented middle-class youth, belie some counterdiscourses. First, popular culture and public discussions are also rife with worry about the consumerism of youth, their lack of interest in the heroic struggles of the anticolonial nationalist generation, and their apathy toward the problems that plague contemporary India. Rather than celebrate the emergence of a consumerist, globally oriented youth, in such discourses there is much anxiety about their roles as committed citizens of the nation. Moreover, neither celebration nor anxiety acknowledges the Kerala students I met who were deeply engaged in contesting visions of India under globalization. Again, one way of understanding this discrepancy is to point to the disparities between the nonmetropolitan, regional, low-caste, semirural social location of these students and the metropolitan, upper-caste elite indexed by the category "zippie."[9] This book not only focuses on nonmetropolitan youth; it argues that globalization does more than simply exclude them from its sphere of influence or straightforwardly include them by "trickling down" to benefit them. They are liberalization's children in their own right.

The discourse of "India Rising" proclaims that the nation has transcended its colonial and postcolonial histories. Working against such triumphalism, this book examines globalization in India as a complex encounter between such legacies and their transformations under liberalization. It refutes the notion that globalization is either a radically new force or simply the persistence of older forms of cultural production generated by colonialism and nationalism. I examine globalization as experience, as practice, and as discourse. Young people at the lower-caste Kerala college where I conducted my research are situated as citizens and consumers at the intersection between development and globalization in particularly salient ways. Located between region and nation as well, they provide a nonelite, nonmetropolitan perspective on the dominant, nationalist trope of generational shift that has come to mark constructions of globalizing India.

Consumer Citizenship

While the discourse of generational shift from midnight's to liberalization's children rightly focuses on the eclipsing of the Nehruvian vision of the nation within liberalizing India, it obscures more than it reveals when it simply highlights the triumph of consumerism.[10] For members of societies that are actively being transformed by globalization, consumer practices and discourses become an increasingly important axis of belonging for negotiating citizenship; in other words, for the politics of social membership, for negotiations of public life, and for an understanding of politics within the nation. Through a careful analysis of consumer citizenship, this book argues that the breakdown of the Nehruvian vision connects with ongoing struggles over the meanings of public life: lower-caste cultural-political assertion; the ascendancy of a Hindu nationalism; reconfigurations of upper-caste, middle-class aspirations; and attempts by the middle class to reconfigure understandings of citizenship in India.

Scholars have drawn attention to shifting articulations between constructions of consumer and citizen, arguing that access to consumer goods and the "freedom to choose" was considered a fundamental political right in the West by the middle of the twentieth century.[11] Within India, earlier nationalist constructions of consumption linked the consumer to the exercise of citizenship through the notion of a "producer patriot" in the service of the nation (Deshpande 2003). For example, as Satish Deshpande argues, the anticolonial Swadeshi movement of the late nineteenth and early twentieth centuries politicized the buying of foreign goods in ways that sought to produce a new kind of nationalist consciousness. For this movement, the consumption of commodities was linked to an image of the economy as a locus of production in the service of the nation (Deshpande 2003). The elite, reformist, modernizing middle class, as the vanguard of the new nation, was sometimes imagined as comprising consumers whose practices of consumption were tied to appropriate forms of modern domesticity and a productivist paradigm of citizenship.[12] Such discourses of consumerism, and the ways they were linked to understandings of citizenship within India, are marked not by arguments about high and low culture, something that characterizes debates about consumption within the Euro-American world, but rather by debates about westernization, tradition, and modernity generated out of the problematics of colonial and postcolonial nationalist cultural projects (Chua 2000).

Increasingly, forms of consumer citizenship in the era of liberalization articulate the citizen through the notion of a right to consume, a right that must be protected through state action. In dominant discourse, the economy is no longer imagined only as a locus of production; it is now more consistently imagined as a marketplace of commodities for consumption, in a shift that also entails a move away from the idea of the citizen as producer patriot to one of a "cosmopolitan consumer" (Mazarella 2003; Vedwan 2007; Deshpande 2003). In the chapters to follow, I examine such claims as they are made by middle-class-oriented civic groups with respect to education, claims that have important implications for understanding politics. Rather than take at face value their image of a depoliticized and privatized citizen-consumer, I examine how consumerism intersects with state-centric discourses and the practices of education, development, politics, and citizenship formation. Rather than see consumer citizenship as simply displacing older notions of citizenship, as these groups do, I examine the articulation between new discourses and practices of consumption and the ongoing productions of public life across the boundaries of gender, class, and caste.

I deploy an expansive anthropological understanding of citizenship in order to explore the crucial role of consumption in the self-fashioning of young people as part and parcel of their negotiations of public life. Moving beyond formal, legal, and constitutional definitions—or, citizenship understood narrowly as rights and obligations with respect to a state—anthropological approaches to citizenship formation have emphasized the everyday practices of belonging through which social membership is negotiated.[13] Here, citizenship is understood as "an on-going process, a social practice, and a cultural performance rather than a static category. It entails . . . struggles over the definition of social membership, over the categories and practices of inclusion and exclusion, and over different forms of participation in public life" (Berdahl 2005, 236). The framework of citizenship is thus a useful entry point for understanding how the changing practices and discourses of consumption, generated by globalization, are reconfiguring the dynamics of public life in India.[14]

The intensification and expansion of commodity flows through the liberalization of the Indian economy have made consumption of goods and mass-mediated images a key site for producing youth identities.[15] Rather than simply view youth as consumers, I examine the contradictions and entailments for young men and women of being marked not simply as consumers but as commodities as well. I focus on the terrain of public culture in India—fashion shows, beauty pageants, ice cream parlors, youth fashions, and movies—in order to argue that it is crucial to pay attention to the ways in which different cultural and political fields shape everyday consumer practices (cf. Appadurai and Breckenridge 1988). Scholars tend to depict the consumer in neoliberalism as a depoliticized and privatized elite in withdrawal from the state. If they consider a wider population, they contrast the sphere of the citizen-consumer with that of traditional citizenship. Nestor García Canclini (2001, 15), for one, argues that consumer citizenship is the reworking of citizenship under conditions of globalization in ways that displace older languages of politics, democracy, and citizenship: "Men and women increasingly feel that many of the questions proper to citizenship—where do I belong, what rights accrue to me, how can I get information, who represents my interests?—are being answered in the private realm of commodity consumption and the mass media more than the abstract rules of democracy or collective participation in public spaces." While paying attention to the dynamics of privatization and changing notions of politics, this book draws attention to consumer citizenship not as a form of "private behavior" but rather as a form of cultural politics at the intersection of history, culture, and power with implications for how citizens negotiate public life within and beyond the boundaries of the elite, nationalist, middle class.

So I consider young people as citizens in the making and colleges as sites where society produces them as such.[16] That is, I situate the ethnography in places—a street, the college hostel, the college compound, a performance stage, corridors, classrooms, an ice cream parlor, a train station, or bus stand—but these "places" are not self-evident sites for the location of ethnography. I variously understand them as representing different kinds of publics—consuming, democratic, political, national, and intimate—which also rely on various notions of the private. I examine how notions of the "public" get linked to conceptions of citizenship, consumption, and politics.[17]

I examine notions of public citizenship within the college that include young women within "civic" conceptions of the public yet marginalize or exclude them from a "political" public, and I consider how liberalizing discourses of consumption address these notions. Such discourses and practices of consumption rework education as a formal institution for the production of citizens, and they also transform the everyday negotiations of public life that mark young women and men's sense of belonging and social membership. I also focus on education as part and parcel of social reform movements begun in the colonial period to "uplift" low-caste communities, in particular the Ezhava caste community in Kerala. I attend to the ways in which a community-based anticaste movement emerges and functions within the putatively secular and democratic space of the college and how such a caste-based college and its students are increasingly oriented toward a transnational horizon of opportunity and aspiration. Thus an exploration of young men and women's participation in the public spaces of college life reveals the gender, class, and caste dimensions of the public sphere and democratic citizenship in India.[18]

Indeed, as I explore these struggles within the realm of education and youth cultural life, I look beyond the nonelite students to consider how the liberalizing middle class envisions the nation in order to lay claim to a state that it considers corrupt and ineffectual within a new global dispensation. I demonstrate how their increasing global orientation has led middle-class Indians to very actively critique the postcolonial state, its legacies, and functioning. They are not simply leaving Indian society by becoming more worldly; they also seek to transform it for the purposes of consumption. For example, some organizations attempt to ban student politics from colleges in Kerala because, they claim, such politics prevents the smooth functioning of educational institutions and the preparation of students for a new global economy. A privatizing educational industry links such arguments to conceptions of education as a commodity rather than a public good; in these conceptions, it juxtaposes the rights of citizens as consumers to a more long-standing notion of citizens as producers for the nation. I explore how this elite, middle-class "consumer patriotism" of liberalization encounters new consumer identities among nonelite, nonmetropolitan young people in the small town in Kerala where this study is located.[19]

In the end, my conceptualization of consumer citizenship has several consequences for understanding globalization and citizenship.[20] Phenomena that transcend the boundaries of nation, such as the extensive circuit of transnational migration, commodities, and remittances between Kerala and the Persian Gulf and the construction of the Non-Resident Indian (NRI), are crucial to the chapters that follow. My work here builds on discussions of globalization and citizenship that focus on the deterritorializing effects of globalization that challenge nation-state–derived conceptions of citizenship. That focus has led to a wide variety of scholarship on "postnational," "cosmopolitan," and "global" forms of citizenship.[21] However, I examine these phenomena in terms of the reconfigurations of region, nation, and world *within* Kerala, drawing attention to the dynamic relationship between deterritorialization and *re*territorialization within processes of globalization.[22]

11

Engendering Youth and Globalization

Female students like Priya have historically enjoyed high rates of literacy, health care, and education in Kerala, making the state a model of gender equality, development, and successful modernization elsewhere in the world.[23] Built into the discourse of "India Rising," however, is the promise of a better path to liberation from traditional family and kinship structures into a world marked by greater gender equality. When she was faced with the destroyed garden, her exasperated remark that "here, there is no modernization" resonated for me with several possibilities: her marginalization from a long-standing masculinist political culture that is central to Kerala's postcolonial development experience, her sense that the celebrations of gender and education in Kerala might obscure its more ambivalent consequences for young women, and her embrace of liberalization as a more promising path toward greater gender equality and class mobility.

While Priya embraces the opportunities of liberalization, there is a wider sense that globalization is undermining Kerala's reputation as a model of development and is transforming the understanding of the state as a highly developed place that treats women well. Priya is a middle-class aspirant of liberalizing India, someone who is studying computer science on the side, along with her regular studies, in the hope of getting a high-paying IT job and the lifestyle that might come with it either within India or abroad. Yet the prevalence and persistence of moral panics about and protest against beauty pageants, fashion shows, and the celebration of Valentine's Day in colleges suggest the ambivalent and contested nature of young women's opportunities in globalized India. Such objections to liberalization reveal how celebrations of liberalization's promises provoke anxious discourses and regulations of young women, their bodies, their sexuality, and their vulnerability. In exploring such debates, I also consider how struggles among young people about their roles as student-citizens and as political actors—as opposed to youth as consumers engaged in an expanding and youthful commodity culture—position women and men and define masculinity and femininity.

A central argument of the book is that anxieties over globalization surface in highly gendered politics about the place of women in public and the specter of sexual exploitation in an ever-expanding commodity culture. A crucial node in the crisis-ridden narratives about Kerala in the 1990s, such anxieties have a long history in the production of modernity in Kerala, and they have become the conditions under which young women and men negotiate globalization. I show that young middle-class women are central to struggles over the cultural meaning and impact of globalization, both on the part of an assertive Hindu nationalism that emerged in the 1990s and the feminist left as it confronts and contests globalization. The middle-class New Indian Woman of earlier articulations of modern gender is now figured as more aggressively public and sexual through her consuming practices, while continuing to be regulated in a variety of ways; at the same time, liberalization has also generated contemporary forms of lower-caste and class masculinity that are newly tied to commodity cultures. These commodified genders become another axis of exclusion for lower-caste and lower-class young women.

In Kerala, the lack of job prospects and extremely high rates of education have transformed life for a large group of young men and women. Instead of moving quickly into marriage and employment, they spend an extended period pursuing one educational degree or course after another, all the while negotiating jobs and marriage prospects at home and abroad. This extension of youth has created a consumer-driven social and cultural world that young people increasingly understand on its own terms. I explore the contours of this sociocultural world in arenas emblematic of youth: fashion, romance, politics, and education. However, I do not render this world as a "subculture" with its own logic, something that has characterized much of the cultural studies literature on youth.[24]

Rather, in order to apprehend these figurations of youth and the ways that young people inhabit them, I reconceptualize youth as a social category that sits at the crossroads between familial and educational contexts, a category that is structured by job, marriage, and consumer markets.[25] It is moreover a category that closely links education and the possibilities of migration and creates the conditions for a complex mediation between consumption and citizenship. Consumer and state-centric developmentalist projects seek to turn people in this category into consumers and citizens, and as a category youth is receptive to global migration and changing ideas about sex and marriage.

In particular, I consider a variety of masculinities and femininities through which young people navigate public spaces of education and a wider commodity culture. While femininity is often equated with "difference" and "tradition," one task of this book is to link such analysis to the ways *modernity* is in turn central to gender.[26] Understanding how gender is modern in Kerala entails a complicated and nuanced mapping of the public/private dichotomy.[27] I consider the gendered demeanors young women and young men deploy as they navigate the public spaces of education and new consumer spaces. I contrast the notions of femininity and masculinity that accompany these demeanors, considering them in terms of the embodied politics of public life.

For example, I track the assertion of new forms of masculinity among lower-caste, lower-class young men tied to fashion and commodities as these forms intersect with reconfigurations of upper-class, upper-caste femininity as aggressively public and sexualized in the aftermath of liberalization. I examine how these terrains of masculinity and femininity, marked by young people's engagements with consumption, deny lower-caste, lower-class young women access to forms of commodified femininity in ways that make their claims on the public spaces of education and commodity culture tenuous at best. Moreover, I show that within the context of globalization, processes of reterritorialization often hinge on the young female form, which bears what I call "the burden of locality" on an increasingly global scale. Thus my analysis of gendered spatial divisions tracks the deployment of class-specific, caste-specific, and gender-specific constructions of masculinity and femininity in ways that unsettle and cross the oppositions between public and private and tradition and modernity.[28]

Finally, I mediate multiple locations for the production of knowledge about gender in India and Kerala. In particular, because I am an anthropologist interested in questions of gender and globalization and am located within the United States, my knowledge production emerges from feminist intellectual and political fields within the American academy and within India. Part of the challenge of writing this book was to pay attention to the complexities of the ethnographic encounter between myself as a U.S.-based academic and my informants in Kerala; to the fields of debate and politics about gender and globalization across Kerala, India as a whole, and the United States; and to naturalized hierarchies of the relationship between these sites of knowledge production.

Genealogies/Sites/Themes

My interest in youth, gender, and globalization in Kerala emerged from my own experiences and that of my family as members of a global Kerala diaspora. I was born into a Christian family in Kerala, raised in north India and the United States, and returned to Kerala as a U.S.-based anthropologist. My religion, nation, class, and gender shaped both my fieldwork and my analysis. In particular, as what the state identifies as a "Non-Resident Keralite" woman, I have lived and negotiated the gendered cultural politics explored in this book, a politics of foreignness shaped by the migratory circuits of the global Kerala diaspora.

The hierarchies of gender, class, education, and geography within my own family—our members are dispersed among Kerala, other parts of India, the United States, Canada, Australia, the Persian Gulf, and Europe —were puzzling and remarkable to me while I grew up. Because my immediate family and I followed a classic U.S. immigrant pattern of social mobility through education, I wondered, even as a young woman, about the role of education as a site for social change in Kerala, with its different histories of colonialism, political radicalism, and migration. As India's emerging reputation as a global power transformed my own experience of being an Indian immigrant in the United States, family visits to Kerala over the years showed me how globalization and experiences of transnational migration were changing what it meant to be young in Kerala.

The central focus of this ethnography is a midsize (3,500 students) coeducational college on the outskirts of a town in southern Kerala. My most intensive period of ethnographic fieldwork there began in the mid-1990s for a period of two years, followed by shorter fieldwork stays over the years. Situated on the national highway that runs through this small yet commercially important town, the college is easily reached by bus, and the railway station is within walking distance of the campus. It is part of a concentration of institutions and businesses that cater to students: several other private colleges, hostels, tutorial centers, bookstores, small restaurants, ice cream parlors, and shops selling drinks, sweets, snacks, and newspapers. While some of its students live in nearby hostels, most come from both the town itself and from the villages surrounding the town. Many travel between one and two hours, sometimes three, to attend college there. The college is one of a large number of private colleges in the state, all of which are affiliated with one of the seven state universities.[29] Founded in the 1950s by a private trust, this institution is an OBC college: OBC refers to other backward classes, the official state category under which the Ezhava caste community is classified.[30] The trust itself is affiliated with the Sree Narayana Dharma Paripalana (SNDP), a social reform movement that challenged the caste hierarchy of the region beginning in the latter half of the nineteenth century from the position of a formerly untouchable caste. It draws a cross-section of students from within the Ezhava caste community, comprising students from middle-class families in town and those from more rural and peasant backgrounds. However, while it is managed by this trust and has a mandate to serve the Ezhava caste community through what is called its "management quota" which allows it to set aside admissions for its constituency, state policies, the college's size and reputation, and the range of subjects it offers, draw a diverse student population from different caste and religious communities. At the time of my most extensive fieldwork, the college granted degrees equivalent to a bachelor's in the United States and offered postgraduate master's courses in a few subjects. In addition, higher education in this college was organized such that the eleventh and twelfth years of schooling were included in colleges and understood as "pre-degree" courses.[31] This meant that the students in the college ranged in age from approximately sixteen to twenty-three years.

During the intensive fieldwork period, I lived in an affiliated student and working women's hostel, run by the same trust and within walking distance of the college. Many of my hostelmates' homes were too far away for them to live at home and commute. While the majority of my hostelmates were students of the college, the hostel also housed women just beyond their college years, who were usually unmarried and working at their first jobs in and around the town. There were also a few older women, sometimes married with children who lived at home while they spent the working week at the hostel and others who were not. Some, like me, came from other parts of India or abroad. Most of my hostelmates were Malayalee (with a few exceptions), Malayalam being the dominant language of the state.

My fieldwork involved living in the hostel, attending classes at the college, and generally participating in the everyday activities of a college student. I also pored over documents at the college library, went to youth festivals, traveled with students for various projects and trips, attended political marches and rallies, and participated in many other activities. I went shopping, attended movies, watched television, listened to music, and frequented ice cream parlors and restaurants. Apart from participant observation, I conducted more systematic interviews with a variety of students, teachers, and administrators. At the time of my most intensive fieldwork, I was only several years older than the oldest students at the college, making it relatively easy for me to navigate the formal and informal spaces of student life. My status as a social scientist from the United States conducting *gaveshanam* (research) was simultaneously apprehensible within an institution of higher education and curious to students, teachers, and administrators. While both students and teachers were extremely helpful, providing me with documentary materials, helping me find places to conduct interviews and participating in them, they were puzzled that I could afford to spend a year or two in Kerala. With little funds available to them for conducting research, especially within non-elite, regional institutions, many were struck by the fact that a funded grant enabled me to do research for so long. I also conducted research among students in the nearby capital city while I lived in a student hostel for several months. That research focused on a student population that was more urban, middle-class, and upper-caste and provided some comparative data that was useful for situating my main ethnographic focus.

Before the ethnographic chapters, chapter 2 provides background on Kerala. The state has a global reputation as a model for development, based on its unusual achievements in the area of gender and education, among other development indices. I show that standard explanations of these achievements draw on elements of Kerala's modern history—largely focused on its historically important systems of matrilineal kinship among dominant castes, enlightened nineteenth-century local rulers, caste and class mobilization, and the rise of the communist left—that elide the emergence of a modern and patriarchal gender regime that structures such development gains. Through various projects of social reform, this regime differentially positioned women along the axes of tradition/modernity and public/private. Through women's increasing assertions into public life, further shifts in this modern gender system through the 1920s and 1930s allowed women greater access to education and jobs, albeit in gender-specific ways. Nonetheless, by midcentury, a modern norm of middle-class domesticity rooted in the nuclear family was established, something that came to buttress the postcolonial developmental state. I trace a modern gender ideology that underwrites social reform efforts across a variety of caste and community reform movements, including the Sree Narayana movement, in order to highlight the emergence and consolidation of a middle-class norm rooted in ideas about modern education. However, this gender norm was differentially articulated and experienced along the vectors of caste, class, and community. This "model" came into crisis in the 1990s through global transformations and the increasing importance of transnational migration, which led to the emergence of discourses and practices that newly fashioned Kerala as a consumer society.

The following four ethnographic chapters focus respectively on fashion, romance, politics, and education. I explore how these emblematic youth cultural and social practices are situated at the intersection of both conceptual and literal spaces defined as private and public, modern and traditional. I examine the ways in which these ideas of public and private mutually implicate each other and the ways in which people live and contest them along the axes of gender, caste, and class through various kinds of embodied performance. I also situate the ethnographic objects within the colonial and nationalist histories of these practices. For example, I examine how a range of clothing styles index particular kinds of femininity and masculinity that enable and constrain young people as they navigate the boundaries between long-standing notions of private and the public and ideas of tradition and modernity in ways that allow differential access to modern, globally inflected publics. The chapters on fashion and romance explore the effects of new productions of consumer identity on highly gendered negotiations by young women and men of the public spaces of commodity culture and education. These chapters specify how the upper-middle-class "modern" girl who is now understood to be more aggressively public and sexual intersects with the production of new forms of commodified, lower-caste and lower-class masculinity in ways that marginalize lower-class and lower-caste forms of femininity.

Chapter 2, on fashion, examines how new, globally inflected patterns of consumption among young people (through fashion, movies, and the staging of beauty pageants) become a new axis of belonging that differentially mediates young women and men's claims on public life. Chapter 3 demonstrates how narratives of modern romance, linked to transformations in the gender regimes of Kerala's colonial modernity, shape how young women understand and navigate their entry into the worlds of education and work, all within the horizon of normative understandings of marriage. Eschewing a sharp distinction between private and public, I examine romance as a form of public intimacy. Given that a college and its environs are one of the few spaces available for heterosocial interaction, the construction of romantic intimacy, more often than not, must be initiated and sustained in public. I track the ways in which practices of romance emerge through a negotiation of the meanings of social interaction between peers within public spaces of education and an expanding commodity culture. Movies turned out to be a key source for mediating the romantic ideal. These and other narratives demonstrate how romance enables and constrains a young woman's entry into and experience of a wider public world.

The next chapters shift the focus to youth practices that are more self-evidently enactments of citizenship: politics and education. I demonstrate how these practices emerge out of colonial and postcolonial configurations of culture and power and how contemporary discourses and practices of consumption are transforming them. In chapter 4, I treat "politics" (rashtriyam) as an objectified discourse and domain of activity in which youth confront the state. As such, politics is a crucial aspect of Kerala's political history and highly salient in everyday life as well as in the workings of the college itself. Although it would be easy for me to construct a narrative of exclusion in addressing the lack of women's participation in this "political public" and in the practices and institutions of democratic citizenship, I instead examine the masculinist underpinnings of the space of student politics, rooted as it is in gendered notions of mobility and traversal. I track a contemporary debate about "politics," in which a privatized, neoliberal, consumerist, and civic-minded public confronts a disorderly politicized public that has its roots in colonial and postcolonial political developments. This debate is crucial to the field of education in Kerala, where education is both an object of political contestation and a place for its enactment. I elaborate how older narratives of Nehruvian nationalism tied to service to the nation are changed by discourses of consumption that reconfigure the very meaning of politics within an increasingly commoditized and privatized educational context. In chapter 5, I turn to education itself, considering it as a strategy of social transformation and mobility. I situate the college within a colonial-era social reform movement for the eradication of untouchability while locating this anticaste project within an increasingly transnational educational trajectory. Taking up the critique of caste that has defined recent South Asian anthropology, the chapter argues for a "post-Orientalist" anthropology of caste in contemporary India that locates caste within the spaces and practices of secular citizenship. Through an exploration of the politics of identity and secularism within this low-caste college, the chapter goes on to examine contemporary transformations of caste, community, and religion in a Kerala increasingly affected by Hindu nationalism. The chapter also examines the politics of the English language in the college.

In the epilogue, I discuss some of the implications of this research on youth and globalization in Kerala for understanding figurations of liberalization's children as well as point to some more recent shifts and continuities in the cultural politics of globalization in contemporary India.

The book focuses on key cultural practices that young people understand, in highly self-conscious ways, to be emblematic of their lives as consumers and citizens. The unfolding of the ethnographic chapters on fashion, romance, politics and education—in that order—develops an argument about the intersections between consumption and citizenship that seeks to foreground consumer citizenship as constitutive of young people's lives in liberalizing India. While the chapters on fashion and romance highlight the gendered stakes of consumption, the chapters on politics and education feature explicit gendered discourses and practices of citizenship. The ordering of chapters also charts a temporal trajectory of entry and exit from the space of youth. Through fashion and romance, we get a sense of what is entailed for young people in gaining entry to and navigating the spaces of college student life, while the focus on politics provides us a sense of how the college is inhabited by them. As the focus shifts to education and strategies for social mobility, the world of adulthood in the form of jobs and setting up households begins to impinge on the highly demarcated zone of commodified youth culture and student politics.

While this book is focused on the region of Kerala within a larger Indian context, my focus on consumer citizenship at the intersection of gender and youth illuminates a wide-ranging and contested set of transformations wrought by contemporary globalization. Consumer practices and discourses of rampant consumerism, especially among young people, have become emblematic of globalization's reach and impact around the world. Through the framework of consumer citizenship, I hope this book will expand understandings of consumption and globalization by drawing attention to the ways practices of consumption and discourses of consumerism intersect with public politics and understandings of citizenship. Moving beyond denunciations or celebrations of consumption as a harbinger of globalization, especially with respect to young people, I invite a more careful assessment of what is at stake in consumer practices for young people, their families, and the nations and states to which they belong. I hope this book will expand our understandings of globalization by drawing attention not only to how globalization structures lifeworlds but also to the ways it becomes an explicit object of contestation and negotiation within everyday contexts. Through the framework of consumer citizenship, paying attention to the cultural politics of globalization carefully contextualized within local and national histories enables a nuanced assessment of both popular and scholarly claims about globalization as a radical new force in the world.

1

Locating Kerala,
Between Development
and Globalization

Both popular and scholarly discourses, within India and on the global stage, have overwhelmingly understood the region-state of Kerala as an exception. Here, K. M. George, the editor of an anthology of short stories written by women from Kerala, describes the unique "customs" and "manners" making up the living "museum" that is the Indian state of Kerala.

Kerala . . . a narrow strip of land on the south-west coast of India, lying between the Western Ghats and the Arabian Sea . . . has been among the most vibrant and problematic states in the Indian Union. . . . Perhaps one reason for this is the combination of high literacy and low per capita income, making the people conscious of their claims for a minimum standard of life. . . . Kerala appears to be a place of paradoxes: the land is fertile, but the people are poor, the percentage of literacy is the highest in India (now 100 per cent), but one comes across the most orthodox and superstitious people along with the most modern and revolutionary kind. The land is very beautiful and so are its people. Its lovely lagoons and backwaters, and its colourful landscape continue to charm tourists. Kerala, very much a part of India, nonetheless has its own distinctive sub-culture with its special customs and manners. (1993, 1)

The author emphasizes the traditional matrilocal, matrilineal system of inheritance among the dominant Nair caste, the history of a particularly oppressive caste structure, and high rates of literacy among women. He also speaks of Kerala's "composite cosmopolitan" culture, with 50 percent of the population being members of the dominant Hindu community and an unusually high percentage of minorities comprising the rest: 21 percent are Christian, 19 percent Muslim, and 10 percent tribals (ibid., 1–4).

George nicely captures the multiple tropes of popular and scholarly commentary across the decades on Kerala, which run the gamut from matrilineality to the "revolutionary zeal" of this communist "bastion" to its tropical beauty to its high levels of literacy. When taken together, these tropes constitute a discourse about Kerala's exceptionalism. Moreover, a range of actors consciously deploy these tropes to construct a specifically regional identity: the Kerala state government does so for tourism purposes; policymakers and development practitioners at the state, national, and international levels do so when trying to explain the state's social and economic development; and scholars and journalists do so when they comment on the region. While this discourse has many registers, it is noteworthy that they oscillate between the idea of Kerala as a space of exotic "tradition," marked as exceptional by its tropical beauty, unique matrilineal kinship patterns, and rigid caste system, and Kerala as uniquely "modern" and revolutionary, indexed as exceptional by high levels of literacy and its communist traditions. For example, brochures published by the state tourism board will juxtapose images of Kerala women in traditionally coded saris lighting traditional lamps with text that proclaims Kerala to be the "most advanced" state in India, with "100% literacy" (Sreekumar 2007).

Specifically, one important thread within the construction of Kerala as exceptional is the trope of development, in which the so-called Kerala Model of Development is held up as an example for other parts of the world. This literature narrates a heroic story of a progressive march from "tradition" to "modernity." Education is crucial to the idea of Kerala as a development success story, particularly the education of girls and women. However, rather than a "black box" that produces various development indicators like "literacy" or "low maternal mortality," as I discuss later, education and its gendering are a contested cultural project where the historical forces of colonial and postcolonial modernity, development, and globalization meet in order to shape the life trajectories of youth.

Given these discourses of exceptionalism, how can Kerala be a site through which we can understand Indian and global modernity? It is not my intention to nest the region within the nation and then within the world, as standard spatial imaginaries of social scales and globalization would have it. As a region, Kerala's experiences of globalization are powerfully mediated simultaneously by the shifting context of India's economic liberalization and through a highly regionally specific trajectory of development and migration. For example, Kerala's development experience must be contextualized at the intersection between a regionally specific history of leftist radicalism that took on an overwhelmingly developmentalist form because of how this history intersected with a Nehruvian and nationalist vision of state-centric development; the figure of midnight's children must be understood at the crossroads between region and nation. Similarly, constructions of liberalization's children assumes a 1990s metropolitan location as the prime example of globalization in India, and discussions of the latter have been dominated by studies of Delhi, Mumbai, and Bangalore.[1] Kerala's experiences of a global flow in labor, commodities, and capital, primarily to the Persian Gulf but also to other parts of the world, are long, expansive, and intense and they predate the liberalization of the Indian economy in the early 1990s. However, this does not, in a straightforward way, make Kerala an exception. The contemporary economic, cultural, and political manifestations of international migration within Kerala intersect with this national moment of liberalization without being reducible to it. The rise of Hindu nationalism during the 1990s and its manifestations in Kerala have provided new conditions in which the politics of gender, caste, and class is tied to transnational migration and its impact. Further, while a regionally specific trajectory of international migration started in the early 1970s, the expansion of consumption and mass media that underlies the cultural politics of globalization I discuss owes much to the nationally driven economic reforms of the early 1990s. Finally, the politics of gender, class, and caste as it intersects with the largely male and subaltern migration circuit to the Gulf is linked to the nationally coded figure of the Non-Resident Indian (NRI), a figuration of consumer identity in the aftermaths of a liberalization tied to a more professional, upper-class emigration to the first world.

Attention to this flexible articulation among region, nation, and world enables critical attention to complex processes of place making generated within processes of globalization over the last century. A close reading of the historical discourses and debates over Kerala, then, offer a map and a context for understanding more recent transformations.

Modeling Kerala

The construction of Kerala as a model for development can be traced to the mid-1970s with the publication of a report by the United Nations (CDS 1975). Its macrolevel data did confirm that Kerala exhibited low per capita income with high levels of unemployment and poverty, typical of poor regions in third world countries with a weak industrial base. However, it also reported that Kerala had high levels of literacy and life expectancy and low levels of fertility and infant and adult mortality, at rates that were more typical of highly industrialized regions of the first world (Parayil 2000; Franke and Chasin 1992; Jeffrey 1993). The report proposed an exceptional development profile for Kerala, centering on a high physical quality-of-life index across a wide spectrum of the population, notably including women and girls. However, this was coupled with low levels of income and economic growth.

This development profile became prominent within international development discourse as it was inserted into a polarized and ongoing debate among global policymakers and scholars of international development about the best way to achieve a higher standard of living for the poor of the third world (Parayil and Sreekumar 2003; Jeffrey 1993). On one side of the debate, the major view asserts that industrialization will generate economic growth that will eventually "trickle down" and raise the standard of living for the general population. This model of development argues, in other words, for rapid capitalist industrialization. On the other side, critics hold that development in the third world requires a highly centralized and planned process that will ensure better living conditions for the poor; this model of development argues for socialist transformation with varying degrees of importance given to industrialization. Both positions cite different aspects of Kerala's development experience for their own purposes. For those critical of capitalist industrialization, the prominence of the communist movement makes Kerala an exemplary instance of what could be achieved in the third world through socialist-inspired mobilizations without full-scale revolution.[2] Others hold up Kerala as an example of what is possible without a socialist revolution in the immediate present with very little expenditure on the part of wealthier nations and international donor agencies (Ratcliffe 1978; Morris 1979).

No one has done more to highlight Kerala's development experience at the international level than the Nobel Prize–winning economist Amartya Sen, whose views fall somewhere in the middle of this spectrum. With various colleagues, Sen has made the Kerala experience important as an argument for his "capabilities" approach to development (1990, 1995, 1997, 1999). Eschewing an economic model that measures development solely through per capita income and economic growth, Sen has instead highlighted what he calls "human capabilities." Constituting a universal standard, the production and nurture of these capabilities are linked to political freedom and social goods such as education, health care, and protection from hunger. Distinguishing between wealth and development, Sen has found the low per capita income levels and high quality-of-life indicators of Kerala important for laying out his vision of development.[3] So important is Sen to the prominence of Kerala's development experience that when he was feted in various forums in the capital city Thiruvananthapuram in 2000, the Kerala governor and the chancellor of the university stated that "by honoring you, Amartya Sen, we are honoring ourselves."[4]

In particular, Sen and others persistently bring to light Kerala's achievements on behalf of women and girls. More than any other aspect of Kerala's development profile, the indicators of female literacy, health, and educational levels are understood to be most noteworthy, particularly given the vulnerability of women and girls within the third world more generally. And, indeed, these indicators are impressive. Female literacy in Kerala, as of the 2000 census, is 87 percent, while that of India is 54 percent, and girls outnumber boys at every level of education (Parayil and

Sreekumar 2003). As Sen notes, "The distinction of Kerala is particularly striking in the field of gender equality" (1997, 13). Although considerable attention is devoted to health indicators as well—Kerala has one of the lowest rates of population growth in the third world and a sex ratio that favors females (the only state in India with such a ratio)—indicators of female literacy and education are seen to be more important because they are understood as causative links with multiplier effects (Sreekumar 2007; Parayil 2000).

Since independence from Britain, the dominant approach of national development has worked from the highly centralized, planned, state-centric Nehruvian view, modeled on the Soviet experience. Yet this approach has always been in contest with (and has sometimes overlapped with) a more grassroots, locally based, small-scale model of development, the vision of India's other great nationalist leader, M. K. Gandhi (Khilnani 1999). Precolonial and postcolonial political and social histories, which encompass state-centric and grassroots mobilizations, have shaped a state-centric development planning regime in Kerala, as they have in other states. Much literature and debate about Kerala centers on picking and choosing from various elements of this complex historical context to explain the state's development profile.

An important theme in scholarly explanations for Kerala's development experience is the role of a politicized, public-minded citizenry in demanding concessions from the state. Robin Jeffrey argues that the "shaping of a new public world" and the "opening out of politics—the growth of a readiness among 'ordinary people' to try to influence decisions" was the key factor in bringing about what is now called "the Kerala model" (1993, 1). Robert Franke and Barbara Chasin discuss the importance of "people's movements" and "political mobilization" led by the Communist Party of India (Marxist), or CPI (M)—the dominant leftist party in the region—in demanding a better quality of life (1992). Similarly, Sen emphasizes the importance of what he calls "public action" and public mobilization in Kerala's development experience (1999).[5]

Debates also focus on how exactly a politicized public comes into being and begins putting pressure on the state. In the literature on Kerala's development experience, some emphasize the role of the "enlightened" and "modernizing" nineteenth-century rulers of the princely states of Tiruvitamkoor and Kochi, two of the three regions that were brought together to form the Kerala state in 1956.[6] For example, Sen argues that those rulers responded to British colonialism and an increased missionary presence by expanding educational opportunities across caste groups in 1817 (1990). Sen sees the spread of literacy through the early expansion of educational opportunities as crucial for the development of a population able to articulate demands and mobilize publicly.

In a somewhat more diffuse way, Sen and others also highlight the matrilineal past of the dominant Hindu Nair caste in the region (Sen 1990; Jeffrey 1993). Asserting that this matrilineal history indicates that society positively appreciated women's rights and positions and gave women material means for survival, such scholars often link matrilineality and the high rates of female literacy that distinguish the Kerala development experience. Others also point to a long tradition of contact with the "outside world" through trade and religious practices, which created an openness to new ideas and a pluralistic culture with large minority populations. The Christian community, in particular, which dates back to the first century, took advantage of missionary educational efforts during the British colonial period to create a vigorous and expansive educational infrastructure (Franke and Chasin 1992; Jeffrey 1993). All of these arguments take the spread of education and the creation of a literate population as the foundation of a public citizenry willing and able to demand the expansion of social rights, such as education and health care, from the state.

Others offer more contemporary explanations of Kerala's exceptionalism, rooted in the state's modern social and political history. Arguing that high rates of education and literacy per se do not automatically lead to an active citizenry, they emphasize the interaction between vigorous caste-based social reform movements and the communist left.[7]

Caste-based social reform movements and the organizations they nurtured began during the colonial period in response to the pressures and opportunities of colonial modernity. In a cash economy fueled by a growing colonial bureaucracy and expanding markets, traditional upper-caste groups such as the Nair and the Nambutiri Brahmin communities sought to retain power through various attempts at internal community reform and modernization and by lobbying for the protection of land and other resources. The Nair-based movement, headed up by the Nair Service Society, was among the most vigorous, one of its most notable achievements being the legal dismantling of its own matrilineal system of inheritance and marriage in the name of producing modern forms of marriage and nuclear families.[8] Social reform among the Nambutiri Brahmin was led by V. T. Bhattatiripad and organizations such as the Yogakshema Sabha.[9] The mobilization of the largest Hindu caste community in Kerala, the untouchable Ezhava caste, began through leadership provided by the first generation of Ezhava to be educated in modern, missionary schools in the 1880s. Later spearheaded by the religious leader Sree Narayana Guru and the Sree Narayana Dharma Paripalana (SNDP), this movement challenged various forms of caste discrimination (in government jobs, schools, and temples), while working to reform and uplift its own community members through the development of its own network of educational, religious, and social institutions.[10] Similarly, among the slave Pulaya caste (who now identify as Dalit), the movement spearheaded by Ayyankali also struggled to challenge caste discrimination and economic, political, and social marginalization.[11]

Rooted in the reform and assertion of particular caste-based communities, these organizations and movements simultaneously entered an emerging terrain of modern democratic politics, adopting and mobilizing the language of modern citizenship grounded in the rights and obligations between states and citizens (Ouwerkerk 1994). A volatile coalition-based politics began during the pre-independence period, with various caste movements aligning in different ways with organizations representing Muslim and Christian minorities for representation within the state legislature. The intensifying anti-imperialist nationalist movement, led by the Indian National Congress, articulated with this caste-based and community-based politics in various complex ways to produce a modern form of democratic politics in Kerala.

The nascent communist movement emerged out of the more radical elements within these caste-based social reform movements, in terms of both the social origins of its early leaders and later the mass support of the Ezhava, already mobilized by the Sree Narayana movement (Menon 1994, 2006; Isaac and Tharakan 1986). For example, the preeminent Marxist leader and intellectual in the state, E. M. S. Namboodiripad, entered the communist movement after being involved in the social reform movement within the Nambutiri caste community. The communists also worked with the Congress-led nationalist movement in these early days, though they split from it in the 1930s and gained regional prominence in their own right.

In 1956, the national government formed the state by bringing together the Malayalam-speaking regions of Malabar, Kochi, and Tiruvitamkoor. The first democratic elections brought the Communist Party to power in 1957, famously making Kerala the first place in the world to freely elect a communist government.[12] More importantly, this election signaled the communists' eschewing of armed revolution and their entry into the institutions of parliamentary democracy. Though short-lived, this government sought to reform education and the land tenure system, raising expectations that subsequent governments across the political spectrum have had to meet. This has led to what Parayil and Sreekumar call "development through modernization"; that is, a vigorous politics of redistribution that characterizes the postcolonial period in Kerala (2003). Despite the complex and contested coalition politics of the post-independence period—dominated by the CPI (M) under the banner of the Left Democratic Front (LDF) and the Kerala Congress Party under the banner of the United Democratic Front (UDF)—these redistribution policies have persisted and become an important terrain for postcolonial democratic politics.

In summary, the dominant understanding of the historical process by which the "Kerala model of development" comes into being tells a particular history of progressivism through which an active and politicized citizenry, engaged in democratic politics, demands social rights that have led to a high quality of life distributed in a relatively egalitarian way across caste, class, and gender. Some scholars emphasize precolonial historical factors such as international contact, a diverse and pluralistic ethos, a history of matrilineal kin and property relations, and modern and enlightened rulers who emphasized and spread education and literacy. Others argue specifically for the centrality of the CPI (M) in producing Kerala's development achievements, while some scholars point more broadly to a vital and pluralistic colonial and postcolonial democratic process that resulted from complex interactions between caste and community-based mobilization, anticolonial nationalism, and the rise of the communist left in Kerala.

Questioning Development

The narrative of modernization assumes that increasing education leads to increasing freedom for women (choice), which leads to better development outcomes (tradition to modernity). Stepping back from the rates of participation in education and levels of female literacy, I would like to ask two relatively simple questions: What are the conditions under which young women gain entry into education? and What are they being educated for? If we pay close, ethnographic attention to the actual process of education and its gendered aspects, contextualized within the historical emergence of modernity in Kerala, we will better understand the complex role of education in young people's lives and the role of young people's lives in larger regional and national imaginaries.

Young women and men attending the low-caste college, in the small district town in southern Kerala where I conducted research, are situated at the heart of a project of "development through modernization" and are central to the Kerala model of development. Their college is situated within a complex of institutions that emerges out of the Ezhava-based, anticaste movement led by Sree Narayana Guru. Postindependence, it affiliated with the university system, connecting it to the larger development infrastructure of the state, and its student politics refracts the wider political culture of the state. Yet the ways in which I approach students' participation in educational processes is a marked departure from the ways in which development discourse understands education as a process of modernization.[13]

Modern educational systems depend on and engender modern patriarchal structures that belie any simple move from tradition to modernity. Attention to the everyday ways in which young women and men participate in the public spaces of education and youth reveal a terrain of caste-specific and class-specific gendered embodiments of masculinity and femininity through which young people participate in the educational process. These embodiments, their contextualization within the historical emergence of modern gender ideology in Kerala, and analysis of their enabling and constraining functions reveal this process to be a contested and contradictory site of social transformation. It should become clear that the dichotomy between tradition and modernity is not a theoretical one for me; it is not simply part of my conceptual tool kit but ubiquitously deployed in the ethnographic material I collected. Further, this dichotomy between tradition and modernity is generated from within an already modern worldview. This is a society thoroughly saturated by modern institutions, in which talk, one might say obsession, about "tradition"—its loss, its revival, and so on—is the surest sign of its modernity. By ethnographically examining the conditions of possibility for women's and men's participation in public spheres of education, I analyze discourses and practices of gender as they relate to public space with the aim of apprehending the conditions under which young women participate in education so as to produce the Kerala model of development.

Such a perspective entails a new way of understanding the history of Kerala's modernity. The narrative of progressivism that underlies these explanations elides crucial aspects of the history of modern social reform in the region and ignores their important and transformative effects (Arumina 2003; Devika 2007a). In particular, the much-lauded relationship between the Kerala model and "gender equality" in the region obfuscates the emergence of a decidedly modern patriarchy that structures much of what is now called the Kerala model. A modern gender ideology has underwritten much caste and community social reform and in fact buttresses Kerala's development profile, yet the rising communist left hardly challenged it. As J. Devika and Mini Sukumar state, "We would even argue that patriarchy in Kerala partly rests upon the agency of the 'Kerala Model Woman'—the better educated, more healthy, less fertile, new elite woman" (2006, 4472).

Central to the genesis and spread of the narrative of progressivism about Kerala is the idea of the liberated "Malayalee woman," whom modernity has freed from the shackles of exploitative and barbaric caste practices and various kinds of domestic servitude into a modern world of education, work, and public life that is eminently more civilized. As G. Arunima charts, within Nair social reform, her rise involves the highly ambiguous process by which young Nair men began, in the middle and late nineteenth century, to argue against the matrilineal system of marriage, kin, and property in which they are relatively disenfranchised, as inheritance is through the female line and property is held by the collective household (taravad) (2003). Drawing on new notions of modesty and sexual morality, they argued that matriliny (marumakkattayam) sexually exploits women, "forcing" them into sexual liaisons (sambandham) with upper-caste Nambutiri Brahmin men.[14] A series of legislative and legal actions legally dismantled matriliny by 1933, in the name of producing modern nuclear families, based on companionate marriage, in which landholdings are divided among the younger members.

Among the Nambutiri Brahmin, a very different, patrilineal set of marriage, kin, and property arrangements prevailed (Devika 2007a). Within the Brahmin joint family and lineage system (illam), only the oldest son was allowed to marry, and polygamy was allowed in order to produce the male heir. Women of such families, called Antarjanam (inner people), practiced strict seclusion and were thoroughly incorporated into their husbands' families. They could not inherit land and were subject to a dowry system.[15] Younger sons were allowed to have alliances with women of other castes, notably Nair. In the 1920s, younger male members started advocating for the rights of younger men to marry within their caste, for female education and dress reform, for the partition of joint family property, for the dismantling of polygamy, marriage of young girls to older men, and enforced widowhood. Among the Ezhava (some of whom practiced matriliny while others were patrilineal), Sree Narayana Guru and the SNDP advocated a patrilineal system of inheritance and monogamous marriage, simplification of marriage rituals and the eradication of various puberty rites (talikettukalyanam and tirandukulikalyanam), and education of females (Velayudhan 1999; Osella and Osella 2000a; Rao 1979).

Thus, among a variety of caste-based movements with different and overlapping traditions of kinship and inheritance, the nuclear family ideal, founded on a monogamous sexual arrangement, became the focus of reform. Each group subordinated women's roles to the production of a new kind of modern family and its attendant domestic arrangements. Each understood this ideal as the "liberation" of women from barbaric caste practices through the workings of a modern and progressive public.

However, this understanding of the modern public ignores the profoundly gendered and gendering nature of the public itself, in which roles for men and women are proscribed anew by reconfiguring distinctions between the public and the domestic. As the modern public expanded and women gained greater access to it, which they certainly did beginning in the 1920s, they were integrated into it as subjects of a new gender ideology centered on modern ideals of femininity. The distinction between tradition and modernity, the public and the private, and new conceptions of masculinity and femininity were central to community reform movements across the caste spectrum and central as well to the emergence of a Malayalee middle-class sensibility that underlies much of what constitutes Kerala as a "modern" and "developed" place.

Gender differentiation emerges through the deployment of a public/private distinction: modern middle-class masculinity must be geared toward producing in the public realms of work, while modern middle-class femininity is geared toward restructuring the domestic. In the production of modern forms of masculinity, a great deal of criticism is leveled at men ensconced within traditional and feudal economic roles tied to the land in which they are happy with a simple and inexpensive life, unwilling to see the necessity for actively improving one's standard of living through the production of greater economic profit and surplus for the betterment of various collectivities, understood as either the community or the nation.[16] At the same time, the modern public is a collection of modern, self-regulating selves. New notions of individuality for both men and women focus on the idea that the modern, self-regulating self has well-developed internal capacities (Devika 2007a; Kumar 1997). This is in contrast to the traditional order, which (in the modern understanding) wastes internal human capacities.

Early expressions of modern domesticity in the emergent public sphere of Kerala, composed of public forums, meetings, newspapers, and magazines centered on the notion that women were not simply vessels for giving birth but active agents who needed to be trained in domestic practices so they could raise children capable of becoming modern individuals within modern collectivities. This idea is prevalent in discussions about women's education from the late nineteenth century onward. Education would harness and properly mold the seemingly natural affinities of women for mothering and their instinctual proclivities to gentleness, care, and nurture; education would make them efficient and productive mothers rather than wasteful and inefficient ones. Training girls and women in useful skills (sewing, for example, as opposed to engaging in idle gossip), or educating mothers to stop filling their children's minds with superstitions and silly myths, were all part of this reformulation of domesticity. Both as wives and as mothers, women were central to social reform efforts intent on producing modern collectivities peopled by modern individuals who were understood to have distinctly gendered capacities and roles.

Although the idea that western education was necessary for properly harnessing women's natural capacities became dominant, another discourse argued that western-style education eroded a woman's natural capacities and made her a wanton imitator of the West. Champions of modern education for girls optimistically stressed a third possibility: an educated young woman who seamlessly blended tradition and modernity. An iconic figuration of such a woman appears in *Indulekha*, the first modern Malayalam novel, published in 1889 by O. Chandu Menon. The novel's eponymous heroine is cultivated in the western style (she plays the violin and sews) yet retains her Malayaleeness in manners, speech, observance of rituals, and dress. Altogether, she is understood in terms of a reformed, modern, and upper-caste Nair identity (Arunima 1997).

By the middle of the twentieth century, the ideal of the modern nuclear family and its domestic arrangements—based on the distinction between public and private, and male and female, domains—had largely consolidated. However, starting in the 1920s, women had also begun to assert themselves in the public domain in an extensive and vigorous way, such that the literal distinction between the public and the domestic became less important for configuring modern gender relations (Devika 2007a; Velayudhan 1994, 1999; Jeffrey 1993). Newspapers and magazines began to report on females who did well in school examinations, graduated with degrees, and acquired teaching posts and other paid employment. The idea that womanly capacities could be harnessed for an expanding set of activities that crossed the divide between home and the world enabled women's entry into a public that largely consisted of schools, hospitals, charity organizations, reform institutions, and orphanages.

In the 1920s, the entry of women into a broader public domain also began to elicit a shifting set of ambivalent discourses, in which the modern women in the public became an increasing source of anxiety. While Kerala's early engagements with colonial modernity generated anxieties about cultural alienation and the imitation of western ways, a largely male narrative articulated a relatively optimistic vision of a blending of traditional and modern elements in which the figure of the modern woman ensconced in the modernizing home was crucial. Now men accused women of not valuing education in and of itself but of rather selfishly seeking education (particularly higher education) for the purposes of gaining employment and thus transgressing the ideal of sexually complementary gender roles consolidated in the earlier vision of cultural modernization: in short, they were now competing with men. As G. Arunima states in a discussion of the shifting views of the city and colonial modernity among upper-caste male elites in Kerala during the 1920s and 1930s, "Even as the Malayali man was desperately throwing off the shackles of barbarism and tradition and willingly entering the modern world of opportunity, he found himself tripping over the unexpected hurdle of the 'modern' woman. . . . Her [modernity] reminded him uncomfortably of his own compromised position within a colonial context" (n.d.).

Within this evolving terrain, advocates of the entry of women into the public domain, including the first generation of Malayalee feminists, argued that it is precisely women's capacities that make them ideal participants within a wider public (Devika 2007a). Drawing on that aspect of modern domesticity that reformulated mothering as a process for creating useful collectivities, they argued that women's capacities were important for conserving and furthering life in the areas of health, nutrition, education, and fertility. They carved out a space within the public in which women could assert themselves while avoiding direct competition with men in occupations mutually understood to be male. For example, the idea that women make good teachers is tied to the notion that a modern, productive school does not discipline through violence but rather through the gentle power of words that women are eminently suited to deploy. The large percentage of teachers who are female perhaps attests less to the direct power of this ideology than to the ways in which it legitimated the teaching profession as an acceptable form of public presence for women. Thus women entered the public spheres of education, health, and social service—yet they were marginalized from an important aspect of it, namely, the arena of public politics (Jeffrey 1993; Lindberg 2001; Mathew 1995; Erwer 2003).

Many state-based and community-based social reform movements and projects are characterized by an interlinked set of organizations and institutions, outside of the sphere of official politics, such as schools, hospitals, orphanages, crèches, hostels, and health clinics that have become an important source of education and employment, carving out a particular domain within the public for women (Jeffrey 1993; Devika 2007a). These institutional networks are also the backbone of the development infrastructure in Kerala, directly linking the mobilization of women within spaces of this public to the Kerala development experience. Further, studies of the postcolonial development state in the areas of family planning and women's empowerment schemes demonstrate the ways in which modern gender ideology underwrites many of these efforts (Devika and Thampi 2007; Devika 2005).

The project of development and modernization that I have been discussing sits at the intersection between the production of modernity in Kerala and more contemporary forces of transnationalism and globalization. During the 1990s, the Kerala development experience came under increasing critical scrutiny from a variety of positions (Parayil 2000). Some focused on sustainability and feasibility, asking whether a development strategy that did so little to encourage economic growth and industrialization could continue to afford its expenditures in education, health care, and the like (Isaac and Tharakan 1995; Franke and Chasin 2000). Others raised questions about those excluded from the benefits of the model, including traditional fisher folk, tribals, female workers, and Dalit groups (Kurien 2000; Mencher 1994; Pillai 1996; Bijoy and Raman 2003).

While these researchers continued to have faith in the larger project of development in Kerala but questioned its feasibility, others began to challenge its assumptions. Using the 1990s fiscal crisis of the state as an entry point, Tharamangalam (1998) argues that the development trajectory in Kerala has been a "debacle" that quashes the entrepreneurial "spirit" of the people by turning its citizens into unproductive welfare dependents of a patronizing state while eroding many civil society institutions. This worry was often expressed as a criticism of the left and the politicization of the state, one that linked this politicization to a stagnant economy unable to provide jobs for its citizens. The ensuing debate, contextualizing Kerala's fiscal crisis in new structural adjustment policies, the liberalization of the Indian economy, and the labeling of Tharamangalam as a "neoliberal scholar," demonstrates the new conditions within which the Kerala model is understood and debated (Parayil 2000).[17] While such positions focus on a stagnant economy as a structural feature of the Kerala model, from a different position, feminist scholarship began to question the model's underlying assumptions (Devika and Sukumar 2006; Devika and Kodoth 2001; Sreekumar 2007).

While the questioning of Kerala as a model of development has come from many different positions, one major reason for the destabilization of the dominant development framework through which the state has been understood is a growing recognition of the importance of transnational labor migration from the region to other parts of the world, particularly the Persian Gulf, and its effects in terms of money and consumption within Kerala. This migration goes back to the 1970s and earlier, but the fall of the Berlin Wall and other shifts of the 1990s—such as the accelerated pace and intensity of corporate globalization and the economic liberalization of the Indian economy—have created a new context in which development in Kerala is understood, debated, and experienced. I now turn to explore the linkages between Kerala's development experience, its history of migration and globalization, and an emergent sense of Kerala as a new consumer society.

Development in the Era of Globalization

In a recent and large-scale study on the scope and impact of emigration from Kerala, the authors make the rather bold statement that "migration . . . has contributed more to poverty alleviation than any other factor, including agrarian reforms, trade union activities, and social welfare legislation (Zachariah, Mathew, Rajan 2001, 63).[18] It becomes immediately clear from such a statement that discussions of this emigration are entangled with debates about the merits of the Kerala development experience. Given the circulation of the Kerala model in international discourse, the links between this migration trajectory and the model have also recently come to the attention of the international press.[19] While arguing that emigration has done a better job than the development state in providing a better standard of living for people in Kerala, the authors also contend that the root cause of the extensive migration of people out of Kerala is precisely the Kerala model of development (Zachariah, Mathew, Rajan 2001, 78), an argument that complicates our understanding of cause and effect. According to the authors, the reduction in mortality that came with development led to a demographic expansion that contributed to emigration. In addition, a stagnating agricultural sector, the rapid expansion of education, and the inability of the state to generate jobs all contributed to the desire to emigrate. Alongside these "push" factors, expanding job opportunities in the metropolitan and industrial cities of India after 1940 and the Gulf oil boom of the 1970s created "pull" factors.

Indeed, any discussion of globalization in Kerala must begin with the fact that this region has had extensive and long-standing linkages with other parts of the world. Kerala became part of a larger Indian Ocean world through religious networks (mainly Muslim, Christian, and Jewish) and spice trade routes that go back centuries. In addition, starting in the nineteenth century, individuals migrated for work to Southeast Asia and what is now Sri Lanka as part of an evolving colonial plantation economy (Zachariah, Mathew, Rajan 2001). Scholars of Kerala point to the enduring significance of such linkages by drawing attention to the importance of "international contact" for the reception of new ideas during periods of radicalization in the modern period, and what the scholar and cultural critic Ashis Nandy calls an "indigenous" form of secularism and pluralism among religious communities in the region (Franke and Chasin 1992; Nandy 2000). These overlapping linkages from the precolonial into the colonial period also integrated Kerala into the global economy by the turn of the twentieth century. This incorporation hinged on the export of primary commodities (spices and rubber, for example) and labor, primarily to other plantation economies such as Sri Lanka and those of Southeast Asia. In this way, Kerala has been a weak link in the commodity chains of the global economy that has nevertheless been a central part of the regional economy (Parayil and Sreekumar 2003). The liberalization of the Indian economy has produced new conditions under which the Kerala economy now struggles. Some have argued that it makes Kerala more vulnerable than ever, as the structural changes in the Indian economy vis-à-vis globalization will not necessarily benefit Kerala because of its specialization in the export of primary commodities and labor (Parayil and Sreekumar 2003). Meanwhile, this round of economic globalization further exposes Kerala to the vagaries of price fluctuations for its commodity exports.

Migration to and from this geographical area expanded after Kerala was created and incorporated into India in 1956. The first phase, and still a very important component, was emigration to other parts of India. However, international emigration overtook intra-India migration by the 1980s.[20] Of the international migrants, an overwhelming number (95 percent) migrate to the Gulf states, with the largest percentage (2 percent) of the rest emigrating to the United States (ibid.). Though the statistical picture is unclear due to the large numbers of workers in the unorganized sector, while Kerala's population is 3.75 percent of the nation's, Keralites make up a disproportionate percentage of the approximately three million Indian migrants in the Gulf (Zachariah, Prakash, Rajan, 2000). After sampling ten thousand Kerala households to track migrants within India, emigrants to other countries, and returning emigrants, Zachariah, Mathew, and Rajan (2001) estimated that 40 percent of the households across the state had some experience of migration.[21] The economic impact of this migration is felt most directly in the form of remittances of cash and commodities sent back to Kerala. One study estimates that throughout the 1990s, remittances to Kerala made up between 17 and 22 percent of the state income and were 2.55 times the budget support provided by the central government to the state (Kannan and Hari 2002).

A significant portion of the migrants are from the Muslim communities of northern Kerala, but extensive migration patterns are also present among Christian and Hindu communities (largely Ezhava) of central and southern Kerala (Zachariah, Mathew, and Rajan 2001). An overwhelming number of the migrants are unskilled, semiskilled, or nonprofessional skilled workers in manual and clerical positions. While this migration is largely male and nonelite, the emigration of females is increasing, and there are important concentrations of female migrants such as nurses from Kerala to both the Gulf and other parts of India (Percot 2006). More than 80 percent of the migrants are between the ages of fifteen and thirty-four, with the average age being twenty-seven (Zachariah, Mathew, and Rajan 2001).

The development state in Kerala is thus intertwined with the state experiences of migration in ways that profoundly affect the life stage of youth. The years of college student life are structured at the intersection of the development state and this migration trajectory. As the authors of a large-scale study indicate, educational expansion, particularly at the higher educational levels, and the inability of the local economy to generate jobs have created a large category of the "educated unemployed" between the ages of fifteen and twenty-five (ibid.). There is a high correlation between higher levels of education and unemployment: more than 40 percent of those with a Secondary School Leaving Certificate (equivalent of a high school diploma) and more than 35 percent of those with college degrees are unemployed, with young women unemployed at four times the rate of young men. Kerala's educational system generates a large pool of educated young people, but many of them are unemployed for many years during and after receiving high school and college degrees, until they emigrate, marry, and either enter or leave the labor force.

Studies indicate that migrants and their families spend much of the money brought back building large "Gulf houses," which pepper the rural, semirural, and urban landscape, announcing a family's connections abroad. Migrants use remittances also to build and buy flats in more urban areas, which, along with the expansion of the state's tourism infrastructure, has generated a speculative and volatile market in land. Migrants and their families use remittances to purchase consumer durables (televisions, cars, refrigerators, washers and dryers) that far exceed those of nonmigrants and make Kerala's per capita consumer expenditure the highest in India (Kannan and Hari 2002). After the liberalization of the Indian economy in the early 1990s, high rates of disposable income and the "sophistication" of Kerala consumers have also made the state a preeminent test market for many companies.[22] In addition to consumer durables, Kerala is a key consumer market for gold in India, a commodity culturally and religiously important for signifying wealth, status, and auspiciousness.

Quite apart from houses, land, gold, and consumer durables, migrant families also spend remittances on the education of children. Most migrants to the Gulf do not get family visas, and children often remain in Kerala with one parent or grandparents. Households with migration connections spend more on education than those without, and successful migration is correlated with higher education levels. More than 40 percent of the migrants abroad and almost 60 percent of the migrants to other parts of India have either a Secondary School Leaving Certificate or a college degree, compared with 23 percent of the general population (Zachariah, Mathew, and Rajan 2001). This often leads to an intergenerational cycle of migration and education as the increased investment in education leads to migration for younger members of the household.

Situated as citizens of a historically important and vigorous political culture tied to the rise of a development state, young people are also now enmeshed in the hopes, aspirations, and trajectories of transnational migration—whether they manage to migrate or not. This migration is not simply people's movement across borders but a complex transnational circulation of labor, money, and commodities that has a profound impact within Kerala through the impact of remittances, the expansion of commodity culture, education, and the structuring of families and intergenerational relations.

While it is the labor of migrants and the transnational circuit of money and commodities it has spawned that most closely ties Kerala to a wider global economy, globalization as an explicit object of political contestation is not debated in terms of this migration. Rather, globalization is painted as an external threat and linked to corporate globalization, the rise of a market ideology, and the machinations of large multinational corporations and international aid agencies. For example, leftist student political parties, intimately linked to the larger party politics of the state, have often rallied against government policies understood to be in cahoots with corporate globalization; a good case in point is the ongoing battle against a Coca-Cola bottling plant in the village of Plachimada in central Kerala.[23] Such spectacular instances of antiglobalization politics sit alongside a more ambiguous negotiation of what is understood to be the workings of "neoliberal" forces in the state. For example, the CPI (M) in Kerala initiated in 1996 what was called the "People's Planning Campaign," a wide-ranging program to decentralize development initiatives and share decision-making power over the allocation of development resources (Isaac and Franke 2002; Heller 2001). Questioning the sources of funding for this initiative, which were linked to international aid agencies, some in the party saw this as a capitulation to neoliberal forces that were undermining the power of the state and transforming its leftist ethos in the name of greater "participation" by the people (Devika 2007b). Equally relevant are positions that contest this characterization of globalization. For example, on a popular blog titled "Dog's Own Country," a play on the popular Kerala tourist slogan "God's Own Country," bloggers discuss what they see to be the hypocrisy of the left with regard to globalization.[24] Discussing the agitation against Coca-Cola and recent allegations that it is unsafe to drink Coke, one blogger wonders why the leftist parties want to ban Coke but not alcohol and cigarettes.

Here, the politics of globalization turns on the consumption of Coke, a commodity that is iconic of globalization and the power of multinational corporations. While the more everyday manifestations of globalization in the form of an expanding commodity culture and its links to youth, family, and intergenerational relations are not debated as explicitly as corporate globalization, a more pervasive cultural politics of mass-mediated consumerism mediates the intimate structurings of contemporary Kerala by the forces of migration and globalization. I now turn to an exploration of the crisis-ridden narratives of Kerala as a consumer society.

The Crisis of Consumerism

While the Kerala model literature and its historical explanations narrated a heroic and progressive march from barbarism into a relatively egalitarian modernity, the breakdown of the Kerala model of development and its reconfigurations through globalization generated a discourse of crisis in the 1990s. As Sharmila Shreekumar has argued, the "utopia" of the Kerala model literature is increasingly countered by a "dystopia" whose symptoms include "corruption, moral laxity, stagnant economy, widespread unemployment, high suicide rates, alcoholism, indebtedness, increasing violence against women and, more recently, AIDS" (2007, 43). Commodification and consumerism are central to these crisis-ridden narratives; the intersection of youth and gender are an important axis on which these narratives pivot.

Increased levels of consumption in Kerala in the 1990s resulted from a convergence of higher disposable income due to migrants' remittances and the expansion of commodities available for purchase after the liberalization of the Indian economy. The expansion of the consumer market also converged with the expansion of the mass media in Kerala. While Kerala has a long-standing and vibrant print culture that includes books, newspapers, and weekly magazines, the expansion of the electronic media, including film and especially television during the 1990s,

44

has generated a palpable sense of Kerala as a mass-mediated consumer society.[25] Within this context, consumerism itself emerged as an object of discourse.

One site of crisis where Kerala's development experience is seen to be undermined by the effects of consumerism is in media discussions of the state's high suicide rates, which according to state statistics are among the highest in India and triple the national average.[26] The media portray several types of suicide victims: indebted farmers, students who have not done well on exams, young women "disgraced" by allegations of impropriety or victimized by sexual violence, unemployed males, and housewives. The pattern of family murder-suicides is understood to have emerged in the early 1990s.[27] Suicide has become such an issue that the state government, for the first time, has set up a special suicide prevention committee. Prominent among the causes cited is consumerism, more specifically, conspicuous consumption in which the pressures of a consumerist and competitive society, linked to migration and the onslaught of globalization, lead to living beyond one's means, which then leads to financial troubles. In addition, the highly publicized suicide of a female engineering student from a Dalit background who could not pay her college fees led to student protests against policies encouraging the privatization of higher education throughout the state and became a crisis for the government—leading to much discussion about the competitive and consumerist nature of the educational system.[28] Articles also cite the "Gulf syndrome," in which migration and the desire for upward mobility, money, and commodities tear apart family social support networks, leaving lonely spouses (usually women referred to as "Gulf wives") and unsupervised children—conditions seen as factors leading to the suicide of wives and youth.[29] This depiction of the family diverges a great deal from the happy nuclear family of the Kerala model literature. In these consumerist narratives of family life (kudumba jivam), young women and men appear as particularly vulnerable.

A second node in this discourse of consumerism is its effects on the leftist political culture. There is a pervasive sense that consumerism is undermining the values of egalitarianism that generated the Kerala model of development and that it has led to the waning of the left. In an analysis of this 1990s discourse about the "erosion of the Left," J. Devika notes:

Participants in . . . the debate often view depoliticisation in Kerala as the erosion of the dominant left, caused mainly by external forces such as global capitalism . . . [while] consumerism in Kerala has been hugely accentuated by migration since the early 1970s. That no section of the left has made any serious effort to analyze Malayalee consumerism . . . reveals that their . . . critique is not a political but a moralistic one, which only serves a sharp and belligerent distinction between inside (leftist Kerala) and outside (global capitalism). Many participants in the above debate view consumerism as cultural-ideological contamination which weakens political subjectivities and accentuates the alleged downward progression of left values. This does not tell us about the specificities of consumerism in Kerala. (2007b, 2467)

While some scholars argue that migration has buttressed the Kerala model of development and its efforts to alleviate poverty, those who bemoan consumerism in Kerala argue that it has shaped a citizenry that has become deeply suspicious of politics and that is uninspired by the goals of equality and justice that had led to Kerala's development achievements. This discourse of depoliticization targets both consumerism and the influence of the mass media, particularly the expansion of television, for creating new forms of political passivity. As Devika notes, such discourses rely on a binary distinction between a new form of global capitalism which is understood to be external and Kerala which is understood to be a safe haven of the left. What such discourses elide are the specific histories and imbrications of consumption within Kerala.

Within this moralizing discourse about consumerism, it is important to pay attention to the continuities and differences between earlier discourses of consumerism and contemporary ones. We know that anxieties about social change are often expressed through anxieties about the consumption of commodities. In particular, the social changes generated by the twin forces of modernity and capitalism are often negotiated through a cultural politics of consumption (Felski 1995). For example, within Kerala, and in India more generally, in the late nineteenth century and after, the shift from caste-based and community-based clothing to forms of dress associated with community reform and modernization generated a critique of wanton imitation, excess, and profligacy, particularly targeting women. The opposition between tradition and modernity, and between public and private, which underwrote much of this negotiation of colonial modernity, is still in play as young people negotiate globally inflected spaces of modernity.

During the late nineteenth century, a discourse emerged in which colonial modernity as a form of "white magic," often linked to glittering modern and urban domestic spaces, was a key trope in the elite male-authored literature of the time. As G. Arunima argues, this discourse did not entail a critique of commodification but was a resolutely positive assessment of entrepreneurial and commercial activity (n.d.). By the 1930s a shifting assessment of modernity emerges in which satires about modern forms of life feature highly gendered critiques of "modern" women seeking to displace men. Though critiques of commodification became more prevalent, the consumption of new commodities was understood to be in the service of a reform-minded, productive household that was part of the emerging modern middle class.

The expansion of economic opportunities through migration and globalization has generated a new politics of consumption in which this productive, reformist middle class is reorienting itself, and newly upwardly mobile communities and groups (for example, young men from the Ezhava community) assert themselves through consumption in ways that far exceed the midcentury productivist domestic paradigm. While I explore these new dynamics ethnographically in the chapters to follow, some initial sense of the broad contours of this reconfiguration is revealed through a brief discussion of popular representations of new consumer identities in newspapers and contemporary mass media and cinema, highlighting youth cultural life and the college context in the region.

A letter to a newspaper titled "Dubai Dreams"[30] provides some sense of the discourse of youth, education, Gulf migration, and globalization from a middle-class male perspective; it also provides some sense of the competitive terrain shared by class-inflected engagements with globalization.

> Throughout our schooling we were an inseparable gang of five. . . . School days over, we began our search for admission to pre-university. . . . Narayanan disclosed that he was unlikely to join us at college as he had been offered a job in Dubai. . . . In Palghat we resumed our mundane lives, the high point being Narayanan's long newsy letters. Very soon we were familiar with Dubai's modern airport, the luxury hotels, the fully carpeted centrally air-conditioned

homes, the duty-free electronic stores and the overstocked supermarkets. Dubai became a cherished dream. A year later Narayanan returned home on holiday. We waited several hours at Madras airport. . . . Once out of the airport he insisted on taking a tourist taxi and retaining it for the whole day. He checked into an expensive hotel and treated us to a lavish meal. . . . Year after year Narayanan's annual visits were eagerly awaited by all who knew him. Time passed and the four of us graduated and set out in search of jobs. I moved to Bombay and started work in an international bank. Slowly and diligently I worked my way up the corporate ladder. I began travelling abroad on business. . . . I transited through Dubai International Airport. Never having forgotten Narayanan, I wished I had had his phone number to call him. During my three hour wait, I entered the spotlessly clean washroom and found the toilet attendant busy with his broom and soap water bucket . . . The toilet attendant moved away from the door and looked up. Our eyes met. I quickly averted my eyes and he looked down again at the freshly wiped floors. I left without hugging or even speaking to my beloved friend Narayanan.

This letter suggests how young subaltern males migrate to the Gulf, circulating in and out of Kerala in the shadow of the figure of the affluent, consumerist Non-Resident Indian (NRI), so celebrated as a "mythological hero" for a globalizing middle class (Deshpande 2003). It illustrates the ways in which youth, education, trajectories of migration, and visions of global experiences are intertwined. The author of the letter follows a respectable middle-class ("slowly and diligently") path into adulthood, climbing the corporate ladder of an international bank that allows him to globalize ("traveling abroad on business"). Here is the middle-class male globalizing through the opportunities of a newly liberalized Indian economy in which international banks are now allowed to function—liberalization's children taking advantage of new opportunities. The attitude of the letter writer toward his beloved schoolmate moves from envy about his friend's experiences abroad and his abilities to consume to a self-righteousness about his own slower career trajectory. It ends with pity and shame as he, finally a member of the globalized, affluent Indian middle class, encounters his friend cleaning toilets at an international airport. In particular, he carefully distinguishes between his own respectable and diligent path into adulthood and his friend's trajectory, which he represents as an illegitimate shortcut (forgoing college) and marked by excessive, enviable consumerism in India and Kerala—yet it turns out that all the while his friend is cleaning toilets in Dubai. The symbolic valence of cleaning toilets—a traditionally coded occupation of untouchable castes—should not be elided here, as it creates a contrasting set of trajectories marked by caste and class associations. Here we have a typical representation of the non-elite Gulf returnee as a transgressive, illegitimate, excessive, and pitiable *nouveau riche* (see Kurien 2002; Osella and Osella 2000).

Such representations are also part of a new genre of comedy films of the late 1980s and 1990s. A brief discussion of cinema will further reveal how youth becomes a site for mediating globalization. Until the 1990s, Malayalam cinema was seen as a vibrant, intellectually sophisticated, socially progressive film culture based on an aesthetic that provided "realistic" depictions of ordinary and everyday life, making it "superior" to other regional and national film industries.[31] With its reliance on a strong and modern literary tradition tied to social reform and the left for themes and stories, Malayalam cinema participated in the larger discourse of progressivism and modernity in the region (Muraleedharan 2005; Rowena 2002; Radhakrishnan n.d.a). During its initial emergence as a full-fledged cinema in the 1950s and 1960s, its major themes included class and caste oppression and struggle, progress, and the rise of a secular and democratic outlook. While themes of disillusionment with state and society, the tensions and costs of social change and transformation, the problems of individualism and existential crisis emerged during the 1970s and after, these remained well within the narrative and aesthetic rubric of a socially conscious and realist cinema. Like the larger contours of progressivism and modernity in Kerala, this cinema too was largely situated in a progressive and modernizing respectable Malayalee middle-class family that Jenny Rowena P. argues "was predicated on the themes of reform and social responsibility almost always shouldered by educated upper-caste male figures" (2002, 33). Heroism in these films centered on a single male protagonist who was more often than not upper caste/class, while men and women of other castes/classes and women of these upper-caste/class families, more often than not, were impediments and objects of reform or were tragic and/or peripheral to the main storylines (Rowena 2002).

The rise of television and internal problems within the film industry have generated a discourse of crisis and decline focused on women and youth. Discussions of mass media in the state point to the abandonment of cinema halls by the middle-class family and women in general who are depicted as glued to their television sets, entranced by hugely popular melodramatic serials such as *Stree* that largely cater to a female audience. While news and sports programming cater to a male audience, studies of gender and television demonstrate the ways in which an increasingly commodified televisual culture targets housewives and middle-class domesticity through talk shows, serials, and advertising (Usha 2004; cf. Mankekar 1999). While youth-oriented shows featuring Bollywood cinema and music have long been available through an expanding set of channels—leading to complaints about the influence of Hindi film culture on youth and regional identity in the state—it is only recently that the youth market has been explicitly targeted, with Asianet, the first private satellite channel in the state, expanding to include a specifically youth-oriented channel in 2005.

More significant than television for the young people I worked with were youth-oriented films that emerged in the late 1980s and early 1990s. These films shift some of the emphasis of Malayalam cinema away from the reformist middle-class family toward the social category of youth outside familial spaces, one that mediates Gulf migration, youth unemployment, and shifting gender, caste, and class relations.[32]

In an insightful study of the emergence of "comedy-films" of the late 1980s and early 1990s, Jenny Rowena P. links these films to a new consumerist ethos tied to Gulf migration. While most film critics dismiss these films as silly slapstick, one that indicates the decline of Malayalam cinema, she demonstrates how these popular films shift the focus from tears, romance, melodrama, and sentiment rooted in the middle-class family home to that of young, unemployed men from a variety of caste and class backgrounds in public spaces—large cities, workplaces, men's hostels, lodges—anxiously pursuing jobs and financial stability within an expanding commodity culture through jokes, gags, various kinds of fraudulence, and slapstick.[33] They have become such a ubiquitous part of popular culture that cassettes of famous scenes are popular and television programs devoted to comedy allow viewers to request their favourite scenes from these films.

In this cinema, the upper-caste/class responsible, reforming hero is replaced by a group of young incompetent men, many of them from lower-caste backgrounds—a shift that marks the assertion of nonelite masculinity through consumerism, social mobility, and the opportunities of Gulf migration. The films are framed by fantasies of wealth, success, and the acquisition of commodities, including the upper-caste/class woman. While the difficulties of performing masculinity by becoming a productive breadwinner were central to the modern, middle-class nuclear family in Kerala, here, in the context of acute unemployment and consumerism, this struggle generates a crisis and competition between elite and nonelite young men. The struggle to gain a stable foothold, Rowena argues, is mediated through laughter and comedy; one that is nevertheless resolved through competition and rivalry that ultimately reasserts the values of an upper-caste/class masculinity in ways that "remasculinize" contemporary Kerala society (2002).[34]

These earlier youth-oriented comedy films focused on unemployed young men, sometimes students and sometimes not, from a variety of backgrounds in public spaces outside the family home; now the campus itself has become an increasingly greater focus of attention. While the college has often been a backdrop in earlier cinema for explorations of romantic love, for example, films such as *Pavithram* (dir. Kumar, 1994), the recent hit film *Classmates* (dir. Jose, 2006), *Chocolate* (dir. Shafi, 2007), and *College Kumaran* (dir. Thulasidas, 2007) explicitly thematized "college culture," bringing together the themes of romance, intrigue, politics, and rivalry within the college context—films that are not as overwhelmingly male-centered as the earlier comedy films.

At the same time, college students are the focus of several perceived crises within Kerala, and the college has become a key site for debates about the privatization of higher education, linked to debates about globalization, consumerism, and their impact. In addition, the moral panic about college students and "college culture" focuses on the sociocultural world of young people, making the college campus and its environs an increasingly important and explicit focus of popular culture and cultural politics. These moral panics focus on what is sometimes called "cinema culture" and its impact on fashion styles and dances understood to be lewd and hypersexualized in college-sponsored fashion shows and youth festivals. These anxieties led the state government in 2005 to officially ban fashion shows, "cinematic dances," and mobile phones from college campuses in an attempt to stem the influence of consumerism and its sexualizing effects on students.[35]

On the other hand, quite apart from college students as consumers, college students as citizens form another site of public contestation. The intensity of student politics on college campuses is understood to hinder preparation for jobs within a global economy, another way in which the leftist ethos interrupts the smooth functioning of educational institutions for the development of the economy and globalization of the state. In these debates, education as a commodity to be consumed is a key focus. Throughout the 1990s in Kerala, various legal cases sought to officially ban politics from college campuses, understood as an instance of a corrupt democratic culture. Youth are to be protected from a predatory, sexualized commodity culture while being prepared for a global economy through an increasingly commoditized educational infrastructure—all the while being reconfigured as democratic citizens. All of this makes consumer citizenship among young women and men a central site for understanding globalization in Kerala.

Region, Nation, World

The notion that Kerala is an exceptional region pervades popular and scholarly understandings. Especially with respect to its development experience, the state/region has been held up as possible model for other parts of the world to follow. As I have discussed, not only does the model itself elide complex histories of caste, gender, and modernity but the discourse of Kerala as a highly developed place has been increasingly undermined by ideas about Kerala as a crisis-ridden, mass-mediated consumer society.

Arguing against the notion of exceptionalism, I have nevertheless pointed to regionally specific histories of modernity, politics, development, and migration that are an important context for understanding youth, gender, and consumer citizenship within the region. Such regional histories are part of a flexible articulation between region, nation, and globe, one that does not make Kerala exceptional but points to specificities that mediate Kerala's experiences of globalization. The young women and men who are the subjects of this book are situated at the dynamic crossroads between Kerala's development experience and larger global and national forces. In contemporary Kerala, a discourse of crisis animates this conjuncture, one that makes youth/college students, gender, and consumption central to anxious mediations and contestations about globalization. Both development and globalization have deep roots within histories of the region—histories that nevertheless persistently mediate nation and globe.

2

Fashioning
Gender and Consumption

It was Onam, an important harvest festival in Kerala.[1] The hostel where I lived, which housed female students of nearby colleges and female employees of various banks, post offices, schools, stores, and government offices in town, was celebrating the occasion. First, we "inmates," as we were called by the hostel staff, sat in rows on the floor of the common room and entrance to the hostel, while the "warden," or head of the hostel, bent down to ladle the rice and curries that make up a traditional Onam meal (sadhya) onto the banana leaves in front of us. My hostelmates met the temporary reversal of hierarchy that this entailed with giggles, a mixture of discomfort and amusement.[2] After the meal, several students presented ritual gifts of saris and cloth (onakkodi) to those who worked in the hostel—assistant warden, cook, sweeper, gardener, watchman. What we were all really waiting for, however, was the mock fashion show that the students had been preparing all week. Within the safe, semiprivatized space of the hostel, it was possible to be playful.

Ajitha sashayed out onto the makeshift stage in a "Garden Vareli" sari as a cassette player belted out the latest hits from Malayalam, Tamil, and Hindi films. This sari was a play on an expensive brand of chiffon saris in floral patterns, often worn by middle-class working women. Ajitha strutted about to much laughter in a red sari blouse that clashed with the pink synthetic sari, from which various actual leaves, stems, flowers, and branches were dangling. Aside from the "garden" on her sari, the sari itself was a source of amusement. This type of sari is often called, in a derogatory manner, "*pandi* style"—referring to the fashion of workers from the adjacent state of Tamil Nadu, who now make up a significant portion of the manual and laboring poor in Kerala. Drawing on the connotations of cheapness that the shiny synthetic sari evoked and deploying the literalness of the word *garden*, Ajitha was able to playfully subvert the status of the Garden Vareli sari as a sign of mature, middle-class female respectability. Next came Meena, who strutted across the stage in a tight yellow top and high heels, wearing "hot pants"—a pair of white trousers with dried red chilies hanging from them. Barely able to stand in the heels, she sashayed about, imitating the stereotype of a hyperwesternized upper-class woman. Following Meena, Lekha skipped across the stage in an "umbrella skirt," holding a huge open umbrella, wearing a very long and wide skirt, a fashion at the time. Tripping numerous times as she skipped, Lekha showed us the impracticality and frivolity of the skirt's design, to great comic effect. Next came Sheena, who demurely walked across the stage in a "half sari." Now out of fashion, this South Indian style used to be popular with young women who would wear it before marriage or paid employment, when they might begin to wear regular saris. The half sari consisted of a long skirt (*pavada*) and a full blouse, with cloth wrapped around the outfit (*kavani*) to resemble a sari. Sheena's version consisted of a full sari that came down only to her knees instead of her ankles. Walking demurely as she coyly showed off her bare calves and ankles, Sheena played with the persona of the good young traditional girl. Finally, there was Anjali, hair up and under a hat, a fake moustache on her upper lip, in a man's shirt. She wore "baggy pants" with four or five purses draped all over her. Prancing about with long, extended steps, chest out, sidling up lecherously to various audience members, Anjali mocked the macho persona of the fashion-conscious hip young man of the street. The show was a huge hit, amusing and to the point. Even the usually dour warden could not help herself, laughing along with us, congratulating the young students on their performances.

These young women are consumers of fashion who are able to mock the commodification and objectification of fashions and the bodily demeanors that go along with them; they are both potential consumers and commodities, subjects and objects of consumption. The oscillation between playful subversions of adult feminine personas, such as the respectable working woman in her "Garden sari" and the hypersexualized, upper-class westernized woman in "hot pants," and younger personas, such as the girl in an "umbrella skirt" or the postpubescent girl in her "half sari," carves out a middle-class space, in between girlhood and full maturity, of young feminine adulthood at the intersection of region and nation, a space intimately tied to the pleasures and dangers of fashion. The contrast between these various feminine personas and that of the strutting young man about town in his "baggy pants" point to both masculinity and femininity as a terrain of class-inflected gendered embodiments that are central to the ways in which young people navigate the public spaces of modernity and globalization. The movement between "Indian" fashions such as the sari and half sari and "western" ones such as the pants or skirt point to the importance of spatial and temporal oscillations between tradition and modernity, the West and notions of "India" and "Kerala" in the production of this gendered terrain.

However, what is being mocked here are not just specific styles and gendered personas. These young women are also playing with the very idea of youth, and young women in particular, as "fashion conscious." What is so humorously scrutinized is not only the content of the fashion show but also its very form—the idea of young people as emblematically consumerist and fashionable. Some of this scrutiny stems from many of the hostel residents' marginalization from cosmopolitan and metropolitan constructions of "modern girls" who engage in such increasingly popular things as beauty pageants and fashion shows. Largely from lower-caste, lower-class Kerala backgrounds, they are marginalized from both local and national articulations of middle-class globalized Indian femininity. In order to so humorously scrutinize the very idea of youth as fashionable and the specific personas that occupy this terrain, they move beyond consumption as a set of practices to focus on consumption itself as fetishized object; something that is created through highly objectified constructions of consumer agency. These personas become condensed and congealed signifiers of consumption itself (see Appadurai 1996, 42).

Although Ajitha, Lekha, Meena, Anjali, and Sheena could turn a critical and mischievous eye toward the dominant understanding of fashion-crazy young people, their performative playfulness is circumscribed. The contrast between the relative safety of the semiprivate hostel and the dangers of the public street, the college, or a public stage compels young women and men to behave differently in the public spaces of consumption and education—spaces that leave less room for such assertive mockery. Further, while they may be able to critique the nexus of youth and fashion in this instance, their navigations of public life require a much more careful and calibrated negotiation of the gendered styles and personas they so amusingly rendered. The gendered terrain I discuss in this chapter helps us understand the enabling and constraining conditions of possibility for women who wish to enter not only public consumer spaces but the spaces of education as well, demonstrating how globally inflected consumption becomes an axis of cultural belonging with implications for how women participate as citizens within the spaces of public life.

India's Beauty Machine

Nowhere is the gendered production of the new globalized youth more evident than the burgeoning beauty industry in India. Key moments in the celebration of India's ascendance to a new role in the global economy include the figures of Sushmita Sen, winner of the Miss Universe pageant in 1994, and Aiswarya Rai, winner of the Miss World contest in 1995, their bodies embodying India's worth on the global stage, their tiaras crowning India's attractiveness in the global market. In fact, with the crowning of Lara Dutta as Miss Universe in 2000 and Yukta Mookhey and Priyanka Chopra as Miss World in 1999 and 2000, India has become, like Venezuela and the United States, a major "beauty machine."[3]

The Miss World pageant of 1996, held in the city of Bangalore, was particularly noteworthy. The mobilization over a two-month period of

12,500 police and paramilitary personnel from city, state, and central security forces was the largest use of state power to help what was essentially a multinational private commercial venture fend off widespread protests from a diverse array of political organizations. The protests came essentially from two sides. Women's groups on the Hindu right opposed the pageant on the grounds that it would import a decadent western culture that undermines "Indian culture." In the words of Premila Nesargi, a lawyer and member of the Bharatiya Janata Party (BJP):

> There is only one common culture of Indians, irrespective of caste, creed, and sex. Our culture cannot be taken away by others, invaded. . . . In India women are not meant to be sold. Women are not treated as a commodity available for sale in the bazaar. If she sells herself, either her flesh, or body or beauty, she is offending every law in India. Commodifying a woman is wrong. You cannot reduce her to the status of a chattel. Beauty cannot be sold.[4]

The left-affiliated and independent women's groups distinguished themselves from the more conservative critics who they felt focused on a unitary and conservative notion of "Indian tradition," "a euphemism for the subordination of women." Rather they focused on the liberalization of the economy and the growing influence of multinational corporations, which they argued had created a climate in which events like beauty contests thrived, demeaning and commodifying women. Brinda Karat, general secretary of the left-affiliated All India Democratic Women's Association, brings a class and gender perspective to bear on the pageant:

> Copycat contests are being organized in neighborhoods across the country. The growing obsession with "looking good" is not a reflection of the growing confidence of the independent-minded "modern miss" . . . nor is it a reflection of "free choice." . . . This constitutes oppressive pressure on young middle class women and distorts their self-worth. The processes of a new type of socialization driven by the market mantra impose stereotypes that are as oppressive and degrading for women as the earlier stereotype of the *pativrata*. . . . With the advent of policies of globalization and liberalization there has been an unprecedented increase in the efforts of the beauty industry to

create a market for its products. . . . There are clear links between globalization and the accelerated commodification of women. . . . The contest was an insult to the vast masses of India's women, who struggle to make both ends meet and are deprived of the right to a decent human life. If there is beauty it is in their courage.[5]

The pageant and such commentary on it demonstrated that consumption is not only one half of a capitalist system but also a discursive site for contesting and imagining the Indian nation in the era of liberalization. This discursive site, which markets to and constitutes a consumer-driven middle class oriented toward the global economy, is centrally imagined through the bodies of young middle-class females. While the beauty contestants themselves illustrate this, the Canadian-born host of the pageant, Ruby Bhatia Bali, brings together the "global teen" and the nonresident Indian (NRI)—two sites for fetishized images of consumer agency—to represent globalizing India.[6] In fact, Bali was a "veejay" on Channel V, India's counterpart to MTV, which also featured Sophiya, a British Indian, and Kamla, a U.S. Indian.[7] Marked by fashionable clothes and an aggressive public persona, speaking their respectively accented English, with occasional forays into exaggeratedly accented Indian English and broken Hindi for comic effect, they personify and market the NRI lifestyle for the new consumer in India. The crucial point to note is this: these veejays are not white Canadians, Americans, or Britons.[8] On the other hand, neither are they children of less affluent migrants to places like the Persian Gulf. The selective appropriation of the diasporic experience of migrants to industrialized, "first-world" destinations not only marks an important aspect of the class character of that particular diaspora itself but points to the class-specific, highly gendered stakes of producing a new consumer subject within India. This production hinges on an equation between youth and fashion that is crucially tied to the female form.

Protests of the beauty pageant contested the construction of this figure through a demonization of consumption, linked to the commodification of women's bodies. The Hindu right and left-feminist perspectives are obviously different in important respects. The conservative position rests on a deployment of tradition that masks gender oppression and patriarchy within as well as outside India. Like cultural nationalists of the late nineteenth century that Partha Chatterjee has discussed, these nationalists of the Hindu right place women under the sign of a privatized tradition that must be defended against the corruption of western materialism. The left-feminist perspective rejects Indian culture as patriarchal. Yet it also rejects simplistic identifications of modernity with the space of women's freedom. This modernity, rooted in the structures of patriarchy and capitalism, collaborates with the patriarchy of continuously reinvented tradition to produce new forms of gender oppression. Both positions, however, are operating in tandem in their rejections of the commodification of women. For the Hindu right, this commodification is associated with an invasive, alien, foreign culture. For the feminists, it is associated with an imperialist form of capitalist oppression. This is an oppression that differentially affects the "modern miss" and those who cannot afford beauty products.

The messy alignments between the Hindu right and leftist feminists around the protests to this pageant reveal the complicated terrain upon which Indian feminism is confronting globalization. Critics of the feminist position have focused on two aspects of the protests against the beauty pageant.[9] First, the feminist position renders transparent the process of commodification, leaving the feminist critique of the pageant outside the circuits of global capitalism. Simply blaming commodification on the West assumes that there is a noncommodified, primordial space, something easily naturalized as the space of tradition within the Hindu nationalist position (John 1998). A more critically engaged interrogation of the actual process of commodification might reveal a more complicated analysis of the dynamics of the beauty industry, something that might enable the beginning of a more nuanced and differentiated political vocabulary. Second, Menon (2004) criticizes the dependence of the protests on nationalism, either culturally or economically understood. The Hindu right's collapsing of anti-imperialism with cultural nationalism was couched in an emotive language that was difficult to address and hard to resist, and cultural nationalism in turn became conflated with the economic nationalism that many on the left relied on to protest the pageant. Further, Niranjana urges us to pay attention to the question of why women's bodies became such a rallying cry for antiglobalization politics (1999). Not only do these processes target women and girls but they also put on public display the "normed upper-class female body," central to the historical consolidation of Indian nationalism. This element of nationalism was not scrutinized by feminists. Recognizing the ways in which women bear the burden of authenticity and the centrality of this role in the operations of nationalism becomes imperative for understanding the dynamics of globalization in India.

What these criticisms do point to is that a rejection of commodification as "western," something that both the Hindu right and the leftist feminists relied on in their critiques of global capitalism, depends on spaciotemporal grids distinguishing India from the West, and tradition from modernity, that are often worked through the figure of the ideal Indian woman. Rather than examine and critique these grids as part of the process of commodification itself, feminists fell in with the Hindu right in relying on such distinctions for the articulation of their position on beauty pageants, thereby relying on an uncritical nationalist platform. Further, the pageant itself relied upon globalized standards of beauty and femininity that simultaneously index locality, as can be seen, for example, in the celebration of these pageant contestants as national heroines. A straightforward dismissal of the pageant as "western" fails to address the ways in which these beauty regimes rely on their own nationalist constructions.

Protests against the pageant took the form of mock "queens" crowned "Miss Disease" and "Miss Starvation" in order to point to basic priorities, such as alleviating poverty and providing health care, from which the state had been retreating while lending tremendous support to this consumer-oriented private venture. The privatization of the state and its withdrawal from social welfare provision under new regimes of economic liberalization are certainly important rallying points for a politics of globalization. However, this form of protest skirts the critical task of examining beauty as a structure of gender, class- and caste-based aspirations, and anxieties; and it also fails to address a feminist politics to young middle-class women, the "modern miss" (John 1998). An insistence on considering the vast majority of women who cannot afford beauty products and who struggle to make both ends meet is an inadequate response to the realities of the ideological and political terrain, marked by an expanding consumer culture across caste and class distinctions, that Indian feminism must now confront.

The recent proliferation of fashion shows and beauty pageants—often sponsored by colleges, youth organizations, stores, and other commercial ventures—and the attempts by the state, educational institutions, and political organizations of the Hindu right and the feminist left to ban or curb their presence inside and outside college spaces have made youth fashion an emblematic and highly objectified instance of gendered consumer culture tied to globalization.

In fact, a shorthand way to mark the advent and impact of globalization more widely is to point to the evidence of "global" youth consuming practices and symbols in often remote corners of the world: the popularity of the basketball star Michael Jordan and his team the Chicago Bulls during the 1990s in the slums of Brazil and in rural villages in Africa, the spread of hip-hop music around the world, and the popularity of McDonald's among young people in China. These examples have a theory of globalization and youth embedded within them: youth is a consuming social group, the first to bend to what is understood to be the homogenizing pressures of globalization, a globalization fundamentally tied to Americanization.[10] Youth consumption practices index the presence and reach of globalization. That fashion shows are available for mockery by my hostelmates and that the state government has attempted to ban them from college events reveals fashion as a highly objectified and potent terrain of cultural distinction for young people, one tied to a moral panic about the onslaught of a global consumer culture, and especially about what women wear.

However, these ways of indexing the salience of contemporary forms of globalization obscure the ways in which new global cultural forms are inserted into struggles over the meaning of modernity in many postcolonial locations.[11] In the context of India, an understanding of the dynamic relationship between youth, consumption, and globalization requires an interrogation of the conditions under which young people engage new spaces of consumption. These conditions are profoundly shaped by long-standing colonialist and nationalist preoccupations with westernization, tradition, and modernity. Globalization works through strategic images of consumer agency that rely on notions of "India" to fashion a young, globally oriented middle-class Indian femininity. If a feminist critique of consumerism and globalization is to distinguish itself from nationalist anticapitalist critiques, of either the cultural or economic variety, it must produce a critical account of the production and circulation of these spaciotemporal grids, so as to reveal and interrogate what I call the "burden of locality" placed on femininity in processes of commodification. Rather than oscillate between the fact of the commodification of young women's bodies by global consumer culture on the one hand, or too simple an argument about the agency of young women within this culture on the other, I draw attention to how globalizing consumer culture is manifest within Kerala through highly selective discourses and constructions of consumer agency that mediate the boundaries between tradition and modernity, the West and the non-West, the public and the private for young women and men in ways that are both enabling and constraining.

Locating Fashion

It seems commonsensical now to say that clothing styles and the bodily demeanors that go along with them become an entry into a world of fashioning gender for young people that is central to the ways in which they navigate new spaces of consumption.[12] This navigation is both fluid and structured, revealing genders and the spaces they operate in to be both enabling and constraining. But this understanding, and these embodied practices, have both a politics and a history: part of the rise of consumer culture, they are the current products of long debates over the role of clothing and the idea of the individual.

Studies of consumption within Europe point to many factors that define the nature of what is called "the consumer revolution" (Miller 1994; Bourdieu 1984; De Grazia 2005). Without getting into the competing explanations for what conditions led to the expansion of consumption within Europe or what the full contours of such a history might look like within India, one large-scale shift is important for the analysis here: a shift from a society organized according to sumptuary laws to a society organized around fashion (Appadurai 1996). This shift entails the gradual replacement of overt regulations on dress, based on ascriptive categories such as age, gender, community, and class, with ideas of choice and change, marked by a more generalized desire to consume.[13] The emphasis on choice and change as a key feature of fashion, which ties it intimately to theorizations about modernism and modernity within the

West, needs to be situated within the larger contours of debates about westernization, tradition, and modernity that characterize the history of clothing styles within India (Tarlo 1996). While differences in fabric, design, and cost can create a whole world of distinction, individuation, and choice within a particular style of dress—for example, the respectable chiffon "Garden sari" as opposed to the cheap "*pandi* style" synthetic sari—decisions about different clothing *styles* are structured by a politics of culture tied to debates about westernization and cultural authenticity that is highly gendered.

In an insightful article that traces the emergence of new discourses of the body and interiority in Malayalam literature, Udaya Kumar discusses the transformations of the late nineteenth century in Kerala with regard to clothing (1997). As has been discussed, caste was a primary source of differentiation. Clothing, along with jewelry, hairstyle, naming, food, and bodily gestures, constituted a sign system that regulated bodies in public. As Kumar notes, "The spectacle of the body in public spaces was replete with caste markers" (1997, 248). Within this context, what became known as the "breast cloth controversy" reveals how clothing gets transformed in the context of colonial modernity in Kerala.[14] One caste regulation involved a prohibition on lower-caste women wearing an upper cloth (*melmundu*), the preserve of upper-caste women on special occasions, to cover their breasts. European missionaries who were converting lower-caste members to Christianity encouraged their converts, in the name of Victorian notions of modesty, to wear a "jacket blouse," similar to what Syrian Christian women wore. In the 1850s, Christian converts began to wear the upper cloth in addition to blouses, a direct challenge to upper-caste norms. This led to tensions between upper-caste and lower-caste communities as they struggled over the changing nature of caste relations. Kumar notes that by the end of the nineteenth century, the blouse ceases to be a simple caste marker and emerges as an object of fashion, something to be personally and aesthetically enjoyed as part of a fashion sensibility (249–50).

This dismantling of the sumptuary and the emergence of a fashion sensibility during the colonial period is an important moment in the genealogy of fashion. However, debates about fashion and style during the colonial period also reveal the insertion of questions of fashion and clothing styles into a new set of contentious debates about tradition and modernity, community and nation; the rise of a fashion sensibility is not simply about choice, change, and variability, though those are entangled within the elaboration of clothing styles. The example of the "breast cloth controversy" is a case in point. The blouse as an object of aesthetic pleasure emerges in a contested reworking of caste relations in the context of colonial modernity that is written onto the female body.

Within a larger context, histories of cloth and clothing in colonial India have demonstrated that dress underwent an important set of transformations for both men and women (Tarlo 1996). At the height of the nationalist period, the most spectacular example of the politicization of clothing is khadi (homespun cloth), the production and wearing of which Gandhi made central to Indian nationalism. Within the realm of the everyday, the contours of these transformations involve changing attempts to define what is Indian and what is western through dress: how to sartorially mark the boundaries of work and education within the modern colonial spaces of office and school, while reformulating what home and the family meant. For men, the adoption of European-style dress in public was easier than it was for women. The debate about what constitutes proper dress for women became a key site for working out new definitions of community and nation. Within Bengal, the dress of the bhadramahila (respectable lady) of the middle classes was extensively debated before the brahmika sari (a form of wearing the sari in combination with blouse, petticoat, and shoes) became accepted as a standard for middle-class women. As Himani Banerjee notes, the sartorial recasting of women within the Bengali middle class involved much more than the introduction of a fashion sensibility (1991). The debate about women's fashion involved a cultural-ideological reworking of the role of women within the community, one that tied the question of women's dress to the dynamics of anticolonial Indian nationalism.

Fashion, style, and consumption have become important sites and metaphors through which we understand the processes of identity formation. They form a terrain of youth fashion, at the intersection of region, nation, and world, tied to embodiments of masculinity and femininity—an intersection that mediates young men and women's differential navigations of consumer and educational spaces.

Masculine Anxieties

An important concept for understanding the association between youth, masculinity, and new forms of consumption in the Malayalam language is derived from a slang word, *chethu*.[15] While it can refer to the stylish nature of many commodities and in some sense can refer to the notion of "being fashionable" in general, it refers most significantly to a kind of commodified masculinity.[16] If a male is dressed in a new pair of jeans and fancy sneakers, he is usually called *chethu*, which literally refers to the activities of slicing, cutting, and slashing and also the traditional low-caste occupation of toddy tapping and the tapper's knife; figuratively it means "sharp," "cool," "hip," or "shiny," something like "cutting-edge."[17] A fancy car, a stylish house, or a new motorbike are all *chethu*. A store dedicated to selling fashionable clothes in town was named Chethu. A fashionable young man is *chethu*, but women rarely are. If a woman dresses in a particularly fashionable way (especially if she is wearing a western-style skirt), she is said to have *gema*, a term that connotes arrogance—something between being a "showoff" and being "stuck up." A young man is rarely described as having *gema*.

One of the more fashion-conscious young men in the college interpreted his sense of *chethu* for me during a long, rambling interview. I never saw Devan in anything but jeans or baggy pants, an oversized shirt that went down to his knees, sneakers, and often a baseball cap with *Boss* emblazoned on it. Somewhat the class clown, he was a curious mixture of anxieties. He came from a lower-middle-class Ezhava family in town. As he tells it, he had been a good student in his well-disciplined Christian school. College was a different story. He did not want to study engineering or medicine, as his parents wanted, saying he found the subjects boring. He had an interest in the civil service. According to Devan, that meant studying something like history, English, or political science, subjects he surmised would give him the writing skills and knowledge necessary to pass the civil service exams. As history was "just the study of dates," he dismissed it. He stated that if one were to study English for the exams, he would need a very high quality of English education from extremely elite schools such as the Doons School or Delhi Public School.[18] English seemed risky given where he was coming from: a marginal college, in a backwater town, in southern Kerala.

So, from his perspective, that left political science, which was what he was studying.

However, he was not very serious about college. He blamed a bad crowd he fell in with when he first got to college, going to three or four movies a week, hanging out at the beach, and spending time at the public library reading Mills and Boons romance novels for titillation. He was affectionately known by his friends as "Mr. Quote" because, as I found out, he punctuated much of his speech with quotes in English, from sources as divergent as Dale Carnegie's *How to Win Friends and Influence People* and Gandhi. Explaining the effect of falling in with the wrong crowd, Devan said, "You are the company you keep." On the importance of friendship, he quoted Gandhi: "True friendship is a rare one. It is the identity of two souls." Caught between his bourgeois aspirations and his desire to have fun, Devan presented a humorous, anxious set of observations on his life and the meaning of being young.

Devan told me that you needed to be *chethu* in order to matter in his college: "It's the *chethu* style: jeans, a Yamaha bike [he had only a bicycle]. You need to have six or seven jeans, Killer jeans [a brand name]. You need four or five cotton shirts, three to four T-shirts, a well-groomed, *chethu*, smart look. A bike. You must have a bike." Having delineated the minimum material requirements for a *chethu* style, Devan went on to describe the masculine persona that signifies and is signified by this style of commodified masculinity by describing some fine nuances. A less common term often used interchangeably with *chethu* is *ash-push*—a term that many said came from English, or the sound of English as it was heard by Malayalam speakers.

> It's just a matter of intensity. *Ash-push* is much more intense than *chethu*. *Ash-push* . . . a life that is in the *chethu* way, you enjoy life. You go to a beer parlor and have beer, that is *ash-push*. A Yamaha bike, money in the hand, a *line* [slang for a relationship with a girl], that's it, in between you go to a beer parlor and you sip two beers, you have plenty of friends, you enjoy life. You enjoy the life. You don't care about what has happened yesterday. You don't care what will happen tomorrow. You are always happy. That is *chethu*.

This notion of *chethu* encompasses within it several aspects of a youthful, commodified masculinity that brings together clothing styles, status, and an attitude about the world based on ephemerality and some notion of fun.

Devan's narrative reveals the aspiration and anxiety that underlie his desire for Yamaha motorbikes, Killer jeans, T-shirts, and beer parlors. One way of contextualizing Devan's reflections and his persona is to link them with the analysis of a film, *Kaadalan* (Loverboy), that was enormously popular with Devan, his friends, and college students in general. In an article about this important Tamil film, Dhareshwar and Niranjana point to new forms of youthful, commodified masculinity produced within this new moment of liberalization (1996). *Kaadalan* helped create a new youth style and aesthetics characterized by *ragga*-inspired clothing (baggy pants, oversized shirts, sneakers, pony tails), rap music, and Michael Jackson dance moves that have come to be the referents for a fashion-conscious sensibility among low-caste young men. Devan's style directly borrowed from this film and other Malayalee variants such as *Street* (see Osella and Osella 2000b). The video and music cassettes of these movies, and those of the *ragga* musician Apache Indian, a UK-born Indian musician popular in the UK, the Caribbean, and India, were the hottest-selling items at many music stores in and around the college. Hit songs from the movie were standard fare at college and youth festivals. Perhaps the hit of the 1990s, this film marked the beginning of a new aesthetic in film, combining MTV-style shots, dance sequences, and rap.

Set in a college-student milieu, as Dhareshwar and Niranjana argue, the film reconfigures the young lower-caste male body, in the figure of its star Prabhu Deva, to mediate globalization, the violence of the state, and the demands of tradition. Under the sign of "fashion" indicated by his desire for blue jeans and sneakers, the body is refashioned as urban and consumerist. This kind of fashioning had previously usually been reserved for the upper-caste male body, as seen in the important and popular films *Roja* (1992) and *Bombay* (1995) directed by Mani Ratnam, in which the space of liberalization is produced through the bodies of upper-class, upper-caste Hindu forms of masculinity and femininity.[19] Previously, it was under the rubric of the "folk" and the "rural" that the lower-caste body had been configured. This film marks an important moment in which globalization and its signifiers attach themselves to the body of the lower-caste, lower-class male.

However, the commodification of the lower-caste male body is not the only element of the chethu style. Devan's reflections on what it takes to achieve a chethu style focus significantly on key commodities and their number, such as six to seven pairs of Killer jeans, four to five cotton shirts, three to four T-shirts, the crucial and expensive motorbike, along with a line—a romance with a girl. Further, this style is about having friends and drinking beer in a beer parlor, which points to assertion and public forms of sociality. The lower-caste male body is commodified through fashion but is also a consuming subject marked by an aspiration for the good life.

An important component of the chethu style is the consumption of public space itself. Other than the requisite jeans, shirts, sneakers, and the all-important bike, Devan insisted that you needed to have money in your hand. When I asked him why, he said it was to karangan. Karanguga can be glossed as "to wander about," "to gallivant." One needs money in order to consume in public. But it implies more than the material ability to participate in spaces of public consumption. Key to this notion is the aimless quality of this mobility—aimless in terms of not having a specific place to go to and also not having a specific goal to accomplish. It implies an ephemerality with respect to both space and time. As he stated, part of having a certain kind of chethu style was an attitude oriented toward the present, not the past or future. When folded into the idea of "wandering about," it implies a kind of aimlessness with regard to not only the past and future but space as well. Therefore, whether the space was the actual college campus, or a beer parlor, movie theater, park, beach, restaurant, ice cream parlor, or bus stand, it was fodder for wandering about. And what was the reason for going to any of those places? The answer would invariably be chumma—for "no reason."

Often, this past and future that one is trying to hold at bay are related to obligations and aspirations—to study, work hard, succeed. Here is Devan describing his desired future:

> My idea of the good life is that you must have a lot of money. Per month, you must get ten to fifteen thousand rupees per month. You must have that. You will see. Living is not just eating. I do like traveling. Prices are skyrocketing. For example, all want to have one car. On average, you can spend two thousand rupees on maintenance of a car. Then there is food, housing, social gatherings, like that. If you want to live and have some savings, at least ten

thousand per month. You see, lots of modern things are coming into our life, like pagers. Life is too short. You must have ten thousand per month. Then, a good woman. If you have money, naturally, all other things will come. Certainly, it will certainly come. If you have a good job and you are drawing this much salary, like that, you can marry from a well-to-do family, I don't mean top-class, but middle-class, like that. You will naturally get a good woman like that. And you can enjoy life.

This movement from the present to the future, in which one is trying to transform the ephemeral enjoyment of consuming in a chethu way in the present into an upwardly mobile and secure form of middle-class consumption in the future, is a precarious journey, something that makes this chethu style problematic. Devan goes on to describe what he calls the "positive and negative aspects" of being chethu, expressing his worries about making such a transformation:

> You have to speak in a chethu style [chethu rithiyil samsaram] and you have to have chethu relations. You are good company for everyone. Then, you study well. If you have all this, then you can say that you have a positive chethu style. But there is also a negative side. You don't care about what has happened yesterday. You don't care what will happen tomorrow. You don't have aim, but you are always happy. That is chethu. There is a negative side. You throw away work and you become chethu. What I mean is that you will walk in a chethu style. But you degrade yourself sometimes. The positive side of chethu is that you should know about what you should do—work. But then you use life as if it's sand. You don't care how much sand came here or how much is there. You don't care what will come in the future and what has come in the past. You will just think about how the sands are flowing now. You only care about the present thing.

All of this reveals many of Devan's own anxieties about having had a little too much fun in college. Approaching the end of his college days, unsure about what to do next, remembering when he did work hard in school, wondering how he was going to make his ambitions of the good life materialize, he wondered about the limitations of aspiring to be chethu as the past, present, and future weighed heavily on his mind.

Devan's aspirations for and anxieties about achieving the good life mediate the many forces that structure his life—his social origins, his education, the space of youth as pleasure and consumption, and the horizon of getting a job, setting up a household, and being a bread-winner. He most immediately aspires to the pleasures of consumption, marked by ephemerality and fun. This present is marked by the pleasures of self-fashioning and the consumption and traversal of public space. While trying to hold past and future at bay, he is plagued by the enor-mous task of having to turn his educated and aspiring self into a model of middle-class stability, respectability, and consumption in the future that is his imagined adulthood.

The three to four movies he sees every week are invariably the youth-oriented "comedy films" that came to prominence in the late 1980s and 1990s in Malayalam cinema.[20] Drawing on the work of Rowena (2002), in the previous chapter I discussed how these films mark the emergence of a competitive and differentiated terrain of masculinities in the 1990s across the caste/class spectrum which she links to the influence of Gulf migration, the rise of consumerism, and the crisis of employment. Here, it is important to note that the masculinity of *chethu* is an assertive and aspiring lower-caste, lower-class masculinity that lays claim to the public through consumption. It is marked by precariousness and vulnerability, both in terms of its lower caste and class social location and the wider world of acute unemployment in Kerala. In the broader consumer cul-ture of Kerala during the 1990s, this masculinity sits at the intersec-tion between the developmental state that educates students like Devan and globalization that structures his consumer-oriented visions of the good life.

Feminine Resolutions?

What is the relationship between femininity and these globally inflected spaces of consumption within Kerala? Again, we can begin to grasp the structures of representation that mark feminine engagements with these new spaces through an analysis of films. While it was rare for the hostel residents to go to films multiple times in a week because of evening curfews, we did manage to occasionally see a film at a theater. We also occasionally watched films within the hostel if we could convince the warden. While some of the films we saw were the youth-oriented comedy films I have been discussing, others were of the more standard type, focusing on family melodrama. The figuration of the young adolescent girl in two such films illuminates the structures of youthful femininity through which consumption and globalization are mediated.

One film we saw within the hostel focuses on a diasporic family of Christian origin; the other, which we saw in a theater, features a Hindu family in a Kerala village. Spanning communities and locales both within Kerala and its diaspora, the resolutions to the crises facing both families converge on the young female form. The key figure for the mediations of globalization is not the lower-caste, lower-class male, as in the film *Kaadalan*, but the upper-caste, upper-class female. These movies take us back to the construction of the "modern miss" struggled over in the politics of the beauty pageant. However, while that representation of a globalized middle-class Indian femininity was a highly contested celebration of an aggressive, sexualized young woman in public, these films reveal the specifically Kerala mediation of that nationally inflected construction, one that is much more ambivalent and regulated. I highlight the productions and burdens of locality at the intersection of region, nation, and globe. The highly articulate and contested politics, on the part of the Hindu right and the feminist left, that marked the staging of the Miss Universe pageant reveals one form of antiglobalization politics. Here, a more diffuse and persistent cultural politics of globalization draws on masculine anxieties about modernity in order to raise the specter of a young woman run amuck in public, one who is eventually brought back into the fold.

In the Malayalam feature film *Dollar* (dir. Joseph, 1993), notable for having been filmed in both Kerala and New York, a Syrian Christian family from the central district of Kottayam struggles with the displacements of migration. The story focuses on a grandmother who goes to New York to visit her son and his family. Amid wide-eyed encounters with escalators, dazzling shopping malls, and the New York subway system, the grandmother bears witness to the disintegration of "family life" (*kudumba jivam*) in America. This disintegration turns decisively on the behavior of the women of the family. The daughter-in-law is a greedy, well-paid nurse who controls the purse strings of the family. Besides making more money than her husband and controlling him, her ultimate act of transgression involves hitting the grandmother in a fit of rage. The couple has a teenage son, a teenage daughter, and a ten-year-old daughter. The rebellious, miniskirt-clad teenage daughter has an African American boyfriend with whom she is seen cavorting in bars and nightclubs, a narrative trope that relies on a racialized imagination of America as a space of criminality and vice. Unable to engage her own son, who is wrestling with his wife for control of the family helm, and unable to talk to the rebellious and incomprehensible teenage daughter (who speaks no Malayalam), the only one the grandmother can talk to is the teenage son (for some reason he does speak Malayalam)—who, while tempted by gangs and drugs, nevertheless listens to his grandmother's lectures. In the end, the African American boyfriend takes the elder daughter hostage and the good son dies trying to save his sister. In the final scene, the father, unable to bear what his family has come to, entrusts his youngest daughter, clad in the *pavada* (full-length skirt) and blouse characteristic of South Indian dress for young girls, to his mother, telling her to take the girl back to Kerala, where she will be raised in the "traditional [*naden*] way."

In the Malayalam feature *Pavithram* (Purity) (dir. Kumar, 1994) Kerala—as a space of the traditional—is in trouble. This is the story of the disruption of a traditional Nair (*taravadu*) household. The first half of the film takes place in a *taravadu*-style house in a village. A baby girl has just been born to a middle-aged couple with two grown sons. The good son, played by the foremost male star of Malayalam cinema, Mohan Lal, remains in the village, while the elder son, a college-educated doctor, lives in town. Tragically, the mother dies in childbirth. Unable to cope with the loss of his beloved wife, the father hands over control of the raising of his baby daughter to the good son. The daughter, Cochu ("little one"), grows up living a simple, idyllic village life with her *chetachan*, a term she herself has coined, which combines *chetan* (meaning "elder brother") and *achan* (meaning "father"). The first half of the movie shows Cochu growing up in this space of tradition. Toward the end of the first half, the space is marked by a scene in which a puberty ritual to mark the onset of Cochu's menstruation (*tirantukuli*) is celebrated by the women of the village. The second half of the movie shifts to the city, where Cochu has been sent to be with her childless sister-in-law and other older brother (after much debate) and where she is to attend college. The sister-in-law, who functions like an aunt, immediately goes to work on Cochu, buying her skirts, jeans, and cosmetics. She instructs Cochu to stop wearing the full-length *pavada* skirt and blouse that mark a traditional regional style for young women and encourages her to go have fun. The rest of the movie follows Cochu's decline as she wins a college beauty contest and comes under the influence of a hard-drinking, rowdy bunch of male students. Eventually, she returns in disgrace to her beloved *chetachan* in the village where, immediately upon arrival, she switches from her skirt to the *pavada* as an act of contrition.

These films provide some sense of how contemporary Malayalam cinema represents the "traditional" and the "modern." Much can be said about the cultural politics of this cinema. For example, film criticism has pointed to the emergence of a potent mix of patriarchy and Nair nostalgia, which is repeatedly deployed to create notions of *Keraleeyatha*, or a collective cultural memory defined in upper-caste Nair terms—one linked to Hindu revivalism in the state (Ramachandran 1995). Therefore, while movies of the late 1960s and 1970s might have stereotyped the collective past of Kerala in terms of a generic peasantry rooted in "village" Kerala, now that "village" is understood as the space of Nair-ness and is thereby upper-caste and Hindu. Further, anthropological celebrations of matriliny notwithstanding, that Nair past is rendered in decidedly patriarchal terms. As G. Arunima argues, "As the cultural nostalgia is cast in distinctly masculine terms, so is the anxiety related to it. Memory here is often an act of gendered erasure, with Nayar women slowly and silently fading away in a world of masculine desire and intrigue" (1995, 165).

Nowhere is this more stark than in *Pavithram*, which literally erases the mother, through her death, thus making Cochu the object of her brother-father's prerogatives. The only remaining Nair woman of significance is the city-bred sister-in-law/aunt who leads Cochu down a path of corruption. This kind of cultural memory is also evident in the film *Dollar*. Not straightforwardly nostalgic for a Nair past, within the spatial imaginary of Kerala's diaspora, the crisis of family and culture links the *pavada*-clad body of the young girl to the idea of Kerala as the space of tradition. In both these films, the production of locality onto the female form becomes key to narrative resolution.

The films *Dollar* and *Pavithram* both make the *pavada* and the skirt central, marking two poles in the inscription of the "traditional" and the "modern" onto the female body. The overall trajectories and the specific twists of the movies' plots move between the two extremes that constitute this binary. In the case of *Dollar*, the ravages wrought by the miniskirt-clad, sexualized, westernized, "modern" elder daughter are trumped by the *pavada*-clad, "traditional" (*naden*) younger daughter. In *Pavithram*, a village girl becomes dangerously modern but comes back again to her traditional ways—a transformation marked by an oscillation in fashion from *pavada* to skirt and then to *pavada* again. The representational absence of the *churidar*-clad female body in these movies marks the ideological absence of any possibility for a viable compromise. Moving between the two extremes of the *naden* and the "modern," instantiated in the *pavada* and the skirt, respectively, these movies fail to represent what might be designated as "the demure modern," the *churidar*-clad female body that is otherwise pervasive in schools, streets, shops, and offices. The masculinity-obsessed anxieties about modernity that drive such cinematic representations either produce an utterly privatized traditional girl or a dangerously transgressive girl running amok in the publicity of modernity.

Dominant representations drape women's bodies with the tropes of the traditional and the modes of the modern, as this brief consideration of recent Malayalam popular cinema demonstrates. But, increasingly, in the public spaces of contemporary Kerala—streets, shops, schools, and offices—young women, whether students, professionals, clerical workers, or shopgirls, neither wear the *pavada*-blouse combination nor commonly wear skirts or jeans. The dress of choice is the *churidar* (what might otherwise be called the *salwar kameez*), comprising trousers worn with a long top that usually goes to the knees.[21] The wearing of the *churidar* among young unmarried women, and now increasingly younger girls as well as recently married women, has increased dramatically in the last fifteen years. Associated with North India, the *churidar* has been understood as a prominent example of an increasing North Indian hegemony and the displacement of a regional identity, and one that interrupts the more simple binarism of the "traditional" and "modern" in women's fashions in Kerala.

The *churidar* came to Kerala in much the same way the one-piece sari did in the 1930s and after: first the dress of "fashionable" middle-class women, it became increasingly popular among women of other classes intent on claiming a place for themselves in a specifically "Indian" modern public.[22] For upper-caste, upper-class women, the one-piece sari, draped over the right shoulder in the *nivi* style, which has become the dominant national style, displaced caste-marked and community-marked clothing.[23] For young women today, wearing the *churidar*, as opposed to the *pavada*, is a matter of adorning themselves in the clothing of an "Indian" public—one that takes them out of a *pavada*-clad *nadu* and yet protects them from the rampant sexualization of a "western"-identified, skirt-clad modernity.

As I discussed in the previous chapter, despite the construction of the private/public dichotomy, women increasingly began to move in the public spaces of modernity, especially starting in the 1920s. The construction of separate spheres did not, of course, mean that women did not traverse these boundaries. Several scholars have drawn attention to notions of "respectability" and "modesty" through which this traversal was made possible.[24] The contemporary wearing of the *churidar* is an embodiment of such notions of modesty in the fashioning of a modern femininity—one that enables and yet circumscribes women's participation in the public. However, the modern public at stake here is a specific, nationally inflected one, an often bemoaned fact within popular discourses about the increasing popularity of the *churidar*.[25] In discussions of the perceived threat to Kerala's regional identity, the displacement of the *pavada* by the *churidar* is a key indicator that North Indian hegemony is spreading through Hindi movies and Hindi-language satellite television.

Students at the college revealed to me the demure modernity of the *churidar* during the early days of my stay in the hostel. With respect to clothing styles, I had to contend with the stereotype of the foreign-returned, hyperwesternized, nonresident Indian woman. Early on, male students who came to know of my presence in the college as someone who had come from the United States would shoot comments my way mimicking my American accent or asking why I was not wearing a mini-skirt. Slightly older than many of the students with whom I worked, I sought to sidestep the stereotype by taking on the status of *chechy*, or elder sister. This made possible my role as a kind of confidante to many young women, initially a somewhat curious and exotic outsider who had few ties to the social networks around them, which made me relatively easy to talk to. Being a *chechy* also made possible a safe, generally innocuous, sometimes joking relationship with young men that helped me to navigate the terrain of male-female interaction. Sartorially, what this meant was that I rarely wore saris, because that identified me too closely with female teachers. Dressed in simple cotton *churidars* that were not too fancy, and never in western-style skirts or jeans, I sought to inhabit the relatively respectable role of the modern and demure young woman. My dress was a subject of some discussion, especially among young women. Some approvingly commented on the fact that I did not "show off" and walk around with *gema* like others who had come back from abroad. Others would sometimes get annoyed with my overcompensation. Why could I not wear something that was nice for once? When was I going to dress like the person I was? Surely, being foreign-returned, I could afford to buy something other than *khadi* cotton? What was wrong with wearing a pair of jeans?

Dressed in a *churidar*, I would walk with my fellow hostelmates to college. After several days, one of my friends came up and informed me that I had to learn how to walk correctly. When I told her I did not understand what she meant, she went on to explain that I walked in an "open" (*thuranna*) way: I would look around and peer at people walking by and at things on the road. Sternly, she told me that this might be acceptable in Chicago, but not in that town. She told me that it would invite *comment adi*—the pervasive practice of men "hitting" women with sexual comments as they walk or ride by on roads, at bus stops and train stations, on buses and in trains. She said I should walk straight, I should not look around so much, I should look ahead of me and slightly down, and I should carry my bag and books close to my body. In short, I should walk in an *oudhukam* way. The Malayalam term *oudhukam* can mean "contained" or "closed." I gloss the term here as "demure." I had to learn to properly traverse the public in a demure manner. In public spaces, I would have to be responsible for my own containment.

There is no simple correspondence between the wearing of the *churidar* and being demure, as I found out. However, the force of the "demure modern" is that it is both demure and modern. A young woman wearing a *pavada* could certainly walk in an *oudhukam* manner but could not claim modernity in the same way. Likewise, a woman in a skirt could walk as demurely as she wanted, but she would still be "modern" in a way that would leave her inescapably vulnerable to aggressive male behavior. The *churidar* provides no simple safeguard, but it qualifies its own modernity with the kind of demure self-containment that enables young women to move through public spaces with some measure of circumscribed confidence. Here, however, let me insist on the instability of the category of a "demure modern," one that mirrors the ever-present instability and vulnerability of a woman in public.

So far, this discussion has focused on the *naden*, the *oudhukam*, and the "modern" as they are embodied through women's clothing and as they respectively index spatialized notions of a traditional memory specific to Kerala, a specifically Indian national modern, or a dangerously sexualized "West." Until now, the distinctly spaciotemporal character of each of these categories has remained largely implicit. But any discussion of these terms (*naden, oudhukam, modern*) must also reveal the space-time dynamics that instructively demonstrate the stark inscription of the contestations of modernity on the female body.

Naden—the pervasive term for "traditional"—comes from the word *nadu*, which in Malayalam usually refers to "native place" or "home."[26] A profoundly locational concept, it can be applied only to someone who is understood to be where he or she does not belong. To ask somebody where their *nadu* is (an ubiquitous question when one is first introduced to someone) implies that they are understood to be from someplace else. In the spatial configurations of Kerala's geography, it can also refer to the "interior" or the "countryside" (*naden purethu*). It is in this way that *nadu* as "native place" comes to be taken as "village" more generically. Insofar as the term refers both to place of origin and the traditional (*naden rithi*—the traditional way), the adjective *naden* therefore can only make sense along a space-time grid that maps "native places" onto "traditional" time. And in the logic of nostalgic memory, *nadu* points to another place and another time. The term *modern* is a similar term. Conventionally understood as the marker of a temporal break, the mutual imbrication of the projects of modernity and colonialism has produced a space-time dynamic where the relations between the non-West and the West are mapped onto a distinction between the past and a present-future. So, *modern* simultaneously refers to that present-future and the "West." Thus, for example, an anxiously modern male subject in the film *Pavithram* expels a *pavada*-clad female body from a place in the present to which it cannot with certainty belong, into a "traditional" past constituted by and also constitutive of its location in Kerala's *nadu*/village; simultaneously, a female body that is marked as incorrigibly "modern" is propelled into a dangerous "West" out there in the city.

The term *oudhukam* does not have the same space-time dimensions. It refers most directly to a different space-time grid—that of bodily habitus and comportment. It refers to the "closed," "contained" body of one that walks with her head down, arms in, eyes averted. It refers to no place "out there" but rather contains the female subject within the body itself. In some sense, the resolution of the tension between an indigenous tradition and a predatory modernity is literally the demure comportment of the female body. The production of locality, in this instance, hinges on the female body.

This point might be better made if we compare the terrain of femininity to the terrain of masculinity. Without entering into a full discussion of masculinity here, it is instructive to examine the sartorial representations of masculinities in *Pavithram*. In the film, one sees a "traditional"-coded, *mundu*- or sarong-clad brother who resides in the village and a trouser-wearing brother who is a doctor in the city. This contrast points to a certain kind of emblematic opposition between traditional and modern masculinities; it also points to class differences. However, in Malayalam, one would rarely refer to a young man as either *naden* or "modern." And one would never refer to a respectably clad bourgeois-type male as *oudhukam*. The absence of a readily available concept for marking a respectably "modern" male thus points to the specifically gendered nature of the term *oudhukam* and its constitutive construction of the female body.

Similarly, if we compare the orientation toward the present of the *chethu* style to the presentist orientation of the demure, the body politics of the production of locality begins to reveal itself. The demure modern repudiates the privatized past of tradition and the sexualized transgressive future of modernity by producing a present that is located within the confines of the female form—the space-time configurations of the body. The past and future of femininities are highly spatialized temporalities, whereas the *chethu* style repudiates a different kind of past and future and produces a different kind of present. This form of masculinity is not one necessarily rooted in a spatiotemporal notion of "tradition" and "modernity."

While the present tense of *chethu* is rooted in an aimless kind of wandering—a restless mobility in search of fun that might or might not lead to a secure future of middle-class respectability and consumption—the present tense of the demure modern is rooted in the body and its containment as it traverses public space. This becomes clear as Devan discusses his idea of the perfect girl by describing a kind of girl that he could hardly imagine: "Imagine a girl going about in an *chethu* style. . . . She moves towards people in a big way . . . towards everybody . . . a big style . . . I mean just try and imagine it . . . she speaks to everybody . . . she makes a lot of noise." His idea of a demure girl is "one who won't go around for no reason. For no reason, just wandering about. She won't wander about for no reason."

The demure female body enables a young woman to enter the public, but in ways that circumscribe her movements. She must be goal-oriented and contained as she traverses a public that is also occupied by young men, whose movements and trajectories are different—aimless and wandering. In a sense, this idea of the demure entails carrying the private, "essential" self into the public. Masculinity "shines" (*chethu*) in public, whereas the demure is contained. A demure femininity in public retains its interiority, which is what allows it to enter the public in the first place. The interiority of masculinity is not rooted within masculinity itself, but in the home, family, and a relationship with a woman. The opposition between public and private that young women must negotiate creates a discontinuous social space that leaves little room for a harmonious, essentialized gender identity that can be easily applied across social fields. This "demure modern" style is both inscribed and performed, one that can be identified, talked about, and contested.

Fun, Embarrassment, and Regulation in Public

The masculinity of the *chethu* style involves a congealing of certain fashions; an attitude about past, present, and future; and a mode of traversing public space in which one is very self-consciously on display. However, *chethu* is a precarious achievement, one that can fail in any number of ways. I have discussed some of this precariousness in terms of a lower-caste/class masculine struggle to turn a presentist enjoyment of consumption into a secure form of the good life in the future. Moving through public spaces, whether the street, a bus stop, the actual space of the college, or the stage of a local beauty pageant, involves for both young men and women a complicated mode of self-presentation and traversal. It is here that we begin to see the ways in which the gendering of the youth/fashion nexus structures the participation of young men and women within the public spaces of consumption and education.

In the town where the college is located, nonfamilial, heterosocial spaces for young people to congregate and socialize were increasing but not plentiful. Often, spaces of sociality were fashioned in and around the spaces of the college along with the trains, train stations, bus stands, and buses that many students used to get to and from college. More adventurous types might congregate at restaurants, ice cream parlors, or the cinema hall; the most adventurous, at a nearby park or the beach. Of course, the sense of these spaces as relatively safe or transgressive is tied to their relative sexualization. These spaces also enable homosocial and heterosocial forms of sociality, full of pleasure and risk. These practices of sociality constitute these spaces as youthful, spaces for friendship and romance. It is instructive here to explore humorous stories about the embarrassment (*chammal*) of navigating sociality and public life, stories that reveal something of its enjoyments and dangers.

In the late 1980s and 1990s, comedy films emerged from and reconfigured comedic repertoires and performative traditions within Kerala. For example, Rowena (2002) discusses the ways that a form of stand-up comedy called *mimicry*, in which pairs or groups of young men perform comedic routines about verbal mishaps and everyday blunders and confusions, began in the 1970s to replace *kathaprasangham*, an oral genre that features a single performer who recites song, poetry, and dramatic narration. Like the fashion show, mimicry routines have become a central element of youth festivals and college events, now intimately tied to cinema. Early stars of comedy films were mimicry artists, an early and important comedy film being *Mimicry Parade* (dir. Thulasidas, 1991). Now, performances of mimicry almost exclusively by young men involve enacting comedic scenes—often depicting everyday blunders and confusions in schools, hospitals, police stations, bus stops, and the family home—from popular films and television programs.

A complex everyday mediation of this genre emerges in which what is highlighted are moments of public embarrassment—indicated by the word *chammal*. For example, on the television show *Chammal in Demand* on the Kairali satellite television channel, viewers are able to request their favorite scenes of embarrassment from comedy films (see Rowena 2002, 161). Sometimes, the term can refer to comedy in general. For example, describing a film or a role as *chammal* refers to its comedic elements. (Rowena also links *chammal* to practices of male rivalry called *para*, in which one is trying to cut one's rival down to size.)[27]

Often, during the evenings in the hostel, our conversation revolved around stories of various kinds of *chammal* that happened that day at work or college. These would include examples of physical embarrassment—dropping a folder full of paper in front of one's co-workers and being made fun of. Other examples involved verbal mishaps—being nervous and giving the wrong answer when a teacher asked a question. I experienced a lot of *chammal* mispronouncing various Malayalam words, to the endless amusement of my hostelmates. Still others involved seeing something that was so outrageous that it caused the viewer embarrassment.

One day my roommate Seema came back from the post office where she was a clerk. She walked in the door, wagged her finger at me, and told me that "my people" had caused her too much *chammal* that day. Seema was full of stories about the *sahibs* and *madamas*, as white men and women are referred to, who came through the post office. Those stories often involved language confusion; their hair, eyes, and color of their skin; and most important, the way they dressed. That day, she said that a woman had walked into the post office dressed in a pair of shorts and a bra. At my and my other roommates' protests, she insisted that she was not confusing a bra with a sari blouse. The woman had walked up to her counter with a long series of tasks that she needed to get accomplished. The shock at the way the woman was dressed was followed by such intense embarrassment on Seema's part that she started to "feel *chummy*" and could not look at the woman while she tried to serve her. This caused further confusion, which led to further *chummy* feelings, because then her co-workers started making fun of her and her situation. *Chammal* happens in public—where one is on display, where the performance of one's public self can unpredictably fail; it is a kind of slapstick comedy of everyday life in public. And it's an amusing kind of failure to which both men and women are subject.

However, *chammal* takes on a particular salience when tied to a *chethu* masculine style, one in which wandering about looking for some fun can often involve embarrassing oneself in a clownish sort of way, laughing at other people's embarrassment, or embarrassing others, becoming an aspect of male rivalry and competition. I discussed various forms of *chammal* with Baiju, a student friend of mine, after he came up to me laughing heartily about something he had just seen. He first described what he called "bad *chammal*," a kind of *chammal* in which one is not relating to one's peers but to authority, and the ways in which authority can embarrass you, administering a dressing down that leaves you looking bad in front of your peers, especially girls:

> You're talking in class. The teacher will tell you to stand up. Then he will start a dialogue: "Boy [*eda*], what is this? Who do you think you are? You have no sense [*bodhum*]." He'll go on for a while. After a little while, you will feel *chummy*.

He then went on to describe a more light-hearted situation, like the one he had just seen:

> Rajiv was going on a cycle. A bus went by with a girl in it whom he knew. Just so he would hear, she said out the window, "Hey boy [*eda*] move out of the way!" He looked up to see who said that. He hit the curb and fell over . . . [laughs] . . . At least he didn't hurt himself.

Then he described other *chammals* he had recently experienced:

> A *chammal* that happened to me. I'm waiting for the bus at the junction. I put out my hand. It drove past me and stopped. I ran to catch it thinking it had stopped for me. It stopped because of a gutter in the road. Then just as I was reaching it, it sped off. Everybody in the back and at the bus stand laughed. That was a *chammal*. I had to walk all the way to the next junction. How could I go back and stand there with everyone else?

Finally, he described a *chammal* that he thought was a really big one, involving a friend of his who had just gotten a brand new motorbike:

> You know the road that runs alongside the college? There is that road. Sunish had gotten a Kinetic Honda, the kind that you don't need to change the gears for. There is that curve in the road. Me and my friends were there. They saw

him coming and he saw them too. He wanted to shine [*chethu*] in front of them. He took both hands off the handle bars and said, "Hey!" The Honda turned and skidded. That's a big *chammal*.

These examples reveal the unpredictability of attempting to present a certain kind of public persona. All of them involve one's management of various kinds of public situations—sitting in a classroom, riding a cycle or a motorbike, running to catch a bus. The stories are funny because they reveal a certain incompetence to manage oneself in public, physically or verbally, in a failure of *chethu*. Sometimes it is your transgression or desire to "shine" that gets you in trouble. Other times, it is the fault of a situation beyond your control. And still other times, someone else does something to embarrass you, like a girl calling out to a boy.

What happens when a man tries to produce *chammal* in a woman? It is here that we begin to see the ways in which women's traversal and occupation of public space becomes problematic. The situation shifts from small incidents of unpredictability in public to a more rigorous policing in which women's sexuality and their containment is at stake. The most pervasive form in which men address women in public is *comment adi*, "hitting" women with sexualized comments on the street, in a bus, or in various other situations. Part of a set of practices labeled "Eve-teasing" in popular discourse, *comment adi* emerges out of masculine practices of fun in public.[28] As indicated earlier, women deploy a demure demeanor to navigate this precarious terrain.

In an interview, Shijo, somewhat notorious for his playboy image, produced his own rationalizations for this practice. He began by saying that he was not as bad as most other guys because he did *comment adi* only as he was walking along the road. He did not stand at the college junction and continuously make comments to all the women who came by. He then went on to say:

> In nature there is this notion, that the opposites always attract. That cannot be realized. Right? To have a conversation about that is why people *comment adi*. Then, you say it to boost up confidence. For example, when I was walking along, I saw a girl. She was a friend. Not very attractive [*resam illa*]. Somebody said something in a way that hurt her. I don't do things like that. You should do it to boost someone's confidence. I will give you another small example.

When I was walking along this morning, I saw a girl. Very attractive. She was good to look at. I am walking this way and so is she. So I go up to her and say, without saying anything dirty, I just want to say that you are good to look at. I like you. Do you think you might like me? Then she will laugh. I know I will not see her tomorrow. I know that. It's just a joke, *tamasha*. It works both ways. I get satisfaction, then her confidence is boosted. I tell her she's good-looking. Her confidence is boosted. There is nothing negative here. That's the way I think about it.

However, other than doing a girl a favor by "boosting up her confidence," he also goes on to blame the manner in which girls behave:

When you walk in an unmindful way, you will get comments. Nobody will like it if a girl walks around feeling a little superior [*gema*]. They will try and degrade her. They will say something in order to lower her, bring her back down.

This idea of "walking in an unmindful way" points to the ways in which young women's traversals of public space are regulated. Further, when a man tries to embarrass a woman in public, the specific regulation of women's sexuality begins to reveal itself. This regulation requires both the production of women as sexualized and the policing of that sexualization. The spatialized terrain of femininities mapped out earlier through an analysis of clothing styles structures the ways young women are enabled and constrained in their negotiation of the public spaces of the college and consumer spaces. A young woman's participation in the public spaces of modernity requires her to mediate her sexuality. This mediation happens through embodiments and negotiations of femininities that enact a cultural politics of globalization within Kerala as women participate in globally inflected consumer culture and spaces of education.

In the earlier discussion of the Miss World pageant, I highlighted the figure of Ruby, a veejay and the host of the pageant. Ruby's traversal of the public (on television she comfortably and aggressively moves through the public streets and beaches of Mumbai) is a completely "modern" one. Standing in the heart of the modern, nationally inflected public, the anxieties that provoke the need for another, more demure "modern" are not represented. Such anxieties are represented in *Dollar* and other such movies of the contemporary Malayalam cinema. The elder, skirt-clad daughter is very much like Ruby—she traverses the public (streets and clubs in New York) aggressively. However, the modernity of her body is hypersexualized and dangerous. This *gema* (arrogance) of fashionable girls is manifested in a relatively new way in Malayalam cinema. J. Geetha demonstrates that in Malayalam movies prior to the mid-1980s, the figure of the vamp and that of the coy, assertive "modern" woman were usually taken up by the daughter of a rich, upper-caste, westernized family (1994). In the 1980s, this role was reassigned to a female character who in the movie was actually foreign-returned. She would sport fancy clothes, drive a car, and have an exaggerated American accent. This construction never included a woman returned from the Persian Gulf, the place of most intense and significant emigration. The narratives of sexual freedom and moral depravity could never apply to countries like Saudi Arabia or Bahrain or Kuwait, where, it is said within the discourses of migration in Kerala, the women who go there—like nurses, servants, and clerical workers—are even more constrained in their movements and expressions than in India. So like Ruby, Kamla, and Sophiya of Channel V, the foreign-returned female had become a trope. But she was not valorized as a public, active figure as on Channel V. She represents a long list of transgressions, and the plots of these movies revolve around her progressive transformation from being a "modern" girl with *gema* to a girl distinguished as *oudhukam* (demure).

This transformation from the "modern" to the demure was forcefully produced by the policing of women's fashions in the space of the college. The outside of the eight-foot wall surrounding the college compound, the side facing the street, was full of advertisements for Killer jeans, three kinds of local sneaker brands, Vespa scooters, computer training classes, and the like. Once one entered the revolving gate of the college, however, "fashion" was to be kept at bay: not the wearing of jeans or sneakers by men, that is, but women's fashionable dress. Many girls reported being harassed and bullied by male students about the clothes they wore when they first came to college. If they dared to wear a skirt as opposed to a *churidar* or *pavada*, they were told in no uncertain terms that in this college the male students did not like "modern" girls.

In order to illustrate this dynamic, let us return to Shijo with the playboy reputation. Getting a bit defensive about our discussion on making sexualized comments to girls, he goes on to talk about the assertiveness of the "modern" girl who has too much *gema* by recounting a story of when he was the target of sexual comments. He locates this story in a more elite college in the capital city, where all the girls are supposedly "modern":

> In Trivandrum [Thiruvananthapuram], I had to go to [that] college for some reason, you know it? Yes . . . I had to go see some friend. You have to walk a lot from the main road. I was alone. I had my two hands in my pockets, like that I was walking, kind of smartly. As I was walking along, there were two or three of them, laughing and going. One said to another, "It seems like he's about to break up and fall. He must need his two hands to be in his pockets in order to help him stand up. What does he think, that it's *chethu*? Oh, it's not *chethu*. He's just got on a pair of stupid jeans." I was shocked. I turned around, angry and hot. I pretended not to hear and I just went on. "Can you see how he struts?" [the girls said]. I just turned and said, "Daughter [*mole*], I have a lot of people to see. Can you just let me go?" I'm telling you. These girls say a lot.

Here, Shijo is constructing a narrative in which his marginalized class status, as someone from a nonelite, small-town college dressed up to go to the city, is mediated through gender, a confrontation with the aggressive "modern" girls of the more elite classes. The narrative plays on tropes of conflict and desire between an aspirational lower-class, lower-caste boy and a newly aggressive upper-class, upper-caste girl that have come to dominate youth-oriented films (Rowena 2002).

When I asked why and how girls in other colleges sometimes wore skirts (in Kerala's capital city of Thiruvananthapuram, for example), I was often told it was because those were rich, Gulf-returned girls. But in fact the great majority of these girls would never have been to the Gulf. Under the highly restrictive labor laws of many Gulf countries, rarely does a work permit include a family visa. Furthermore, noncitizens are not allowed into the Gulf countries' university systems, so children are commonly left behind for school. Young women who wore skirts were not recently returned from the Gulf, and their families may or may not have had connections to the Gulf, but their bodies bore the burden of "foreignness." Further, the relationship between the Gulf and the "West" is a complex mediation that is elided in such markings, where the libertine sexuality associated with the "West" is foisted on a woman associated with the Gulf (even though most women who have been there complain of having had to wear a *burqa* for the first time and point to having been highly restricted in their mobility). Such situations reveal the ways in which class and urban-rural resentments come to be focused on the female body.

While this example reveals the negotiation between the "modern" and the "demure," the other end of the boundary that marks the "demure modern"—namely, that between the "demure" and the "*naden* traditional"—is also policed. Beena and Lena were two close friends from a village two and half hours away by bus. They were students on a scholarship for the children of the lowest-caste communities, their fathers being fishermen. Within the college, the state, and everyday talk, they were "SC/ST" students, referring to the bureaucratic categories of "scheduled caste" and "scheduled tribe," the lowest categories of communities in the state-derived classification of caste hierarchy, linked to programs for redressing caste inequality in jobs and education. Acutely sensitive to their marginalization, they had a strong sense of the difference between *naden purethu*—their village, the interior from which they came every day—and the city. They understood themselves to be *naden* and dressed in a *pavada* and not an expensive *churidar*. They were particularly appreciative of teachers who were welcoming and kind, and angry about teachers who seemed distant. College was a difficult and threatening place for them, but they managed to have their fun—sticking with their friends from their village, occasionally and illicitly spending their stipend money on an ice cream instead of a notebook. And they were more assertive than most about the ways in which they were targeted. Beena was especially angry about being threatened by a group she and others called "the bad boys," a group of six male students that had formed the previous year, going around "*chethu*-fying" as Beena scornfully put it.[29] They were of the city, four had motorbikes, and they were known for targeting girls inside and outside the college. Many in this group were from middle-class Ezhava families in town, and one could see in their personas the workings of a more general "OBC" (other backward classes) caste- and class-assertive and commodified masculinity. Beena contrasted them to the nice, respectful boys of her *nadu*, boys she called *pawam*, possessing a simple and humble kind of masculinity.[30]

I ran into Beena and Lena one afternoon as they were leaving at two o'clock to catch a bus. I started to tease them about skipping class, wondering what their parents would say when they came home so early. Beena immediately got defensive. She declared that she was fed up and tired and wanted to go home. She complained about the long commute, which usually meant getting home after dark. She said her parents did not know what she went through every day. Then she recounted an incident that had happened that morning in their classroom. While the teacher was out of the class, the president of the student union had come by to announce the start of a book fair. Beena and Lena were sitting on the windowsill. After the student president left, a member of this "bad boy" gang started berating them for not sitting properly at their desks while the announcement was made. He yelled at them and asked if the classroom was their family home (*kudumba sthanam*), where they could sit any way they wanted. Beena said that they paid no attention to him and continued to sit on the sill. When the lecture started, she moved to sit at her desk. "Why should I have to respect him?" she asked angrily. She vowed she was going to file a complaint with the principal, bitterly noting that it would do no good. For today, she had had enough and was going home.[31]

The male classmate had deployed a contrast with the privacy of the family home to try to make Beena, already marked under the sign of a privatized tradition, behave in a properly demure manner in public. This particular move from the traditional to the demure modern is one that she resisted. But sometimes a young woman wants to make that shift and is prevented from doing so.

Shoba was one of a group of students who came from the surrounding villages to attend college. Like many of them, she came from a relatively poor, peasant Ezhava background. She stood out among this group of students for several reasons. She was the "dancer" of her class; for every college function, it was Shoba who performed the obligatory bharat-natyam dance number. She wore cosmetics and jewelry. She also wore *churidars* while the other girls of her background would usually come to college in *pavadas*. Although Shoba sought to embody the demure, she was also the special and persistent target of male sexual harassment. A year prior to my arrival at the college, it had gotten so bad that a boy on a bus had actually tried to rip off some of her clothing. It was then that she filed a complaint with the school. This sort of behavior occurs in many forms every day, and most young women do not complain. When pressed to answer why she was so singled out, she would simply say

"Boys are like that." When boys were pressed to explain, or teachers, or other female students, it always came around to her uncle in the Gulf. Shoba lived with her widowed mother and sister in a village outside the town. In conversation after conversation, her style, clothes, and body were directly and explicitly linked to the money her uncle sent back for the family. She was often said to have too much *gema*, or arrogance. No matter how hard she tried to enter the space of the "demure modern"— wearing *churidars*, studying *bharatnatyam* (that emblem of the cultured, demure middle-class young woman)—she had transgressed. Needless to say, she had never left Kerala, but her body bore the burden and the traces of that journey abroad, a journey that engendered transgressions of class and caste hierarchy for which she pays the price.

This example demonstrates the ways in which the space of the demure modern is exclusionary and points to the production of locality on the unstable boundary between "tradition" and "modernity." I end by exploring how girls understood to be "modern" negotiate ideas about tradition/*nadu* in the context of a "Miss Kerala" beauty pageant. Notions of fashion and fun and their negotiations reveal tensions between the idea of the "modern" and notions of tradition/*nadu*.

As in the rest of India, the beauty industry in Kerala is thriving. From the proliferation of beauty parlors to the presence of fashion shows at almost any youth or college festival, the practices of fashion and beauty have come to redefine what constitutes femininity for middle-class young women. It is within this context that the Miss Kerala pageant was staged in December 1994 in Thiruvananthapuram, the capital city of the state.

The contest was but one of several Miss Kerala pageants held in various parts of the world. Held under the aegis of the World Malayalee Federation, along with Miss Keralas from such far-flung places as Abu Dhabi, London, Chicago, and Houston, the Thiruvananthapuram Miss Kerala would travel to New York for the final level of competition, thereby mapping Kerala's own diaspora. The contest was held in a large auditorium in a palace of the former maharajah of Travancore, a Nair royal family. Consistent with its location, the beauty contest went on to define a hegemonic Kerala femininity in line with its upper-caste Nair trappings. The contest had some very precise specifications. There were to be three rounds, each with a different style of dress. In the first round, the contestants wore the *pavada*-blouse combination. In the second round, they wore the sari, most of them a Kerala sari, distinguished by white cotton cloth and gold-thread borders. For the third round, the young women wore the *mundum-neryathum*, a two-piece garment worn to resemble a sari. It is the traditional attire of mature, upper-caste Nair women.

In each round, a local television celebrity asked them several questions. The questions were quite specific, focusing on Kerala dance, drama, poetry, history, and literature. In round three, the round in which they wore the *mundum-neryathum*, they came out one by one, carrying a large *villaku* (lamp), in the Kerala style, which they carefully carried to the front of the stage and lit. (As one contestant put it, "It was really heavy.") This mirrors the lighting of the lamp by brides during Nair marriage ceremonies.

Gita, a young woman who was in the audience, stated:

> OK so this is what they thought. She should look like a Kerala girl. The typical Nair. People consider that to be the middle, you know not the highest caste. . . . And it's not the lowest where poverty comes. It's for the middle-class people. With the *pavada* and blouse, the long hair. You get the picture? That's the way it is, in the Nair class.

In describing to me what she thinks the organizers were looking for, Gita links Kerala with Nair, the "middle," long hair, and the *pavada*. This nostalgic production of a specifically Nair femininity is in line with a broader movement of cultural remembering defined in upper-caste, Nair terms. However, within the rubric of the global Miss Kerala competition, the Miss Kerala from Kerala is but one of many the world over. She has an equivalent position with respect to other Miss Keralas. Her Kerala-ness is not privileged with respect to the diaspora; in fact, her equivalence with them is required by a certain cultural politics of globalization. The structure of a globalized middle class makes it possible for there to be an equivalence between the likes of a Miss Kerala from Kerala and a Miss Kerala from New York. The contest reveals starkly the production of locality on a global stage. Miss Kerala must be a *naden pennu* in her dress, comportment, and knowledge. Written onto the female bodies of a proliferation of Miss Keralas, the *nadu*, locality itself, becomes transportable and transposable.

So far, I have presented an analysis that would trace the body of the

woman as object, tradition commodified: a body inscribed and consumed by a patriarchal middle-class masculine gaze. But in many ways,
the Miss Kerala pageant was seen as a failure. In order to examine why,
we must move from the structure of the event to its performative aspects.
The beauty contest can be conceptualized as a literal and figurative stage
for the enactment of gendered identities. Judith Butler points to the
possibility of a breakdown of replicability—a "failure to repeat"—as a
way of understanding gender identity as a real but tenuous construction
(1990). It then becomes possible to view a woman's body as not simply
inscribed and commodified but also performed and enacted.

During the public performance of gender identity that took place during Thiruvananthapuram's Miss Kerala contest, certain dissonances appeared. The main problem emerged during the questioning. In short, all
ten contestants had trouble answering questions about Kerala history,
poetry, literature, dance, and drama mainly because they simply did not
know the answers, sometimes because they did not know the highly
Sanskritized Malayalam necessary to answer. The problem became particularly acute during the third round. After walking slowly across the
stage with the traditional lamp, laying it down, lighting it, and then
walking over to the questioner, many of the women could only answer,
when asked who had won the Kerala Sahitya Akademi award for poetry
two years prior, "Sorry, I don't know," at which point the audience,
laughing and heckling, would shout back, "Then why did you come?" or
"Go home, girl!" It became comically clear that there was a mismatch
between contestants and contest standards.

I asked Gita her assessment of the problem. She said,

They felt this is what Kerala is about. And we need a girl who is about Kerala.
But they forgot that there is no one like that. Do you understand that? There is
no one like that who is going to get up and go onstage. . . . Most of them
had done these things before, I mean other modeling things. I'm sure they
thought this was going to be one of those things. Like other contests. They
have easy questions. You know, like "What do you think women should do?"
Most of them had some title, Miss Coimbatore, Miss Ernakulam. One girl
was in the movies. So, they walked like they were in a fashion show, except
they were wearing a *pavada*.

For Gita, the source of the mismatch was a contradiction between form and content. The form of the pageant was part of a whole repertoire of practices—acting, modeling, fashion shows—which constitute a "modern" and globalized feminine consumer space; a form of publicity that only "certain girls" engage in, the "modern middle-class miss" as characterized by Brinda Karat of the All India Democratic Women's Association. The content required a performance of the "traditional" comportment and habitus in a public space that collided with other ("modern") bodily demeanors—walking as in a fashion show, but somehow doing so while wearing a *pavada*. From Gita's perspective, the failure of the pageant stemmed from the contradiction between a "traditional" Kerala girl and the modern, globalized form of a beauty pageant. She found the expectations of producing "tradition" unreasonable, highlighting the fact that a truly *naden* girl would never participate in a pageant.[32] Gita went on to say,

> I was laughing, they [people in the audience] were laughing. It was so bad. But I don't blame them. They didn't know the answers. And the Malayalam. See, they make fun of it because the kids just don't know. Do you blame them? Some Malayalam words are really difficult. Because it is like when you ask a kid to talk in really high-tech English; it's hard too.

She is in many ways articulating an imbrication between two structures of patriarchy. One is rooted in the patriarchal family formed through India's colonial and then postcolonial, nationalist modernity into a binarism between tradition and modernity. This intersects with the patriarchal structures of emergent spaces of public consumption that commodify women at the same time that they target them as consumers. Gita struggles to articulate a sense of agency, albeit a consumerist sense of agency within this mutual imbrication.

> They say fashion is bad. So they have the girls wear the *pavada*, the sari, and all that. But what's wrong with fashion? I'm not saying fashion is a big deal. I don't say like other girls, you know. In the magazines the girls say, "Fashion is a really important part of my life." I don't say that. It's just a little fun. That's all it is, just fun.

It is difficult to formulate precisely how one can rescue the "fun" of fashion from its simultaneous demonization by the protectors of "tradition" and by critics of capitalism who locate "fun" as a mere diversion, a market-driven, middle-class consumer subterfuge. Throughout this analysis, I have highlighted the production of locality as a key feature of the process of the commodification of women's bodies and their circulation. In this beauty pageant, the failure of the replicability of gender identities is founded on a collision between highly spatialized notions of tradition/modernity and India/West as young women's bodies wrapped in clothing commodities move across the public stage of beauty.

The idea of "fun," marking experiences of pleasure, desire, and leisure, then, becomes one lens through which to understand the differential relationship that young women and men have to new, globally inflected consumer spaces. If we go back to the idea of *chethu*—understood as a masculine, fun-loving, consumer identity—and compare it to the ways in which Gita struggles to articulate her desire for "fun," it becomes clear that the spaciotemporal grids that underlie those two notions are very different. The ephemerality of *chethu*, located as it is in the here and now, marked by its explicit rejection of the future, unburdened by a sense of the past, shapes the roving, fun-loving persona of a young man in his jeans, riding his motorbike, drinking beer. This is a lower-class, lower-caste masculine consumer identity marked by desire and aspiration. The "modern miss," interested in fashion shows, modeling, and beauty pageants, is a middle-class object of desire that must ultimately be tamed and disciplined. Burdened by tradition, preyed upon by modernity, she must learn to navigate these new spaces of consumption respectably and modestly. Her notions of "fun" are situated in and through notions of tradition and modernity, public and private, that make her claim on these new consumer spaces tenuous.

Further, it is important to note the social categories that appear under the sign of "fun" and those that do not. In this iteration, we have the classic and stereotypical contrast between the lower-class, lower-caste aspiring masculine subject and the upper-caste, upper-class feminine object of desire. Analyses of important films of the 1990s such as *Roja* and *Bombay* have demonstrated the ways in which an upper-caste, upper-class masculine subject is reworked through discourses and ideologies of liberalization.[33] What is absent in this structure of representation that marks "fun" in the public spaces of modernity is the lower-class, lower-caste young woman. Here, if we go back to Beena and her friend Lena, we begin to see how their aspirations for "fun" in public struggles against their privatization under the sign of tradition. Within the structures of representation that I have elicited through analyses of filmic narratives—ones that reveal forms of consumer subjectivity that are gender, caste, and class specific—nowhere do we have a lower-caste, lower-class young woman marked by an orientation to and desire for consumption (see Rowena 2002). There is no need to represent her consumer agency and subjectivity, because she is so thoroughly privatized under the sign of tradition through the intersection of her gender and class and caste status that she can make little claim on a modern public, either as a threatening or entitled figure. While she emerges within feminist discourse as the heroic woman outside the fold of consumption—"struggling to make ends meet"—the lack of a consumer identity linked to her social location in liberalizing India marks the boundaries of exclusion and inclusion through which consumption has become a new axis of belonging and social membership.

Conclusion

Youth consumption practices have become an easy way to index the reach and extent of globalization. An analysis of how young people in Kerala apprehend and negotiate new globally inflected spaces of consumption, particularly the youth-fashion nexus, reveals these spaces to be structured by specifically postcolonial preoccupations about tradition and modernity, public and private that have differential consequences for young women and men. These spaces have created new consumer identities—for example the lower-caste male marked by consumerism and fashion—and reworked the respectable, middle-class woman as aggressively sexual, confident, and public. Young men and women in Kerala embody, negotiate, and contest a caste- and class-inflected gendered terrain of masculinities and femininities under both an enabling and a constraining set of conditions for participating within educational and other consumer spaces.

3

Romancing the Public

On February 14, 2006, the state general secretary of the Akhil Bharatiya Vidyarthi Parishad (ABVP) in Kerala, the student political party most closely aligned with the BJP, the Hindu nationalist party, issued a statement urging students to boycott celebrations of Valentine's Day.[1] The ABVP's proposed boycott and its charge that Valentine's Day was the creation of global capitalists intent on marketing their products were part of a wider set of protests that Hindu nationalist organizations began during the 1990s against the growing popularity of the holiday. Within metropolitan locations, upscale restaurants market Valentine's Day as an opportunity for specially packaged romantic dinners; bars and clubs promote special disco nights. More widely, an expanding consumer culture marks the day through the buying and selling of flowers, special television shows, dedications of love on radio programs, letter-writing and poetry-reciting competitions, and most generally the exchange of cards. Increasingly, all manner of commodities, from mineral water to frying pans to ball point pens, have been marketed as part of the celebration. In turn, Hindu right organizations such as the Shiv Sena, the

Bajrang Dal, and various ABVP chapters throughout the country have protested the increasing popularity of the holiday, sometimes violently: attacking card shops, rampaging through restaurants, and burning Valentine's Day cards.

While the ABVP spokesman names the role of global capital in the marketing of Valentine's Day as the chief reason for boycotting the occasion, I argue that it is the link between consumption and the display of sexuality that is at stake. While beauty pageant protests focused on the commodification and public display of young middle-class women, the protesters of Valentine's Day target the young, heterosexual couple on public display, evidenced by several incidents in which young couples have been attacked in public places. Further, while the dangers of romance and sex in public are tied to the (heterosexual) couple, the display of female sexuality is the most problematic; hence the renaming of Valentine's Day as "Prostitution Day" by the Lucknow chapter of the Shiv Sena.[2] Globalization here is once again linked to consumption and the increasing sexualization of public space.

Critical discussions of these protests have highlighted how practices of modern romance, notions of choice, freedom, and possible miscegenation across the lines of community and caste, threaten Hindu nationalist valorizations of tradition, community, and the patriarchal family (Menon 2005). Indeed, young women negotiate romance as a space of choice and agency, one that is situated beyond the confines of the family yet within the temporal horizon of marriage. Within Kerala, the modern understanding of romance (premam) emerged during the colonial period through a male-authored reformist narrative that sought to constitute a new role for women in which the ability to choose one's own partner was asserted as a key civic right. Education was an important means through which these ideas were articulated and women's access to modern publics mediated; indeed, the idea of an educated wife was central here. Ideas of modern romance reconfigured the changing space of emergent middle-class ideas of marriage, infusing it with ideas of emotional bonds and companionship within a newly constituted idea of the couple that more often than not retained the conventional boundaries of caste and community.

Women's contemporary negotiations of romance must navigate new discourses of consumerism linked to globalization and sexualization of the public. Just as with moral panics about youth fashion, a contested negotiation of globalization is manifest in discussions about the increasing sexual exploitation of, and increasing violence against, women, particularly the exploitation of young women and girls. Within the context of these circulating discourses, the young women I encountered linked a long-standing male-authored, colonial-era narrative of romance to their own pleasures and anxieties about romance in a contemporary and expanding commodity culture. Here, romance emerges as a very fraught kind of public intimacy, even as it structured young women's access to and navigations of the public spaces of work, consumption, and education within the impending horizon of marriage. Like fashion, romance emerges as a key site for negotiating consumer citizenship, constituting an important nexus for a cultural politics of belonging through which young women's claims on the public are structured, negotiated, and experienced.

"Gender Paradox" in Kerala

The leftist political culture of the state has historically incorporated women as economic and class subjects, for example, through participation in the trade union movement and in discussions of poverty. However, when women are understood as gendered subjects, in situations involving rape, sexual violence, or harassment, the left and the right collude in seeing these as a question of women's virtue, morality, or individual victimhood. The left also sometimes sees these as "middle-class" concerns that deflect from considerations of women's class exploitation (Devika and Kodoth 2001).

This avoidance of women as gendered subjects began to change in the middle 1990s (see Sreekumar 2007; Radhakrishnan 2005; Devika and Kodoth 2001). Several key legal cases became a focal point of public discourse, highlighting the gendered sexual politics of the public in Kerala and galvanizing women's organizations (Radhakrishnan 2005). The "Ice Cream Parlor" case and the mass media discussions of it drew attention to the sexualization of the ice cream parlor as a libidinal space of romance and sexuality, linking politics and the sexual exploitation of girls. A young woman complained that an ice cream parlor near the Kozhikode beach hospital was a front for a sex ring that catered to important public figures, including a prominent minister. A coalition of women's organizations under the banner Stree Vedi (For Women), in particular the organization Anweshi co-founded by the veteran activist K. Ajitha in the city of Kozhikode, brought the issue into the public realm by pursuing the case.[3] The dramatic Suryanelli case is another key example. In this instance, a young woman from a remote district town filed a complaint in 1996, saying that she had been lured into a sex racket in which she had been trafficked all over Kerala and neighboring Tamil Nadu, being raped by as many as forty-two men. The vigorous investigation of this incident, the dramatic conviction of thirty-five men and women, including prominent public figures, the eventual Kerala High Court reversal of the lower court ruling against most of the convicted, and the move to have the case heard in the Supreme Court of India have made this case a focal point of discussion about sex, politics, and exploitation. Once again, highlighted here is the vulnerable young woman in public, both sexualized and sexually exploited. The woman at the center of the Suryanelli case was allegedly lured into the sex racket through a relationship with a bus worker who promised her a "love marriage" but instead handed her over to members of a sex ring. Much public commentary on this case focused on her naiveté and gullibility in matters of romance, while the legal proceedings focused on her character to question her motives and desires.

These spectacular cases of rape—and others involving sexual harassment—have shocked and titillated journalists and the public sphere of Kerala.[4] Several commentators have argued that these cases point to consumerism. The headline of a newspaper article is telling and typical: "Strong Consumerism Plus Loose Ties Lead to Suryanellis."[5] The reference to "loose human ties" is particularly interesting for its reference to the impact of consumerism on the breakdown of a community and familial network that should monitor and protect vulnerable young women.

Women's organizations such as Anweshi also highlight economic and cultural globalization but do so in a way that focuses on "sex tourism" rather than the breakdown of the family, which from their feminist perspective is not a violence-free and protective safe haven. For example, Anweshi's Web site situates the organization's focus on gender and violence in a contemporary Kerala that is facing the "bitter fruits" of economic and cultural globalization. They state that dowry deaths, suicides, and sex tourism are on the rise, linking Kerala to other key places for sex tourism like Thailand. While there is little research to determine whether Kerala has become a site for the global trade in sex, it is important to note that while commentators analyze the impact of globalization and consumerism, the behavior of prominent male politicians and figures is a persistent focus in these cases and the discourse that surrounds them. In the introduction and chapter 1, I discussed a form of antipolitics linked to middle-class consumerist discourse that depicts the political culture of the state as undemocratic and corrupt, a discourse that demonstrates how conceptions of citizenship are being mobilized to critique the postcolonial state in liberalizing Kerala (something I explore more extensively in chapter 4). Here, this corruption of politics happens through its sexualization, linking politicians to globally inflected libidinal consumer spaces in ways that make them appear hypocritical, lustful, and corrupt. Whether it is a feminist discourse that seeks justice for exploited young women and girls in a patriarchal legal establishment tied to a hypocritical political culture within the context of a predatory process of globalization or a wider public that is simply titillated by the allegedly prurient sexual escapades of key public figures, at the center of this discourse is the vulnerable young woman in public. Far from the "emancipated" and "liberated" woman of the Kerala model, we now have the rise of the victimized, unprotected, and exploited young woman —her high "status" with respect to development indices undermined by a pernicious and predatory globalization, leading to formulations of "gender paradox" that have now replaced the optimism of the Kerala model literature (Sreekumar 2007). I now turn to explore how young women draw on long-standing narratives of romantic love to mediate their anxieties and pleasures about romance within an expanding commodity culture.

The Modernity of Romance

Many journalistic commentaries on the popularity of Valentine's Day and the protests against it remark on the ironies involved in celebrating or eschewing love via Valentine's Day in the land that gave the world the Kama Sutra and has its own well-developed indigenous language of love.[6] Their characterization of a contemporary western capitalist notion of romantic love pitted against indigenous traditions of love, eroticism, and sexuality obscures the complex role of romantic love within colonial modernity. Romantic love emerged under colonial modernity as a site for a complex reworking of tradition and modernity, one that pitted traditional marriages arranged according to caste and community rules against companionate ones in which the idea of the modern couple becomes central. Indeed, much as it does for fashion, scholarship draws an important link between romance and modernity. Fashion replaced ascriptive sartorial rules as part of the larger narrative of increasing individualism. Similarly, western notions of romantic love, situated most often within the courtly traditions of the European Middle Ages, arise as part of a subversive, antihierarchical tradition that places love outside the confines of marriage, which is understood in familial and practical terms. As modern marriage was reconfigured to meet the requirements of a new social contract based on individual rights, love within marriage emerged as a key site of individual subjectivity and authenticity. The reworking of community, understood as either the overcoming of caste and religious differences in the name of a secular modernity or the social reform and modernization of community norms, became an important aspect of romantic love. Love's subversive potential to transform ascriptive community and family-based control over the institution of marriage into one in which two individuals are free to express desire and consent has become a key aspect of the story of modern romantic love.

Just as, in the domain of fashion, feminists have critiqued this modernist narrative of emancipation, pointing out how modern individualism reworked hierarchical norms to produce a modern gender ideology, a generation of western feminist writers saw in romantic love a form of patriarchal false consciousness that was seductive and disenabling (Beauvoir 1973 [1949]; Firestone 1970; Greer 1970).[7] Within Kerala, love, or premam, plays an important role in the emergence of the monogamous marital union that underlies the modern nuclear family. In chapter 1, I discussed the novel Indulekha, a nineteenth-century love story set in the northern Kerala region of Malabar, looking at its heroine as a new type of modern woman that embodies many of the elements of a modern gender ideology. Here, I discuss the novel more extensively to provide an analysis of a male-authored and modernizing view of romantic love that young women negotiate, linked to education, generations, gender, and sexuality. My discussion draws heavily on G. Arunima's insightful reading of the novel (1997).

First published in 1889, Indulekha was written by O. Chandu Menon, a district judge in the colonial courts. It was well received and has been reprinted more than seventy times; it is now part of the tenth standard school syllabus for Malayalam studies. It is, therefore, a canonical text for understanding the emergence of modernity in the region. In the novel, Madhavan, a young educated Nair, falls in love with his cross-cousin Indulekha, a beautiful and talented woman. The plot revolves around their desire to marry and Madhavan's attempts to obtain money to educate one of his younger male cousins. Both of these projects put Madhavan in conflict with Indulekha's guardian and grandfather, Pan-chu Menon, who controls the finances of the household. He tries to prevent the marriage by attempting to arrange a marriage between In-dulekha and a rich, lascivious, and womanizing Brahmin named Suri Nambutiri, a union that conforms to conventional caste marriage prac-tices. With the right mix of missteps, heartache, and separation, the love story has a happy resolution. The novel ends in marriage between Madhavan and Indulekha, and the couple and their two children live happily ever after in the colonial city of Madras, like many other aspiring Nairs of the middle classes.

The novel has often been read as an imitation in an Indian context of Benjamin Disraeli's Henrietta Temple, an ordinary and predictable love story (Menon 1997). However, while Indulekha was being written, read, and translated, a section of Kerala society was engaged in an intense debate about the absence of marriage within the dominant matrilineal Nair community, and this changing dynamic of property, marriage, gen-der, and generational relations gives the novel's argument for monoga-mous marriage a different valence.

As part of a larger movement of social reform, young men from Nair joint families argued that the prevailing "polyandrous" practices of Nair women, in which these women lived in their maternal homes and had multiple sexual partners who had few rights over the children that might follow, condemned the community to a barbarous tradition marked by sexual depravity. At the same time, they also argued that Nair women were being sexually exploited by higher-caste Brahmin men who were their sexual partners. Marriage reform was seen as an important step in "emancipating" women from such practices and modernizing the community (Jeffrey 1976; Arunima 2003). They argued for monogamous marriage tied to procreation and the formation of nuclear families; a project to end the sexual exploitation of women in the community was also linked to taming female sexuality.

Arunima pinpoints generational conflict within families as the key to understanding *Indulekha* in its social and historical context. Younger members of the household, particularly young men, were financially dependent on the head of the household (*karnavan*), usually the mother's brother. Conflicts over land ownership, the right to funds for education, the rights over rooms within the household, and the right to marry a partner of one's own choice all became matters of public, legal dispute. *Indulekha* brings together two areas of generational conflict—education and sexuality. Modern education becomes a civilizing influence to which the younger generations should have access. The unbridled sexuality of women under traditional community customs is tamed by an educated and modern sensibility in which monogamous marriages, driven by romantic love, prevail. "Love marriage" is a defiance of community norms, one opposed to rampant female sexuality.

In this way, modern romantic love becomes about the management of its Other, sexuality. As J. Devika has outlined, in late-nineteenth-century and early-twentieth-century discourses, *premam* was persistently counterposed to *kamam*, or lust, as a purer and more refined kind of love that provided a more solid grounding for monogamous unions (2007, 68; cf. Kaviraj 2007). O. Chandu Menon creates Indulekha as heroine through the positive valuation of *premam* over *kamam*, love over lust. While unions based on unbridled sexuality are linked to notions of women as passive and exploited victims, Indulekha is created as an agentive and strong woman, full of the animating powers of romantic love. First of all, she is an effortless blend of tradition and modernity—a refined lady with European accomplishments who continues to be firmly rooted in Malayalee culture. That is, the author specifically mentions that apart from being well versed in English and Sanskrit, she has also learned to play the piano and the violin, as well as mastering needlework, drawing, and the other arts in which "European girls are trained." However, this does not prevent her from being a "Malayalee lady" who observes all the required caste rituals, performs religious ceremonies, behaves reverentially to her elders, and wears clothing appropriate for her caste. Second, she is capable of choosing her own partner. What English education does for her is to give her a mind of her own, one that will allow her to exercise her all-important right to choose a marriage partner. In his introduction to the English translation, Chandu Menon strongly commended the "refining and liberating influence of English education" and made a strong plea to provide Indian women with this tool, which would enable them to "conduct [themselves] in matters of supreme interest to [them], such as the choosing of a partner in life" (Chamdumenon 2005 [1889]). In the novel, Indulekha's uncle, Krishna Menon, is very particular that she complete her education so that she will be able to marry a man of her own choice. Having the choice to determine ones own husband is represented as a civic right for women.

As Arunima notes, at a time when "rights" were being articulated by young men—including the right to property or more political rights such as the demand for a legislative assembly—within male-centered projects for social reform, social reform movements offered women the right only to choose their own partners, a right that in many cases they may never have been able to exercise within the constraints of family decision making. While education provided young men with money, autonomy, and independence (as in the case of Indulekha's love interest, Madhavan), for women it held only a promise of independence through marriage to such educated men. Once she has declared her love for Madhavan, Indulekha is displaced as the central figure in the novel. The agency for transforming love into marriage vests in the man, and the transition of Madhavan from lover to husband also marks the transformation of matrilineal or avuncular authority to patrilineal or virilocal power (Arunima 1997). This narrative of love successfully turned into marriage is usually glossed as a generational narrative of freedom, the freedom to choose. The choice is a proper, monogamous marriage, one that depends on the construction of the "educated wife": a woman sufficiently assertive to desire love and a man of her own choosing, but demure enough to be his loving and fitting companion.

The romantic ideal of the couple was endlessly narrativized in literature and increasingly onscreen but was hardly practiced. With respect to *Indulekha* it is important to note that this story of modern romance takes place well within the boundaries of caste and community, reflecting internal reform efforts. The Special Marriages Act of 1872 allowed for marriages based on individual choice, but community, family, and kin norms continue to dominate marriage practices. This has led to the juxtaposition between "arranged" and "love" marriages that are now at the center of modern novels and films that focus on romance. Also, increasingly arranged marriages and the discourses and practices that surround them are interwoven with the idioms and repertoires of the modern romantic ideal.

Now films importantly mediate everyday understandings of romance and love (see Dwyer 2000; Mody 2007)—one that explicitly links romance to consumption and mass mediation. While romance is understood as a privatized emotion, it is a very public form of consumer behavior. Young working women's leisure practices in turn-of-the-century New York, "dating" in the United States, capitalism and the structuring of emotional lives—in all of these domains, we see links between the expansion and commodification of leisure, the emergence of heterosocial interactions and their commodification, the reworking of public consumer spaces as spaces of romance, and the reworking of class and gender relations in the context of a commodified romantic culture (Peiss 1987; Bailey 1989; Ilouz 1997). Given that a college and its environs are one of the few spaces available for heterosocial interaction among the students I encountered, the construction of romantic intimacy, more often than not, must be initiated, negotiated, and sustained in and through the public spaces of college student life, one that is also mediated by mass media and its constructions of romance.

Indulekha in the Era of Consumerism

Hostel Day is a celebration held every year to commemorate the laying of the hostel's foundation stone. The culmination of the day's events was an evening program put together by students of the hostel. The evening celebration began in fits and starts due to power outages, with a speech by a student leader in the college. Meera, a member of the Student Federation of India (affiliated with the Marxist party) was a fiery speaker. In order to placate the hostel warden (as she told me later), she began by talking sentimentally about how the hostel was a second home, the warden was like a mother, and hostelmates were like sisters—the trope of kinship being a persistent way of producing the hostel as a home away from home. She then quickly moved to her real theme: the relative lack of freedom for women in Kerala and their need for liberation. She exhorted her classmates to fight for their independence and told them that, contrary to what most people said about the relative emancipation of women in Kerala, they were not free. Meera urged her audience to recognize that while they were being educated, women in Kerala had very little control over their lives, marriage was still the prevailing norm, and suicide rates among Kerala women were on the rise. She went on to name some women who were the exception to the rule, women who might stand as examples for those assembled: Indira Gandhi; two prominent political figures in Kerala, Gowriamma and Ajitha; and the special guest for the Hostel Day celebrations, the new superintendent of police, a twenty-six-year-old woman who had just taken her post. For Meera, more than for the majority of her audience, the figures of Gowriamma and Ajitha were figures of aspiration, their lives examples of the possibility of an engaged, public political life for women in Kerala.

A brief examination of K. R. Gouri's life reveals the gender and caste terrain that Meera herself will need to navigate if she makes good on her stated ambitions to become a politician. K. R. Gouri (otherwise known as Gowriamma) made history in 2004 by being, at the age of eighty-five, the oldest and longest-serving legislator in Kerala history, until quite recently a minister of agriculture. She also holds the record for winning twelve assembly elections, having been defeated only once, in 1977, and for being a minister within various ruling governments six times. Her political career is even more remarkable given the dearth of women engaged in public politics in Kerala. Born in 1919, Gowriamma came from a wealthy, land-owning Ezhava family, much like Meera.[8] She became the first Ezhava woman to graduate with a law degree and joined the Communist Party in 1948, the same year she went to prison for her political activities. In the Communist government in 1957, she was the revenue minister who spearheaded the crucial Kerala Agrarian Relations Act, marking the beginning of her career as an able administrator and formidable legislator. However, her career within the party was checkered. Though mentioned several times as a possible candidate for chief minister, she was never chosen and was never part of the higher-ranking party committees. Her private life has persistently been a subject of great scrutiny. It is alleged that after the Communists won in 1957, the party instructed her to marry her lover, T. V. Thomas, to avoid scandal. When the Communist Party split in 1964, she joined the CPI (M), while her then former husband remained with the CPI. It is said that her former husband threatened to resign as minister in the 1967–69 government if she were made chief minister and he had to serve under her. Whatever the truth of the matter, it is clear that her status as woman and wife has played a key role in her political fortune.

However, it is not only with the politics of gender but also its intersection with the politics of caste that her political career has been entangled. In 1993 she was expelled from the party for a complex set of reasons, and in 1994 she formed the Janithipathiya Samrakshana Samithy (JSS), aligning herself and that party with the Congress-led United Democratic Front (UDF). In forming the JSS, Gowriamma created the first party explicitly dedicated to the political articulation of Ezhava concerns. Many said she was tired of delivering the Ezhava vote for the party while being treated as a second-class citizen by its upper-caste leadership.

While Meera's invocation of Gowriamma points to the caste and gender trajectories that someone like Meera will have to negotiate if she enters public politics in Kerala, the other woman Meera invoked, K. Ajitha, is an example of a different trajectory, one much more explicitly focused on the politics of gender and sexuality outside mainstream political domains. Ajitha's political career begins in the Maoist-inspired, armed Naxalite revolutionary movement, which she joined after dropping out of college and which gained prominence in Kerala and elsewhere during the 1960s and 1970s.[9] Jailed for nine years, Ajitha was released in 1977, only to find that the movement had faded. By her own reckoning, she returned to a "mundane life," marrying and raising a daughter. Always critical of the treatment of women within the movement and full of "feminist feelings," during the late 1980s she was inspired by a conference of women's organizations and decided to help shape the creation of a women's organization in Kozhikode, in northern Kerala. Anweshi was founded in 1993 as a counseling center for women that centered on gender and violence, particularly focused on domestic violence and sexual harassment. For one moment, the careers of Gowriamma and Ajitha intersected when Ajitha joined the JSS with the understanding that it would represent the interests of women, tribals, and other lower castes.

She indicates that she left the party in a falling out with Gowriamma over the Ice Cream Parlor case, in which Gowriamma chose to protect a minister because of her stakes in what Ajitha calls "power politics."

For Meera, the figures of Ajitha and Gowriamma, along with the new superintendent of police, gesture to both the possibilities and the difficulties involved in the "emancipation and liberation" of Kerala's women. Struggling to insert a language of gender politics into one based on family and kinship, Meera articulated a structure of aspiration at odds with that of higher education and marriage. While her speech struck a dissonant chord in the evening's otherwise light and entertaining events, the ensuing, more ambivalent staging and exploration of gender that was to follow resonated with Meera's assessments of the current state of young women's lives in Kerala.

After Meera's discussion of the high suicide rates for women in the state, the evening's entertainment began, a mélange of the traditional and the modern. The students performed several folk dances: a Rajasthani dance set to a popular Malayalam film song, and the Thiruvathirakali, a dance that has become synonymous with Kerala's "traditional" heritage. There was a "modern" song-and-dance sequence, with women wearing "modern" clothing (skirts, etc.), borrowed from a popular Malayalam movie, and comic impersonations of famous Malayalee film stars—Mohan Lal, Mammooty, and Shobana. This was all standard fare for many such youth functions.

The final event of the evening was a stage enactment of *Indulekha*, which, in the hands of the young women who performed it, went through some crucial mutations that spoke cogently to the ambivalence with which young women view romance in their lives. In order to collapse the narrative into a few short scenes, the novel was presented through key scenes of the Malayalam film *Pavithram* (Purity), which I extensively discussed in chapter 2.

To briefly recap, this is the story of the disruptions of a traditional Nair household (*taravadu*) resulting from the behavior of a young woman in the community and the ultimate recuperation of community through her disciplining. A crucial part of the film is the decline of the young woman as she goes to live in a hostel, wins a college beauty contest, and comes under the influence of a hard-drinking, rowdy bunch of male students.

The skit takes the character of Indulekha and inserts her into the narrative of *Pavithram*. Using the song-and-dance sequences of the movie, it transposes Chandu Menon's novel into a narrative in which Indulekha goes to live in a hostel, wins a beauty contest, and, having chosen the wrong man, ends up devastated and unhappy. Drawing a link between their own location within a hostel and Cochu's experiences with hostel and college life, the students refract *Indulekha* through the second half of the movie's plotline.

The skit begins with Indulekha, dressed in the traditional *pavada* and blouse, meeting her love, Madhavan, dressed in the traditional *mundu*, discussing their impending separation: Madhavan must go away for a three-month computer course. Indulekha will stay in a hostel while he is studying. He asks her what she would like for him to send her as gifts. Shyly, she tells him to send her whatever he would like.

Rather than follow Madhavan on his journey as the novel does, the performance focuses on Indulekha's experiences in the hostel, quite appropriate for Hostel Day. She is bewildered and overwhelmed, much like Cochu in *Pavithram*. All the other girls are dressed in modern dress— shorts, skirts, and so on. They laugh at Indulekha, a *naden pennu*, or traditional village girl. The resolution of tradition and modernity that is the refined, cultivated, westernized yet perfectly Malayalee and Nair Indulekha of Chandu Menon's imagination is nowhere in evidence; here Indulekha simply indexes unfashionable "tradition." Madhavan sends her his eagerly awaited present, which consists of lemon pickle and oil for her hair. The other girls make fun of her and these traditionally coded, unfashionable commodities, and Indulekha begins to feel depressed and dejected.

For these young women, situated as they are within the "modern" space of the hostel, the repudiation of the traditional enables an engagement with the pleasures of modern consumption. While the film depicts Cochu's engagements with modern fashion and consumption as morally degrading and repulsive, the skit renders this engagement as one of great camaraderie and fun. In its longest and most elaborated scene, the girls of the hostel decide to make a project out of Indulekha. Having cut her hair and transformed her into a skirt-wearing modern girl, they enter her in the college beauty pageant, which she joyously wins.

However, the skit does not end at this point. If it did, it would be an unusually unapologetic celebration of fashion and fun. What happens next begins to lay out the ways in which the spaces and practices of modern consumption become sexualized and the dangers of romance revealed within a sexualized public. Indulekha's inability to use romance to manage her sexualization is the focus of the rest of the skit and points to these young women's perception of the dangers involved in negotiating modern consumption and romance.

Suri Nambutiri, the seedy man whom Indulekha's male elder wants her to marry, is here transformed into a lascivious judge of the beauty pageant, wearing gold chains and a flashy white suit, speaking in stilted, stylized English, waving his gold-rimmed fake Ray-Ban sunglasses in exaggerated gestures of lechery. Played by a woman in this all-female skit, this depiction of Suri Nambutiri combines the fairly traditional stereotype of the lecherous Brahmin with that of the newly rich young man on the prowl, the exemplar of chethu masculinity. In fact, Suri Nambutiri states that he has just returned from abroad, making him the stereotype of the gulfan. Indulekha is (improbably enough) somehow smitten. Suri Nambutiri visits her in the hostel, and they strike up a romance. It is important here to note the difference between the skit and the novel. In the Nair and male-authored novel, elder members of the Nair community foist Suri Nambutiri on Indulekha and then her female cousin, enacting a kind of generational exploitation from which the young male members seek to liberate their sisters. Here, Indulekha freely desires and chooses Suri Nambutiri, taken in by his nouveau riche flashiness. Her desire for consumption is sexualized through her desire for Suri Nambutiri.

The dynamics of Indulekha's desire for Suri Nambutiri have important gender and caste/class connotations. As I discussed in chapter 2, the commodified, chethu style, linked to Gulf migration, is tied to the assertion of a lower-caste, lower-class masculinity. The figure of the lascivious upper-caste Brahmin intersects with the disreputable consumerism of the lower-caste, lower-class young man about town to produce a figure of comic, predatory sexuality that ensnares the innocent, respectable Indulekha. It is her desire for this commodified and sexualized figure that lands her in trouble.

In the next scene, Madhavan returns to visit his beloved, bearing as a gift a piece of cloth for a pavada. He is stunned to see the new, modern Indulekha. She throws his gift to the ground and kicks him out. She then phones Suri Nambutiri and asks to meet him in the park—the stereotypical space of romantic meetings. There, she asks him when they will get married. He laughs and tells her never, that it was all just for fun. In the last scene, Madhavan, now a high-ranking police officer, comes to visit the hostel on official business and treats a dejected Indulekha with contempt. Having finished his studies, he is now a full-fledged adult with a secure place in the public spaces of work, while Indulekha remains distraught and stuck within the semiprivatized space of the hostel, with nowhere to go.

Much feminist writing on romance, focused mainly on the West, has explained its popularity and appeal in terms of its very narrativity (McRobbie 1991; Pearce and Stacie 1995). The narrative scripts the life cycle of a woman into a temporal, maturational logic leading to heterosexual coupling. In this skit, however, romance is not a wholly acceptable form of coupling; it marks a discontinuous break, that between the space-time of tradition and the space-time of modernity. Public spaces of schools, hostels, parks, and restaurants become particular sites for the possibilities and ambivalences of romance—a form of public intimacy. This traversal marks the temporal movement from tradition to modernity.

The young women of the hostel have transposed the novel onto a highly contemporary site for the production of youth identities: beauty pageants, signifying the impact of an increasingly transnational commodity culture. Depictions of masculinity and femininity are also contemporary: the commodified, *chethu* masculinity of the judge, the contemporary fashion of the "modern girl." Within this commodified context, education and romantic love are fraught with corruption, danger, and ambivalence for these young women. This ambivalence is filtered through the idioms of modern Malayalee cinema which, as is discussed in chapter 2, expresses its own masculinist anxiety about the dangers of modernity, rather than its triumphs, by disciplining its female subjects. These young women took on that anxious male narrative in order to express their own anxieties about the fraught space of romance.

One possible reading of the skit is that the young women who enacted it were simply reproducing the masculine narrative of the novel and the film, which ultimately disciplines the female subject. They made it relevant to their lives by refracting the figure of Indulekha through film narratives that index the contemporary context, but the overall disciplining of female desire remained intact. However, such a reading obscures how the young women redeployed these male narratives in order to create a space for expressing their struggles, desires, and choices for both commodities and men, all of which are persistently structured by the sexualization of their presence within the public.

The dangers of romance for young women are also part of a larger discourse of gender and sexuality that has emerged in a new way in Kerala. The skit tells a cautionary tale about a young woman's desire for romance and consumption that is situated within a larger discourse about the sexual exploitation of young women. While within the original novel it is tradition that sexually exploits women, here the potentialities of exploitation are linked to the desires and seductions of consumption.

The skit demonstrates the consequences of making the wrong choice, which is really no choice at all but a moral fall from grace. Education is not a highly prized route to refinement and civility, as in Chandu Menon's novel, but a space of consumption and corruption. This corruption is expressed through the instability of negotiating constructions of female sexuality through romance. In a narrative that somehow tries to manage female sexuality, romance is always susceptible to sexualization.

While the original Indulekha chose an appropriate partner of her own caste and community, within this skit the female subject who exercises her will is ultimately chastised for having rejected her community by choosing Suri Nambutiri over Madhavan. Indulekha is now forever marred by a romance with Suri Nambutiri, who will not marry her. She went a little too far, meeting him in a park, alone. In this story, the attempt to manage expressions of her consumer desire for fashion and fun, sexualized through her affair with Suri Nambutiri, cannot be made respectable through the codes of romance and marriage. He is not condemned for being fickle; rather, she is in the wrong for being too trusting, gullible, and desirous.

Once again, this parable for the present has important gender and caste/class implications. The respectable upper-caste- and upper-class-coded Indulekha chooses Suri Nambutiri, who, while Brahmin and upper caste, is also semiotically represented through the codes of a lower-caste masculinity. We are confronted again with the juxtaposition between this complex mediation of lower-caste masculinity and the upper-caste, upper-class female, both commodified and assertive in public. The skit becomes a cautionary tale about the pleasures and dangers of an expanding commodity culture, told through a plotline that enacts a caste/class form of discipline that simultaneously transgresses and erects the boundaries of caste and community through Indulekha's fall from grace. This cautionary tale explicitly warns against the potential miscegenations of caste and community within spaces of romance.

If love does not lead to marriage, as in the original novel, there is no proper place for Indulekha. Without marriage, Indulekha cannot move back into the private. She is to be forever stuck in a sexualizing public. Just as the skit displaces the resolution of the novel, so it also displaces the resolution of the film. In the film and others like it, the female subject is not stranded in the sexualizing public she has willfully entered. She is transformed into the disciplined, traditional girl. In the skit, Indulekha has nowhere to turn. She is left in the semiprivatized hostel, rejected by Madhavan. It is in the space between love and marriage, a space of public intimacy, that the specter of female sexuality is raised and disciplined, producing an anxious and ambivalent space of romance.

Meera's opening speech challenged the claims of the Kerala model of development, in which liberation for women is straightforwardly achieved through education, by asserting an alternative path of liberation rooted in public politics. Her hostelmates' skit worked through registers of pleasure, desire, and sexuality to render romance within the spaces of college life as fraught, precarious, and ambivalent. If Meera's speech struggled through a language of public politics against the figure of the demurely educated Indulekha, refined, cultivated, and married, the skit resituated Indulekha within a highly sexualized contemporary commodity culture, one in which there are no easy resolutions. A palpable sense of danger and transgression goes hand in hand with the pleasures of consumption and romance in public. Shame, aggression, violence, desire, pleasure, and intimacy collude and collide as young women and men negotiate romance within the public spaces of college student life. Especially for young women, public spaces are suffused with fleeting and targeted, sometimes innocuous, sometimes aggressive and sexualized heterosocial interaction. I now turn to how they negotiate their presence in such contexts.

Romance in Public

Meera's pro forma invocation of the hostel as peopled by mothers, daughters, and sisters rehearses the cliché of the hostel as a home away from home. For college students and working women, the hostel is often a semiprivatized zone that they inhabit during the working week, after which they go home to their families. A base for their engagements with the public world of work and school, it is a liminal space. The duration of their studies determines how much time the students will spend in the hostel. Working women are usually in the hostel because their employers have temporarily transferred them to a post in town, usually at a bank or post office, or if this is their original posting, they are waiting for a transfer that will allow them to live at home. Unmarried working women mostly live there with the expectation that their hostel days will end upon marriage, migration, or a combination of the two.

So the intimacies of friendship and life in the hostel are both precious and precarious. These intimacies take many forms, as the residents live three and sometimes four to a room, sharing beds, clothes, food, magazines, and books. More important are the sharing of stories, debating of issues, expressing of worries. In this home away from home, it becomes possible for women to develop friendships with a variety of women from different backgrounds, but such friendships are shot through with the solidarities and divisions of caste, class, and community and the sense that they will not sustain themselves in the face of family and marriage commitments.

There were also other, long-standing members of the hostel, who, unable to make their stays temporary for a variety of reasons, appear to be anomalous, public women unattached to family, kin, or the normative horizon of an arranged marriage. The different resources of family support that young women bring to their time in the hostel become a dividing line between them. Mini had been living in the hostel for five years, one of two or three working women who lived there in a semipermanent way. She started living in the hostel as a student and then got a job as the manager of a tire store in town. Given her father's gambling debts, a mother who seemed to her weak and ineffectual, and a sister who had somehow managed a "love marriage" that did not require a dowry, Mini often talked about how she had to manage on her own. She had no family constantly searching for a suitable partner, setting up meetings with potential suitors when she went home for the weekend, which was not very often.

Being a long-standing "inmate" of the hostel, she was treated by other hostelmates as a source of authority in matters relating to doing things in town. The warden, staff, and other members of the hostel treated her with a great deal of affection but also suspicion. Questions swirled around her. How did she get the job in a tire store? What relationships with men did she develop as the manager of that store? Why did she come back after curfew on so many occasions? Mini dealt with these suspicions with a great deal of humor and righteous anger. For example, if the store closed on some days at 6:45 p.m. and there was traffic on the road, why would she not be late for the 7 p.m. curfew?

While the sexualization of her relationship with men was prevalent, her relationship with women would also be sexualized. The intimacies of friendship between women are sexualized, more often than not, as a form of discipline. One of the ways in which the warden sought to monitor the women of the hostel was by keeping track of and inquiring about the phone calls we received, the only phone being strategically placed in her office. At a certain point, Mini started receiving regular phone calls from a female friend who had lived abroad but was now in the nearby city of Kochi. During that time, Mini had come back to the hostel after the curfew on several occasions. One day, as she walked in, the warden started haranguing her about this and suddenly demanded, in front of several other people, "Who is this woman who is calling you? I have gone into your room. Why is your bed so close to Ranjini's [Mini's roommate]? I can read the papers, I know what all goes on in hostels." Mini was furious, bitterly denouncing the impropriety of such insinuations. She was also defensive, explaining to us that her friend in Kochi was someone she knew from childhood. Also, her bed was set apart from that of her roommate. What about all the other rooms in which people actually put the beds together to save space? What were women doing in those rooms?

While the sexualization of relations between men and women and occasionally between women themselves was a feature of life within the hostel, outside the semiprivate hostel the sexualization of heterosocial interactions was even more persistent. One of the most palpable ways in which young women experience the sexualization of their presence in public is through *comment adi* (being "hit" with sexualized comments) and the fondling and illicit physical touching, usually initiated by young men, that takes place, particularly on buses and trains going to and from college. So fleeting and routine is the touching that, a hostelmate once joked, half the time it felt as if ants were crawling up the side of her body or a fly had landed and flown off. She added that comments whizzed by her ear; she barely heard and understood them before the speaker moved on. It was only afterward, when she processed the words, that she began to feel shame (*nanum*) at what had been said, even though she had done nothing to cause such a feeling.

Sometimes, men make comments that are more directed, pointed, and repeated at the same time and place, targeting a particular young woman. Women apprehend them as funny and witty or disgusting and aggressive, depending on many factors, including whether a young woman knows the young man or not, whether she is interested in furthering the interaction, what threshold she has for understanding such comments as humorous, and whether she feels she can give as good as she gets. For example, while Mini would come back to the hostel full of stories about the funny, barbed "dialogues" she had with men who gave her *comment adi*, Sindhu would come back tired and dejected, sometimes crying, because of similar comments that were made to her. "Dialogue" here refers most directly to the dialogues of a film, but in more common usage it refers to performative and often witty repartee between speakers in various social situations. At one point, Mini thought she might teach Sindhu how to respond to sexualized comments in a way that was equally cutting. Many funny attempts involving sexually explicit references to body parts and activities ensued to help her practice. Unlike Mini, however, Sindhu had difficulty in mustering the courage to say such things in public.

Women understand touching or fondling in less playful terms, more often than not as aggressive sexual behavior. In general, they respond in a variety of ways, spanning the spectrum from inaction to retaliation, the latter by sometimes sticking pens and pins into the arms and legs of offending males (many young women would not go to see a movie without safety pins that they held in their hands) or going up to bus conductors and demanding that they force the offending male to get off the bus. Another way that some women try to manage this threat, in a less confrontational manner, is by deploying the language of kinship. To counter aggressive sexual behavior from young men, a young woman would sometimes attempt to familiarize herself in relationship to the man, asking him to imagine her as his sister or mother. I was told to do this if someone's behavior got to be too much. Relying on the idea of family as a protective space free of violence, this language tries to blunt the aggressive sexualization of the public through an attempt to shame the initiator of the encounter, but it rarely has much effect.

Quite apart from the interactions between strangers on buses, roads, and trains, the college also deployed the language of kinship, against both the fractious politics of students and college romances and their possible miscegenations across caste, community, and class. The college administration initiated various projects to try to bring the college "closer together"—a cultural program and the building of a garden were two examples. At every meeting or event, the college as family was emphasized. The teachers were like parents or aunts and uncles. The older students were chetans (older brothers) and chechys (older sisters). The younger students were aniyans (younger brothers) and aniyathis (younger sisters). Yet the strained notion of the college as family hardly kept politics or romance at bay. And sometimes it would be used ironically against the college administration, as was the case one morning as I walked past a department office and saw Sibi, Nisha, and Seema storming out. Earlier, the department head had apparently called one of them in to reprimand her. A teacher had seen the student talking to a few older male students from another department inside the front gate of the college and reported this to the department head. Gossip had it that this particular female student was in a relationship with one of the male students, she from a low-caste (SC/ST) rural background, he from a well-established Ezhava family in town. The teacher who saw her knew the family of the male student, and there was a clear sense on the part of the reprimanded female student that he was trying to nip trouble in the bud. The students had filed a complaint, something that was very unusual. While male students, often under the aegis of a student political party, might protest the actions of a teacher, individuals and female students rarely did so. Further, they filed a complaint on behalf of not only the reprimanded student but all of them, as female students, objecting to the idea that they should somehow not be allowed to speak to male students. Seema turned angrily to me and said, "Chechy, you were there during Freshers' Day. Remember when they said we were all a family? Well, apparently, we can't even talk to our *chetans* [elder brothers]! She got called in for talking! Why can't we talk to anybody outside our class? If we talk to them, are we going to marry them?" Seema was clearly angry about the reprimand and said she would abstain from any participation in the next department event. Sarcastically echoing a journalistic cliché about the decline of "traditional values" in Kerala, she said, "The family has disintegrated [*kudumbam nashapichu*]!"

Students romanticized other spaces within the college. The garden that was continually being planted was imagined by the teacher as a companionate space where students could congregate and discuss, a space of platonic civic virtue. However, several students linked this garden to the possibilities of romance. Raju, who was known to be a singularly unsuccessful flirt, would try to chat up his female classmates, to much derision and laughter on their part. Raju blamed his lack of success not on his own ineptitude or insensitivity but on the girls' supposed inability to respond to him, which he in turn blamed on their "fear" of boys, which he linked to the violence of student politics:

> Look, girls are afraid in this college. This college is full of hitting and violence. When the girls enter in the front and they see a crowd of boys, instead of seeing some boys that they may want to talk to, they become afraid. They think maybe there's a fight going on. I don't know how they manage to get past all this.

This made the girls "closed," "not open in their minds," not "free" or "frank." The garden, he thought, might begin to change all that: "During free time, boys will come out. Girls will come out. We will sit together in the open. Boys and girls should mingle freely, talk full." This vision of romance is in line with the gendering of civic citizenship in which the romance is imagined as demure, appropriate, and companionate. For Raju, this notion of free talk between the sexes is rooted in a sense of the demure. As he put it, "modern girls" were not really "free" or "frank." They just "showed fashion." The girls he had in mind were demure: they participated in the cultural life of the college separately but equally. He went on to say that the college, like nearby colleges, should have things like Sari Day, Women's Day, and a whole host of cultural programs in order to include female students in the life of the college. Presumably, this kind of atmosphere would also make him more successful when he "freely" and "frankly" chatted up girls.

Women who did try to occupy spaces of civic virtue found themselves constantly negotiating the sexualization of their presence. Asha was a studious and energetic young woman, active in college and in various organizations. She took part in debates and writing contests and engaged in public speaking at youth festivals as part of a group of students from the college linked to the YMCA in town. After classes, this group of mostly male students, with two or three female students, often congregated at the meeting halls of the YMCA, spending an hour or two joking around, talking, trying to see who could be persuaded to pay for another round of tea. Sometimes there was more official business to attend to: preparing for a debate, listening to an invited speaker, and contesting elections within the organization. Asha was self-conscious about often being the only female in these public activities and tried to protect herself in various ways. She was demure to a fault, never crossing the line by going someplace that was too sexualized. She refused to go to ice cream parlors, even in a large group. In an almost frantic way, she referred to all her male friends as *chetans*. Those who were relatively equal in age she would say were just like her own "cousins," for which she was teased. Sometimes, she would use a kin term in a sentence three or four times, until finally the "*chetan*" would start to laugh and tell her to knock it off.

The limits of her ability to manage her presence in public became abundantly clear after she went on television as a discussant on a youth program, something she was very excited about. About a week after her appearance, I began to notice that Asha was coming around less and less. If she came, she would come with a female friend in tow, do her business, and leave. There was no more chatting and joking over cups of tea. When I asked her male friends what was wrong, they became angry. They said that her uncle had seen her on television and had indicated that no matter how "proper" it was, that kind of exposure was too much. Apparently, he told Asha that she needed to stop these "outside activities" and focus on her studies. Her friends read her withdrawal as an instance of caste snobbery: she came from a well-educated Nair family, and as one male friend sarcastically put it, her uncle probably told her she should not be mingling too much with her Ezhava "cousins." They interpreted her uncle's admonishments as a way to police the boundaries of caste that Asha was transgressing, possibly, from her uncle's point of view, for romantic reasons. Almost to a comical degree, Asha used her respectable, upper-caste demure femininity to transgress boundaries of caste, class, and gender that were ultimately, in this instance, unsuccessful. She worked hard to find a space not only to participate in all these "civic activities" that were somehow going to help her do well in the future (as she endlessly justified it) but also to develop and maintain friendships that had become important to her. While they made fun of her desperate attempts to turn them all into innocuous brothers, those attempts revealed her difficulties in navigating a sexualized public at the intersection of caste, class, and gender hierarchies.

Though always susceptible to having their presence sexualized and policed, young women participated in spaces and activities of civic virtue in college and in youth organizations. Other sites for youthful social interaction were understood by them, their classmates, parents, and teachers more straightforwardly through the categories of sexuality and romance, not kinship or civic participation. While the beach is most overtly sexualized, the ice cream parlor is better understood through a code of romance, one that by its very spatial organization tries to manage a precarious public intimacy. It might be disastrous for a woman to be seen going into an ice cream parlor by parents and other elder relatives, but it was a risk some women would take for the sake of spending time with a romantic interest, for several reasons. First, an ice cream or drink is cheap. Second, one could go there with other female friends as a group and manage to pull it off as a social situation between friends if one had to. Third, the space could protect your privacy to a certain degree. In conversation with the owner of a newly opened ice cream parlor in town, I learned the logic behind its layout. It was dimly lit, with booths that faced the back wall of the parlor, away from the street. If one looked into the parlor from the street, all that was visible was a series of bamboo walls that formed the backs of the benches of the booths. Each booth could accommodate one couple; none of the patrons were visible to passersby on the street. This form of public intimacy created a space for romance while shielding one from the gaze of the street.

So far, I have examined dominant narratives of romance, linked them to mediations of globalization and consumption, and explored the pleasures, anxieties, and dangers of heterosocial relations in public spaces where young women's presence is persistently sexualized by men. I now turn to explore how young women navigate romantic desire in such contexts.

Love in the Shadow of Marriage

Romance in South Asia rarely leads to marriage (Mody 2007; Osella and Osella 1999). Romantically involved couples who desire to marry rarely obtain parental approval, especially if they cross community norms, and elopements are rare. After a few years in college, when one may engage in friendships and romances that exceed the boundaries of family and community norms, arranged marriages fold most young people back into their kin and community networks. This, however, does not mean that young women can easily disentangle romance from the question of marriage. Even when a young woman explicitly disavows an interest in marriage, this requires the negotiation of marriage, and negotiations of romance within the spatiotemporal context of college life are shot through with the ideas, imaginings, expectations, and structures of marriage as a normative horizon.

An aggressive verbal approach from a male on the street or a bus, no matter how many times repeated, rarely leads directly to a positive expression of interest on the part of a woman. Even if a relationship begins that way, it is usually mediated by a discourse that is more often than not rooted in some sense that the possible love interest is not a complete stranger: one has friends who know him, a cousin has said that his family is a good one, someone once met his sister and she seems nice, and the like. Calculations by a young woman about moving forward into romance often hinge on attempts to understand the character (sub-hawam) of the romantic other and often emerge through contexts in which she tries to find out who that other person is. While all of these impressions may be wrong, the mediation of the unknowability of the other through such a discourse reveals romance to be a complex set of calculations through which one produces and manages romantic desire.

On a long bus ride to her home, which I was visiting for the weekend, Manju discussed with me the decisions she felt she had to make about the possibility of moving forward into a full-fledged romance with a young man at college who was also a neighbor in her distant village. In this conversation, she considered many things as she wondered about moving from some low-level flirting to possibly developing what, in youth slang, is called a *line*. The use of the English word to denote a more fully formed, romantically inflected relationship nicely captures both the fragility and the flirtatious nature of such liaisons. She started seeing him frequently on the long ride to and from college. At first, he was nonchalant and would say nothing to her on the bus. Then, one day, he asked her if she knew when the exam schedule would come out. She gave him the answer, and their friendship slowly proceeded from there. He talked to her more frequently and asked her about her brother in the Gulf, about whom he had some vague knowledge. Then he started giving her letters with love poetry in them, cards, pieces of candy. He watched for her in college, trying to catch her eye. She responded, making eye contact, accepting the letters, making sure he saw that she ate the candy he had presented her. In her narrative, he emerged as a sweet, funny, flirtatious young man who had enlivened her bus ride home. It now seemed that he wanted something more; he had begun asking her to meet him to talk in private, and she was not sure whether she should do that. While she enjoyed her encounters with him and thought he was a *pawam*, sweet boy, she was not sure that he was very exciting. She was contemplating how to proceed with the relationship.

In our conversation, she situated her simple enjoyment of these encounters in a set of considerations that encompass family, college, and her own desires. One thread that ran through the discussion was her sense that the young man was someone who understood her because they both came from poor village backgrounds that made them both marginal within the college. He and his friends watched out for her and her friends in the college, where it was always possible to be bothered or insulted. On the other hand, she came from a Christian family, and he from a Hindu one. He was also an active member of the ABVP on campus. When I asked her how he could be a member of the ABVP and be developing a relationship with a Christian, she said that politics was one thing, love another. That was not what bothered her. The real issue was how much she really wanted this in the face of all that might unfold. Should she pursue this? What if the question of marriage emerged? Was she willing to go against the wishes of her parents if it came to that? If she was not, should she meet him in private?

While Manju negotiated romance in the present with marriage as a possibility in the future, Aisha's negotiated romance with marriage as a more imminent possibility. A classmate was wooing Aisha. He wrote their names on a wall behind the department office, and everyone was talking about them. She told me about him, saying that she had not responded to him but was wondering what to do. It was clear she was excited by the prospect. Aisha came from what she called an "orthodox Muslim family." Her father and uncles had been putting increasing pressure on her to get married. She said she argued with her father almost every day, saying she wanted to study, and refused to agree. She said she would like to get an M.A. and a law degree. Her father was worried that if she got too many advanced degrees, it would become too difficult to get her married, and he was now actively pursuing marriage for her. Proposals came to the house almost daily now. She told me she fought them off. When I asked her how, she explained, with a twinkle in her eye. Any time a proposal arrived, she came up with some story about the person. Usually, she told her uncles and father that the young man was a known troublemaker in school, he chased women, made comments to them, or the like. They had no way of checking whether it was true since they rarely left the village and she was the one with access to that kind of information. Those kinds of stories played on her father's fears for his daughter (as she put it, "I am his pet"), and even if her uncle said that they should check her stories out, he refused the proposal. So far, she had gotten rid of three proposals this way. But she wondered how long she could keep it up.

Marriage, as an imminent or a future possibility, impinges on the pleasures or desires for romance in the foregoing narratives, which reveal the ways in which young women weigh their participation in romance. Ideas of romantic love and marriage are also intertwined in male narratives of romance, ones that produce an ambiguous notion of companionship. Unlike O. Chandu Menon who introduced romantic love within the confines of caste and community, the young man in the following case was willing at least to fantasize about the possibility of romance across the boundaries of community while upholding the notion of a demure and companionate wife.

Prasad discussed with me his idea of the perfect woman, explaining what he liked about the heroine of *Bombay*, a movie he had seen four or five times with his friends. *Bombay*, directed by Mani Ratnam, is a love story that centers on the relationship between a Muslim heroine, played by Monisha Koirala, and a Hindu man, played by Aravind Swamy.[10] Prasad and his friends were not interested in the upper-caste, upper-class Hindu man with the respectable middle-class style. They were interested in the heroine.

> Shaila Banu. They create her in the style of a perfect woman. There are many things involved in that. In order to marry, for a permanent union, they will only choose someone like that. In all these films . . . they all touch on a demure girl. She is more like a child. Perhaps it may be a fantasy. But we all liked it.

Prasad went on to describe all the things he liked about her: her walk, the way she danced, her facial expressions. The gist of the movie, according to Prasad, is love:

> In blind love, no restrictions matter. This is Shaila Banu. . . . She was raised in a purely orthodox tradition. But when love comes, she throws away certain orthodox traditions. Not just the *burqa*. She goes alone to Mumbai. She goes to Mumbai alone. I mean, she has no interactions with anybody growing up. But when it, love, comes, she throws it all away. And when the time comes, she has the strength to face reality. That is what Mani Ratnam shows. Mani Ratnam is showing that love is blind. She's orthodox but she goes up to Mumbai. It's unimaginable if there is no love. Right? Then, there is her devotion to her husband. Right? When I say her devotion, I mean . . . after the marriage . . . the happenings in the house, then she is more or less like a child, she is childlike. It's perfect . . . she's mature when she needs to be. . . . I mean it's just the fantasy of a man, right?

While Manju and Aisha weighed the possibilities of going against the wishes of their families, Manju especially wondering how "blind" her love could be, Prasad held out the image of a love that is blind to everything, including community. Love enables the heroine to assert herself into the modern public, which is conflated with traveling alone to Mumbai to be with her lover. But once she gets there, she is quickly able to retreat into the modern privacy of companionate marriage and household duties. She is his fitting companion, childish or mature as necessary.

This perfect companion should not only be "blind," loving, and devoted; she must be educated but inferior. Prasad went on to outline that she must not have a degree that trumped his. If he had a Ph.D., she must have only an M.A. If he had an M.A., she must have only a B.A. Her family must not be of a higher status than his, and she must show respect toward him. His narrative reveals the mutual imbrications of the ideology of romantic love with the persona of the educated, wifely companion. It was this that Aisha was in danger of becoming: an overly educated young woman who could not adequately "respect" the husband that might be found for her.

With marriage on the very immediate horizon for many young women, their fantasies of the perfect husband are mediated by anxieties and questions. Prema, a fellow hostel "inmate," was notorious, rarely attending classes, instead lying in bed with a stack of four or five Mills and Boon romance novels, finishing them by the time tea was served in the late afternoon. She pulled me into her room one evening where, with a group of five friends, she was trying to develop a questionnaire for potential mates. She was soliciting advice on what kinds of questions one might want to ask a potential husband. While it was a somewhat silly exercise with lots of laughter involved, there was a very serious side to it for Prema. Her slightly older sister was in the marriage market. When she was asked to meet potential husbands, she was so shy and tongue-tied that they rejected her. Prema was determined to not be that way. She thought developing this questionnaire might help her appear more assertive and well spoken. Not only did she solicit questions; she asked her friends, very specifically, about wording and the appropriateness of asking this or that question in an interview, with an eye toward actually using the questionnaire. However, the consensus of her friends was that that would be inappropriate. After all, this was not a job interview.

There were twenty-four questions:

1. Are you fussy about food?

2. What type of dress do you think is appropriate? [That is, what style of dress does he think a woman should wear? Only a sari? Can she wear *churidars* after marriage, skirts sometimes?]

3. When do you want to have a child? Could it be after five years? [They all laughed at this highly optimistic notion.]

4. What do you think of women working?

5. Do you do any cooking or washing? Do you clean up after yourself?

6. Would you respect my parents?

7. What do you think of makeup? Do you approve of it?

8. What books, music, and movies do you like?

9. What do you think is a romantic evening?

10. What is your idea of marriage?

11. What is your religious faith?

12. Do you know how to dance?

13. What kind of outdoor activities do you do? Camping, sports, jogging? [This question seemed unimportant and silly to everybody but Prema, several friends pointing that nobody did those kinds of things in Kerala. She said it was important to her because when she lived in Canada, between the ages of one and four, she saw many people engaging in such activities. It was what she remembered about Canada. If she married a man and lived in India, maybe, she thought, they could do that sort of thing in a hill station in North India.]

14. What are your personal habits? Do you smoke or drink?

15. Character: Are you an extrovert or an introvert? [There was much discussion about whether one could come right out and ask this.]

16. What kind of person are you looking for?

17. What is your idea of a good vacation?

18. How do you sort out problems? Do you share your feelings and talk it out with others, or do you do it on your own?

19. What are your vices?

20. Do you like children? And would you clean up after them?

21. What is your idea of splurging? Do you fight to hold on to your wallet?

22. Where would you like to settle and live? Near my parents or yours? [A big discussion ensued about this question. Prema said she did not want to live near any parents; others said people should try to be near their parents. After much debate, somebody asked her, in exasperation, why she was bothering with this question. Most likely, she was going to end up in the United States anyway. Hopeful at the prospect, Prema laughed and denied its possibility.]

23. Do you have a sense of humor?

24. Can you show me your hands? [After much laughter about the sexual implications of this, the more serious notion was that hands reveal much about character. One would not be able to actually read his palm, but if his hands were gentle, he might be so.]

There was no discussion here of "love," its absence, its presence, whether it was blind or not, and no discussion of attraction, chemistry, or sexuality. This narrative of romance is rooted in scenarios—romantic evenings, dances, vacations, sports activities—spaces of romance that can only be entered through a connection to a man, hopefully one who is gentle, emotionally available, funny, open-minded, egalitarian, and generous with his wallet. Here, Prema was injecting her fantasy of the companionate husband into the structures that guide her "choice" of partner.

It is a middle-class fantasy in the form of an anxious question. This move from fantasy to question reveals several anxieties. One set reflects something of the uncertainty, risk, and vulnerability of a woman in the institution of marriage. Will he be kind? How can she tell? This move from fantasy to question also occurs as the fantasy is injected into the structure of the lives of these women as the daughters of middle-class Indian families, dependent on their husbands for what their futures hold. What will she be able to wear? What will her household duties look like? Will she be near her parents? How soon will she have to have a child? Will she be able to work?

Further, she is not going to meet her potential husband in a London office as the resourceful secretary to a tall, dark, and handsome English business mogul. Nor is she going to meet her romantic hero on a Greek island as the nanny to the motherless children of a handsome and volatile Greek tycoon. Those are the plot lines of the Mills and Boons romance novels Prema read so incessantly. Nonetheless, her world—one might say Indulekha's world—is now transnational. Perhaps her husband will be a computer specialist from the United States, or an engineer in Canada, or a doctor in Dubai. However, the structures of middle-class social reproduction are intact, and this marriage will be well arranged along the lines of caste, class, and community.

Prema was trying to inject some sense of choice into a process that affords her little agency. The narrative of romantic love structures the choice. One chooses one's own partner. However, within the arranged-marriage scenario, there is no question of a preexisting love that drives the choice. This is not a "love marriage." Prema tried to individualize and personalize the process through the idioms of romantic love—is he an extrovert or an introvert, what are his likes and dislikes, does he know how to be romantic? Prema, considering herself an extrovert, could only imagine being with someone who was talkative.

While Prema tries to inject romance into an arranged-marriage scenario, others struggle with college romances where the possibility of marriage was raised and then deflected. Bina's narrative is one of a college romance gone wrong, one that did not lead to a "love marriage." It takes us back to the skit in which romance in college cannot be turned into marriage. While the skit used this narrative structure to sexualize and discipline a desire for public consumption and romance, here we see the effects of romance on engagements with the public worlds of work and occupation. A hostelmate, Bina worked as a bank officer in a small bank in town, though she had studied engineering. She met her boyfriend in engineering college; they had been together for several years. During their last year in college, Bina had gotten a well-paying job in Mumbai while he had not. Bina went, expecting that he would find some kind of job and they would eventually be together.

However, even before she left, she could feel her boyfriend withdrawing from her. He was "cold," as she put it. She went to Mumbai anyway, thinking they would work it out somehow. She wrote him letters every day but got no replies. Meanwhile, she was miserable in Mumbai. She knew no one, the women in her hostel were nice but not very friendly or helpful, and the work was hard. She was sad, lonely, and afraid. The day she actually fell off a train, she called her father and told him she was coming home. She did not tell him why, just that she needed another job. The experience taught her that she was not as tough as she thought she was. As she put it, "I'm not so thick skinned. I'm not so tough, I learned. I used to think nothing bothered me. It was just all too much."

When she got back, her boyfriend would barely speak to her, even though, from her point of view, she had given up the job to come back to him. Finally, he told her that it would not work between them, since they were from different communities. She scoffed at this reasoning. She argued that she knew it was a lie since she was very close to his family. She surmised angrily that he was really upset about her getting the job. Why had he told her he loved her? He had never said that they would marry, but she was treated like part of the family. His mother made special curries for her; they watched videos at his house. If there was a strike that day, she would spend the whole day at his house. How could he now say that they were from different communities? He had told her that his grandmother might not approve of her, but as she put it, "What am I supposed to think of him telling me that when he is sitting across from me in an ice cream parlor?" She bitterly concluded that he had surmised that her family did not have a substantial dowry to offer and he had gotten greedy. He was to marry someone else next month.

The narrative of Bina's entry into the public world of work and her experience in Mumbai is mediated by a fraught and uncertain romance. While Prasad fantasized about his perfect mate, one who could assert herself and journey to Mumbai alone while remaining a demure and companionate wife, here we see a different journey to Mumbai, one that fractures the notion of a romantic love that is assertive and nurturing at the same time. Bina's uncertain romance did not support her entry into the public, it disrupted it. In the end, she came home. She said when she thought about it now, it did not upset her. It embarrassed her. "Blind love," to use Prasad's phrase, had blinded her, but now that it was gone she could see clearly once more.

Conclusion

These women's negotiations of romance demonstrate how understandings of romantic love structure the ways young women experience their entry into and belonging within modern publics. The "civic right" to choose one's own partner is negotiated in a variety of ways, mediating women's entry into, claims on, and withdrawals from spaces of education, work, and consumption. An expanding commodity culture has increasingly linked romance and consumption, with significant implications for young women's understanding of themselves as consumers. In these ways, romance becomes another lens into the productions of new forms of consumer citizenship.

These narratives of romance in the shadow of marriage demonstrate the precariousness of intimacy in publics that persistently and sometimes violently sexualize young women, with sometimes far-reaching consequences in the temporal trajectory of a woman's life, where, as Meera put it, "marriage is the norm." While middle-class colonial male narratives proclaimed love marriages to be the path to increasing freedom for women (so that males could assert their own rights as the heads of modern nuclear families), women's narratives reveal a more ambiguous space of freedom in which it is possible to have some choice but little agency, a sexualized space in which one can be stranded if love does not turn into marriage.

While male colonial narratives of romantic love stressed the role of education in the creation of companionate marriage, contemporary narratives by young women render education as a space of consumption and desire that is fraught with possibility, aggression, and danger. Globalization here is tied to the spread of a commodity culture that is sexualized and corrupting. The simple pleasures of heterosocial romance and friendship within the normative horizon of marriages more often than not arranged are a precarious and tenuous achievement.

If we pull back a bit and focus on the figure of Indulekha in my hostelmates' skit as emblematic of a particular understanding of Kerala's modernity, it becomes possible to bring into view the ways in which contemporary discourses of consumerism are anxiously invested in globalization. Like Indulekha herself, the optimistic and reformist language of modernization, implemented through the developmental state, is being seduced by a predatory globalization that leaves Kerala betwixt and between. These larger discourses operate in and through the spaces of college student life, producing new forms of consumer citizenship that structure social membership and collective belonging. These processes unfold through inscribing themselves onto gender-, class-, and caste-specific bodies that reveal a contested negotiation of the cultural politics of globalization.

4

Politics, Privatization, and Citizenship

When I first arrived in the mid-1990s, I would walk to the college daily from the student hostel where I lived, only to find it closed and largely empty, a situation that lasted for months. Kerala was touted to be an "education miracle" with a nearly 100 percent rate of literacy and high mass participation of both boys and girls at every level of education—all said to be crucial to the Kerala model of development. However, students routinely went on strike, closing the college in protest over the government's attempts to privatize higher education. This particular strike was part of a larger mobilization of students and political parties against the government's economic liberalization policies and what they called the "commercialization" and "privatization" of higher education. At the end of the first day, after most of the students who had shown up for the day had left, the teachers were still hanging about, reading the newspapers or gossiping. They could not leave if they wanted to be paid. Shaking her head as she watched a political procession (*jatha*) of male students move through the corridors, shouting "*Inquilab Zindabad!*" (Long live the revolution!) as they raised clenched fists into the air, a female teacher laughed and said cynically, "It's not democracy, it's demo-crazy."

Over the last century, a new kind of democratic public, linked to education and youth, has been central to Kerala's developing narrative of modernity.[1] Discourses of politics construct this public as a "political public," driven by the agency of revolutionary or revolutionizing young men. Modern publics in Kerala have included girls and women to a very high degree in the public places of work and education through its highly touted educational system, but they have also been excluded from this "political public." The college attempts to contain this masculinist political culture with a Nehruvian discourse of "service to the nation." As the college administration struggles against the persistent and fractious presence of student politics, education itself has become a key object of this political public. Educational institutions are long-standing spaces for constituting modern public spheres and central to the production of citizens in modern nation-states.[2] What happens to the politics and practices of gendered democratic citizenship in an educational setting when neoliberal economic reforms that constitute globalization newly reconfigure education as a commodity?

The Politics of Privatization

Privatization is a set of discourses and policies that portray the state as pitted against the market, in which the state is "public" and the market is "private."[3] While privatization arguments often hinge on the quality of services, supply, and demand, what is most at stake in debates about privatization are competing notions of the public, underwritten by competing visions of citizenship.

In Kerala, as elsewhere, debates about privatization usually revolve around two competing arguments. On the one hand, some herald privatization as the engine of economic growth and prosperity, relieving states and their citizens of the draining effects of huge state bureaucracies and inefficiencies. On the other hand, others oppose privatization on the grounds that the withdrawal of the state from social services, together with the concomitant rise of consumption and market ideology, leads to increasing inequality. Despite their substantial differences, both sides make claims on the state. Moreover, while both positions target consumerism, little attention is paid to *how* discourses of consumption work to reconfigure politics, citizenship, and democracy.

That is, the state-market nexus structures the educational field in Kerala; the meaning of education and citizenship are debated and reconfigured through a persistent yet transformed entanglement of various conceptions of private and public. Importantly, discourses about "politics" (*rashtriyam*) pervade college life in Kerala, marking the reformulation of citizenship via discourses of consumerism in the contemporary context. Students and others struggle over the meaning of democratic public life, pitting a political public, rooted in the anticolonial struggle and postcolonial nationalist politics, against a civic public that Partha Chatterjee links to the emergence of middle-class bourgeois nationalism (see Chatterjee 1998, 2000, 2004). Students actively pursue political activity in an already constituted public space of politics, linked to masculine forms of sociality and mobility. The tension between different citizens' freedom to occupy and traverse public spaces in the discourses of both a "civic public" and a "political public" is grounded in competing, class-inflected masculinities.

This civic public now articulates with new discourses about the freedom of the market. The "private consumer," through discourses of consumption, lays claim to the state by trying to construct a "civic public," based on notions of efficiency and orderliness, in opposition to a "political public," deemed to be unruly, disruptive, and sometimes violent, in ways that are reconfiguring politics, democracy, and citizenship under conditions of globalization. This is a wide-ranging middle-class discourse about mass politics as a form of corruption, a politics that needs to be reclaimed through new forms of civic and political participation (Chatterjee 2004; Vedwan 2007; Fernandes 2006). Nowhere is this discourse of politics more palpable than in discussions and debates about student politics: college administrators deploy a Nehruvian understanding of patriotic service to hold politics at bay, even as a new middle-class discourse of antipolitics works to eradicate this same politics through the construction of education as a commodity that the state must allow its citizens to efficiently and properly consume.[4] As a liberalizing Indian middle class and its aspirants, particularly nonresident Kerala parents in the Gulf, seek to privatize higher education—so as to prepare their children for global employment—administrators and others target student politics in particular for educational reform. Within the more pervasive and diffuse discourse of antipolitics that takes place in higher education, privatization is part of a set of struggles about the place of colonial and anticolonial traditions of politics within liberalizing India, struggles that have also involved specific attempts to ban politics from colleges.

Political Protest, Youth and Masculinity in Kerala

In July 1994, a group of middle-class businessmen belonging to a consumer organization staged a *jatha* (political procession) down Mahatma Gandhi Road in front of the State Secretariat in Thiruvananthapuram, the capital city. Unlike most *jatha* participants, however, they did not march on foot but drove cars, motorbikes, and scooters, not only because they had the financial means to do so but, more pointedly, because they wished to assert their right to use the road. This was part of a larger mobilization to initiate what they called an "anti-*bandh* culture" in the state (*Indian Express*, July 3, 1994). *Bandh* is a commonly used Hindi word that literally means "closed," but it can refer more specifically to a general strike, usually called by a political party, in which workplaces, schools, colleges, transportation, and shops come to a standstill. A petitioner also filed a case before Kerala's high court asking that an injunction be issued against the frequent *bandhs* initiated by political parties. Although that was not initially successful, the Kerala High Court officially banned *bandhs* in 1997, and later that year, this ruling was upheld by the Supreme Court of India. In 2003, another petitioner filed a writ before the Kerala High Court arguing that the government and various other organizations were getting around the 1997 ruling by renaming *bandhs hartals* (*The Hindu*, March 28, 2003). The word *hartal* is often used interchangeably with *bandh*, although it usually refers to a strike that is called suddenly, a more delimited form of protest in duration and scope. The petitioner, who was the president of an organization called the International Society for the Preservation of Human Rights and the Rule of Law, argued that *bandhs* or *hartals*, however one chose to name them, violated the rights of citizens, specifically the constitutional right to equal protection and the right to life.

A consumer magazine, along with a civic organization, organized a conference in the city of Kochi to promote this anti-*bandh* movement. Conference speakers condemned the violence *bandhs* did to people and property under the "cover of democratic dissent." Several acknowledged that at one time general strikes were necessary and genuinely expressed the will of the people. The general strike in 1907 to protest the arrest of the nationalist leader Bal Gangadhar Tilak by British authorities was "spontaneous." Mahatma Gandhi's fasting and Non-Cooperation Movement was "nonviolent." But they drew a distinction between these leaders' use of *bandhs* and *hartals* during the independence movement and political parties' abuse of them in postindependence India. Today's *bandhs* "victimized the public" and "[were] no credit to civilized society." Conference speakers cited the large sums of money lost due to property damage and the undermining of the work ethos due to the interruption of business. They contended that people observe *bandhs* (by not going to work or school and by closing down shops) not because they always approve of a protest but often because of fear of violence. By "forcing" people to stay indoors, *bandhs* are not an expression of democratic rights but violate the people's "fundamental right to move about freely," hence, the "anti-*bandh*" *jatha* on the public roads of Thiruvananthapuram. Although the ruling United Democratic Front (UDF), led by the Kerala Congress Party, was chastised for not doing enough to prevent the *bandhs*, the blame was squarely placed on the leftist parties. The veteran communist leader E. M. S. Namboodiripad of the CPI (M), the opposition party at that time, fired back that *bandhs* were an expression of the people's fundamental right to protest and that to ban them was "fascist" (*The Hindu*, June 25, 1994). Whether they were legal or not, such agitations would always take place. Asked about the violence associated with strikes, he stated that it was a part of the struggle itself. After all, he contended, during the freedom movement many had lost their lives.

This rather striking contestation about the forms of Kerala's political culture brings to light a set of cultural and political struggles tied to notions of the public in which the space of politics (*rashtriyam*) is mostly understood to be occupied by the left. At one level, this speaks to the centrality of the communist movement in the state. Many people in Kerala believe that to be critical of politics is to be critical of the left, and that to be critical of the left is to be critical of politics. In this way, the

politics of antipolitics is mapped onto a set of political distinctions between left and right, pitting, in the anti-*bandh* demonstration, middle-
class businessmen driving down roads lit by the headlights of cars and
scooters against the ordinary folk (*sadharannakar*) of conventional *jathas*,
walking the roads lit by the fire of handheld torches.[5]

The *jatha* has a long history as a mode of political protest. The Punjabi
word entered the political vocabulary of Malayalam in the 1920s, when a
jatha of supporters came to Kerala from the north to join the Vaikom
Satyagraha, a pivotal moment in the struggle to constitute an egalitarian
public (Menon 1994).[6] This *satyagraha* (nonviolent struggle) challenged
the caste-based social geography of space, whereby low castes could not
enter the temple or walk the roads around it. The protesters mobilized a
notion of a unified Hindu nationalist community, which they defined in
largely upper-caste terms, against caste regulations based on exclusion
(Menon 1994). Caste regulations that produced not only untouchability
but unapproachability[7]—regulating the visibility of and distance between
people of different castes—were challenged by the *jatha*, in which members of different castes marched together. Thus protestors traversed
a caste-based understanding of place to produce an egalitarian public
space. Moreover, *jathas* were also central to the production of Kerala as a
regional identity. The *jatha* became a potent political mode in the 1930s:
in agitations over temple entry, salt marches, peasant protests, and various forms of civil disobedience, *jathas* mapped a cartography from Malabar in the north to Trivandrum in the south. *Jathas* traversed the Kerala
landscape vigorously and persistently. The "*jatha* idea," as the communist leader A. K. Gopalan called it, has become emblematic of Kerala's
political modernity (Jeffrey 1993, 121).[8]

The political public instantiated in the *jatha* is intertwined with education. The success of the educational system—spreading education at all
levels across the population—evolved through a process in which, historically, education has been both a key object of political contestation and a
crucial space for the development and enactment of a vigorous political
culture. One could not write the modern political history of Kerala, indeed the history of modernity in Kerala, without writing about education
—either as an object and site of contestation or as an institution that has
produced key political actors, namely, students and teachers. As Robin

Jeffrey has argued, "Most Keralans have first encountered government—and, indeed, public politics—through a school system that has become the heart of the new Kerala" (1993, 153).[9]

Furthermore, the very political history of Kerala has a strong gender and generational narrative. The "youthfulness" of politics was one of its key features, a youth understood to be militant and masculine. For example, like many of his contemporaries, E. M. S. Namboodiripad, the now-deceased veteran leader of the CPI (M) in Kerala, embarked on a life of politics straight out of college. Having arranged a successful boycott of his history class, he left education for good. In 1932, he was arrested, and in his autobiography he wrote: "With this my life had taken a new turn. My transformation from a boy . . . to a youth dedicating his entire life to active politics became complete" (Jeffrey 1993, 64).

The early history of student politics in the region was intimately connected to the nationalist movement. Gandhi's Non-Cooperation Movement of 1920 was the first to draw substantial numbers of students into politics, which increased during the Civil Disobedience Movement of 1930. While some organizations were linked to the nationalist Congress Party or the Congress Socialists, others such as the Student Federation, which formed in 1936, were purely student-run (Altbach 1966). During the Quit India Movement in 1942, students were pivotal. They disrupted British administrative outposts, published illegal newspapers, operated clandestine radio stations, and took over leadership when adult leaders were arrested. Thousands were jailed and dismissed from colleges. However, by this time splits also began to emerge among students, between those who were oriented toward communism and those who were more Gandhian and socialist.

Students emerged as political actors through the nationalist movement, in which young militant sons were seen to drag their elders into a new Kerala. The campaign in 1938 for responsible government in Trivandrum is a case in point that many would argue cemented the form that public protest would take on the Kerala landscape. What was unique about this protest, the largest that Kerala has ever seen, was that the elder, upper-caste members of the dignified Legislative Council, who usually dressed in western suits and ties, had donned khadi (homespun cotton) to march in the jathas, shouting slogans at the goading of student and peasant groups (Jeffrey 1993).[10] In this way, youth and education as a space of masculine political agency has been central to the articulation of public politics in Kerala.

Finally, the masculine gendering of this space of youthful politics is illuminated if we closely examine the family romance that underwrites it. Plays were central to the spread of the leftist movement in Kerala, perhaps the most important one being *You Made Me a Communist* (*Ningal Enne Communist Aaaki*), by Thoppil Bhasi (Zarilli 1995). The play has been performed more than two thousand times and continues to be staged today. It was also made into a successful film (Bhasi 1970). It is estimated that during the 1950s it was regularly staged four times a day. While actors play the characters today, in the 1950s it was activists, many of them students, who took the various roles: the play was first staged in 1952 by the Kerala People's Arts Club, which was founded by a group of student activists intent on raising popular awareness of sociopolitical issues like land reform and caste inequality. In 1957, when the first communist government came to power in Kerala, many attributed that victory to this play.

Like many of its kind, this play involved a transformation of consciousness on the part of a central character, Paramu Pillai, who is "made a communist." An older man of a declining dominant Nair family, he is shown the error of his feudal ways by his communist son Gopalan. By the end, he asks to join the party, and in the final scene he raises the red flag as slogan-shouting youth march against another injustice. In between, various struggles over land and the dishonoring of an untouchable girl form the plot of the long play. These are interwoven with the story of Sumam, the daughter of the capitalist landlord, who escapes from her feudal and patriarchal oppression (her father tries to marry her off) through romance with the communist Gopalan, a modern romance that also teaches her the evils of capitalism. The lower-caste female character is primarily understood through her sexuality, which the communist youths protect from dishonor by a capitalist landlord. In all cases, the youthful agency at work here is a revolutionary or revolutionizing young man, one that is also linked with the singular masculine, reforming, and responsible hero of Malayalam cinema discussed earlier. Often, this young man is an upper-caste male—either a decadent young man who gets politicized, as in another of Bhasi's plays, *Prodigal Son*, or an already politicized upper-caste youth showing his elders the error of their feudal ways. If the young man is not upper-caste, the narrative presents a lower-caste young man who moves from being servile and humble to being aggressive, disciplined, and militant. The family romance that structures this narration of the emergence of a political public demonstrates the gendered and caste politics of youth and of the youthfulness of politics.

In 1924, the satyagraha in Vaikom had focused on the rights of low-caste members to use the roads surrounding a temple. The attempt in the 1990s by middle-class businessmen to erase the prevailing conception of the political provides a stark contrast, by mobilizing around a rhetoric of antipolitics through the assertion of their rights to use the roads. The idea of the public being contested in the *jatha* of middle-class businessmen is both literal and conceptual. Literally, it is about the functioning of roads, shops, schools, and workplaces. These public places are linked to the conception of a space of the public, through the language of rights, democracy, the people, property, and politics. Literal places are linked to contested conceptual notions of the public by the ways in which they are used and occupied. Their contestation over the dominant forms of political culture in Kerala touches the heart of Kerala's self-identity as modern and revolutionary and reveals the larger contours of a debate about the very meaning of democratic politics and citizenship in these globalizing times. The *political* public, a conception of the public rooted within a tradition of public politics that emerged out of the colonial period, is now confronted by a privatized citizenship linked to a conception of a properly functioning *civic* public.[11]

What is being contested here are two notions of the public, both linked to the functioning of literal spaces deemed to express the nature of the public that constitutes them as "public," and the use of which somehow expresses "fundamental rights." Crucial to the constitution of a civic public is the erasure of the political through the assertion of the well-mannered and orderly use of this public space and through the respect for property by those deemed to be citizens. "The people" are disarticulated from these spaces as these are used and occupied to rearticulate a relationship between people, property, and place in a way that argues for a new conception of public space defined in terms of consumer citizenship. It defends the rights of its citizens to consume public space, seeking redress in a consumer forum.[12] The lack of freedom is linked to being forced to stay indoors, to not being able to move around freely due to a fear of violence. In this conception, the public has been forcibly privatized—incarcerated in the home—by politics. Revealing the gendered stakes of new forms of consumer citizenship, while the privacy of the home is understood as an incarceration, the privacy of the market is glossed as the freedom to choose.[13] The privatizing logic of the market asserts its claims on the public through the logic of consumption. The freedom of consumption is linked with the freedom to move in an un-inhibited way through public places. Thus the "public citizen" merges with the figure of the "private consumer." For the civic public, the limit of a genuinely democratic public is violence and fear of violence. For the political public, on the other hand, violence is not a limit as such; when justifiable, it lies at the very heart of politics. The public is not constituted by lack of fear and well-mannered behavior but by the "right to protest" as a popular expression of political legitimacy.

The Politics of Emptiness

The case of P. Rajan, a student who was later understood to be tortured and killed in 1976 by police during the "Emergency" declared by Prime Minister Indira Gandhi, was a pivotal moment in Kerala's postcolonial history.[14] The son of a college professor, and a student at an engineering college in the northern Kerala city of Kozhikode, Rajan was suspected by police of being a Naxalite sympathizer; the Maoist-inspired movement drew many students who were at odds with not only the Congress Party but the CPI (M) as well. The Congress government at the time waged a sometimes violent battle against the movement, but the fallout of the case, which was widely publicized, eventually led to the resignation of a chief minister and other police officials. The Rajan case is still invoked today as an example of the heroic self-sacrifice made by student youth to uphold democratic values, which were severely tested during the Emergency. His story was made into a highly acclaimed film, *Piravi* (dir. Karun, 1988), and the memoir of his father, who brought a case against the government, was released by the Asian Human Rights Commission a few years ago (Varier 2004).

While the Rajan case projects the image of a heroic and vanguard student political movement, politics in the everyday life of the college is more routinized, both in its formal and informal registers. The empty college is a product of the contestation between a civic and a political conception of the college and the practices of democratic citizenship that define it. As with roads, shops, schools, and transportation systems, the college is an embattled terrain, a technology of citizenship in which struggles over its proper functioning constitute a struggle over the meaning of democratic citizenship. However, the persistent emptiness of the college resulting from student strikes emerges from a complex everyday struggle over the presence of politics in the college and the various ways in which students relate to this struggle. Formal student politics must be understood as part of a set of cultural and social practices that mediate gender and generationally specific forms of navigating public spaces.

Officially recognized student politics is almost exclusively structured by the larger political culture; the college system and, increasingly, schools are integral to the reproduction of this official political culture. The most important student parties are the Student Federation of India (SFI), the student wing of the CPI (M), Kerala Student Union (KSU), the student wing of the Congress Party, and the increasingly prominent Akhil Bharatiya Vidyarthi Parishad (ABVP), a separate student party with strong ties to the Hindu nationalist party, the Bharatiya Janata Party (BJP). Very often, it is the student wing of the parties that is called upon to do the hard labor of political grass-roots mobilization and education and to be at the forefront of larger political demonstrations. Student leaders and cadres are socialized into party politics, and they move up the party ranks. Thus, in very straightforward ways, colleges reflect and reproduce the official political culture of the state.

Organizationally, the most important incorporation of student politics is the student union and its election. Many politically involved students would invoke the first student strike in the college in the early 1950s as the democratization of their institution. That strike forced the college administration to acknowledge an independently elected student union, that is, one that was not appointed by the administration. Many students also linked it to the larger struggle by the left in Kerala as it entered parliamentary democracy, winning state elections in 1957 and becoming the first freely elected communist government in the world. The communist-affiliated SFI has dominated the politics of the college since then.

A civic public would define an independently elected union very differently from the way a political public would. For a civic public, the student is a citizen in the making, a pedagogical subject who must learn the proper way to participate in democratic processes. The student union and its elections are not instantiations of politics as such but rather pedagogical exercises in preparation for future participation. The official duties of the union include many "civic" activities to enhance the social life of the college and teach students how to participate in civic life: sponsoring and organizing art and book fairs, producing a college magazine, and organizing students for university-wide youth festivals and competitions. In contrast, for the political public, students are political actors in their own right. The student union and its elections are not educational practice for a deferred future of political participation; they are that participation. While students may value and engage in the "civic activities" that the union sponsors, those activities are folded into a definition of the student as citizen and political actor in the present.

Nowhere was the clash of these perspectives more evident than during the election for the student union. While the politicized students certainly saw themselves as student-citizens engaged in democratic politics, the administration tried to run the election as a "civic exercise," a kind of learning exercise for a more innocuous notion of student-citizen democracy. This democracy was orderly; the student-citizen, respectful. Against the incivility of undisciplined masculine politics, the administration tried to institute a civil, procedural election. Fed up with years of violence and fighting, the principal hit upon the idea of an oath, what he called a "code of conduct," which every elected candidate would have to take in front of the entire college as he or she was being sworn in. After being garlanded by the principal, the student would accept his/her induction into the union by reciting the following:

> I [name, office] student of the college union, solemnly pledge to discharge my responsibilities to the utmost of my ability by obeying the rules of the college and by striving to realize its motto—creation of a community above caste and communal differences where knowledge is given prime importance, and I undertake to work sincerely for the welfare of the student community, for the Indian nation and for the entire mankind, respecting the concept of "unity in diversity."

The oath links obeying the rules of the college to proper participation in democracy, invoking the slogan of democratic, secular India: "unity in diversity." This precarious notion of a civil politics is asserted against an understanding of democratic politics that does not necessarily view the rules of the college as a standard by which to judge proper participation within a democracy.

A highly controversial court case demonstrates how contemporary student politics is now linked to the broader debate about the corruption in Kerala's political culture. In the court case, the proper functioning of educational institutions and a ban on student politics are associated with a need to reform and retool Indian democracy. In 2003, the Kerala High Court, in the Sojan Francis case, ruled against a nineteen-year-old college student from a private college who was barred by his principal from taking a college exam because he did not have the requisite attendance record. The student filed a case against the college and principal, arguing that he was being unfairly treated because he was an active member of the SFI. After all, the argument went, many other students with poor attendance records—especially those involved in sports—sat for year-end exams. Moreover, the principal had banned strikes, meetings, and demonstrations within campus walls, in the name of maintaining "discipline," unless those meetings were recognized by the college administration as official. The justices ruled for the principal, providing a lengthy opinion. In addition to citing other court judgments that found that the presence of politics obstructed learning and the proper functioning of institutions, the court likened students to government employees who are banned from political activism in their places of work (*The Hindu*, May 27, 2003).

Reflecting the larger contours of the debate between the civic and the political conceptions of the public, this opinion generated much controversy. On the one hand, there were those who supported the ban on politics, arguing that students were simply the dupes of political parties and that politics got in the way of learning. Some argued that principals needed to take control of discipline in their campuses in order to create a good learning environment and to teach students how to participate "properly" in politics. Some opined that the current structure of student politics tied to political parties did not allow for any dissent. The ban might actually open up the space of debate within colleges. On the other hand, some were alarmed at the ban on politics, arguing that it curtailed a fundamental democratic right to assemble. As in the debate about *jathas*, editorials that disagreed with the court's opinion wondered what these judges would have to say about the Indian struggle for freedom, which would have been incomplete without students acting politically in educational institutions throughout the country. They also pointed out that this simply sanctioned the politics of the administration as "official" politics. However much the college administration presented itself as a neutral entity for supporting "learning," they said, most managers of private colleges that hire the principal and teachers are enmeshed in their own ties to political parties. All parties to the debate read the ban against politics as a form of politics that pitted the leftist SFI against a center-right administration and judiciary. Finally, several discussions high-lighted the silence of the judges with respect to the politics of teachers and their unions.

This legal battle over student politics is mirrored by attempts to check the presence of politics in the everyday life of the college, particularly in the way that student strikes are handled. As a policy, the principal will recognize a strike call only if it has been sanctioned by the statewide student organization. The principal is notified before 9 a.m. One ring of the bell indicates a strike; two rings indicate that classes will be con-ducted that day. A group of male students will march through the cor-ridors, shouting slogans, and then the day proceeds. The students who did not read the newspaper that morning and showed up for classes will disburse, and the faculty and staff will spend the day at the college in order to maintain their attendance so that they can be paid. Quite liter-ally, the college becomes an empty place through its routinized politici-zation. Threatened by a politics that will not confine itself to processions around the college corridors if the strike call is not heeded, the college becomes an evacuated public place.

Moving beyond the formal registers of politics in the college, the conditions for a possible *jatha* in the space of the college lie in the restless navigation of public space by young men. That is, the everyday life of politics (*rashtriyam*) is situated within the struggles of young men as they restlessly navigate fun, friendship, and romance in public. Re-member that the notion of wandering about (*karanguga*) distinguishes masculine forms of sociality and mobility. Indeed, masculine forms of mobility, rooted in the notion of "wandering about" or "gallivanting," involve a restless, aimless movement of those looking for fun, romance, and friendship. Combined with the idea of *chethu*, the term that incorporates a notion of aimless wandering in navigating the public spaces of consumption, we find that politics can enable masculine forms of sociality in public.

For Biju, a particularly energetic young man, the emptiness of the college enabled all of these things. He related to me that he was everywhere in the college, but never in the classroom. It did not matter to him whether class was conducted or not; it was all the same to him:

> I have been at this college for five years and never had one year of full attendance. I have a very strict schedule, but it is my own. I study from 10 p.m. to 1 a.m. at home. I know the syllabus, so I read on my own, take my own notes. Then there is tutorial in Modern College to help me. But I come to college every day. I will wander about [*karangum*]. I will see what is happening. I start on the top floor, then I come down to the first floor. I never stop. I just say hello to everyone, my friends. Then I'm on my way. By that time, it's noon. Time for lunch. I eat lunch; then I leave the college. Sometimes I go to the public library to read. OK, sometimes I go to the movies. Or wherever my friends might go.

I asked Biju how he could maintain such a poor attendance record since it was impossible to sit for end-of-the-year exams without having attended a certain percentage of classes (attendance was taken by the office clerk every day). He said there were many ways of getting around that, such as bribing the office clerk.

An actual strike call offers a particular kind of opportunity for dedicated and politicized students. Unlike Biju, who steadfastly refused to be affiliated to a student political group, Sissan fits the typical profile of a supporter of the SFI. A first-generation college student from a poor peasant background, he was a hard worker and unusually sincere and passionate in his dedication to the ideals of the party. One day, I saw him on the road, running toward the college. I told him he could stop: he wasn't late—a strike had been called and there were no classes. He had come an hour and half by bus to get to college. He laughingly said, "It's only when there is a strike that it's worth it to come to college. That's when you must come to college." If there was nothing to do for the party at the college, he would often go to the district office of the SFI and do whatever was required of him there or attend a few sessions at what are called "parallel colleges" nearby to keep up with his class work.

In the postindependence period, parallel colleges such as the Modern College, a private tutorial center that Biju attended, have spread all over Kerala as a set of institutions for tutoring, registering to take exams, and so forth. For many politically oriented students, recourse to a parallel institution to cram for two months before an exam allows them to turn the college into an empty place where no formal learning happens. From the perspective of a civic conception of citizenship, colleges as spaces of civic virtue and the public consumption of services are held hostage, incarcerated by politics: the endless strikes that last a day, a week, or sometimes a month, as well as fasts and demonstrations.

The emptiness of the college is experienced differently by young women. Like the street, the beach, or the bus stand, a strike renders the classroom a gendered space of sociality. Women students stay inside the classrooms, rarely venturing into the corridors and open places of the campus. They can only traverse public space with goal-oriented, demure comportment: if there is no class, they usually go home. Sometimes women do stay and hang out with their friends at school and then go shopping, or if really adventurous they go to an ice cream parlor or the India Coffee House. They may also meet their lines on the road behind the college, where they hope no one will see them. In cases where there is no official purpose to her being at the college, however, a woman's presence in public is precarious, for she cannot be "too free" in her movements. Being too free, of course, means that men might see her as sexually available.

For example, one of the more notorious incidents involving Rajeev (a known troublemaker) concerned a female friend from another college whom he brought to this college the day a strike was called. Rajeev got her a fake ID card (all students must carry an ID) and attempted to take her to the top of the reference library building but could not because some teachers were walking by its entrance. He then took her to the roof of the history department. Someone saw him going up there and informed a male teacher (who later told me the whole story). When the teacher went up, Rajeev ran off, leaving the young woman. The teacher then asked her to call home, so that he could hand her over to her parents. She stalled, saying that she had no home. Then he told her he would call the police. She finally relented. In an eerie echo of the typical plotline of a Malayalam movie, her uncle turned out to be a prominent advocate and her father the circle inspector of police. Her most immediate transgression was entering the college without a proper ID card. However, it was the sexual implications of her presence within the empty spaces of the college that hovered over the incident; and the shame of getting caught was compounded by the public profile of her family.

Even for young women who are successfully active in formal student politics, the navigation of the college, in either its civic or political modes, involves the very specific mobilization of a demure femininity, one that reveals it to be both enabling and constraining. Typically two out of the thirty-five candidates for various positions in the student union were women. They ran for posts that were usually held by women—the vice-chair of the union and the Arts Club president. The head of the SFI stated that it was necessary to have some women; otherwise it was difficult to capture the votes of the female students, who made up nearly 50 percent of the college rolls.

Dhanya was passionate and articulate about her politics. She came from a politically prominent leftist family and had been involved in student elections for the past three years. She was running for vice-chair this year. While she was excited about her candidacy, she was also nervous. It was clear she was going to win; none of the other parties had put up anybody to oppose her. But she was going to have to do some campaigning, at the least going from classroom to classroom letting people know who she was. She came to me and said that it would be important for me to write about student politics in my study. Therefore, would I want to come and see her campaign?

I soon saw that she needed me as much as I needed her. Like most other women students, Dhanya was used to spending most of her time in the classroom or the library. Rarely had she moved through the corridors and open spaces of the campus. Tightly holding hands, not looking this way or that way, we quickly walked along the corridors and entered classrooms, where she gave a short speech, hurriedly making her points. She said that education made one self-sufficient, so it was important to study. But one also had to care about society and its problems. Social change was necessary to cure the problems of society. She ended by saying that she hoped that they would vote for her on election day. In almost every classroom, male students booed and heckled her. By the time we had navigated all the corridors and classrooms of the college, stiffly and quickly, we were both exhausted. Back in the safety of her department library, I asked her why it was so difficult. She looked at me as if I were a little stupid and said, "Well, we women are not supposed to do this." Dhanya had asserted herself into the public space that was allowed her: the regulated space of a student election. What both enabled and constrained her presence in that public was her demure comportment, a kind of shield she wrapped around her assertiveness.

Thus, student politics is ambivalently tolerated and incorporated into the everyday life of the college and experienced in different ways by a variety of students. While Biju's narrative emphasizes his freedom to wander about, which he associates with fun and friendship, Sissan's narrative is one of dedicated, disciplined political work. But these forms of mobility are not easily disentangled. The masculinity of wandering about freely in an undisciplined way is the condition of possibility for producing a masculinity in which movement is disciplined (as in the jatha). They are intertwined in the everyday life of the college. For young women, the presence of student politics can sometimes mean a circumscribed assertion into the public spaces of the college, as in the case of Dhanya. For others, it creates an empty place in which the sexualization of their presence makes their attempts at fun and romance more difficult.

Disciplining the Public

Another way of describing the entanglements of different registers of politics is to note that incidents of politics are rarely separable from a problem of unruly "(in)discipline." The college administration confronts rashtriyam in the college both directly and indirectly. Many incidents that become procedurally marked as disciplinary cases get entangled with the structure of student politics. In addition, the administration tries to foster activities that might dissuade students from joining political organizations on campus.

One form of indiscipline involves damage to college property. A good example involved Prabhu, who was brought before a disciplinary committee. He was charged with running through the corridors with a bunch of his friends, shouting, slamming and breaking windows, doors, and shutters. He also stood accused of having run into the botany department classroom and breaking the blackboard. When a teacher came into the classroom, he took off on his motorbike, but not before he was identified. Prabhu was often mentioned as a member of the gang of "bad boys." As Lena, whom they targeted, said, they were constantly "chethu-fying." The link between Prabhu's chethu persona—he was one of the few students who owned a motorbike—and his political participation demonstrates how, for some, politics becomes a terrain of lower-caste, lower-class masculine assertion.

The college estimated that Prabhu had caused about 20,000 rupees worth of damage and filed a legal case to retrieve the money from his guardians. They also immediately suspended him, and he in turn petitioned to have his suspension lifted. The meeting to resolve the issue was a rapid-fire question-and-answer session in which Prabhu stood in front of the seated disciplinary committee, composed of three teachers and two students; his head was bowed with eyes to the ground and hands clasped behind his back.

The first teacher who questioned him tried to establish his poor credentials as a student. He asked him how he had gained admission into the college, establishing that Prabhu had secured admission through a sports quota that did not require good marks on his exams. He then grilled him about his attendance:

Q: Do you come to college every day?

A: In a week, I come three or four days.

Q: Aren't you supposed to come to college all days?

A: Yes.

Q: Do you actually attend class or do you wander around [karuga]?

A: I will often sit in the front of the college.

The teacher then probed for other incidents in which Prabhu was involved:

Q: Do any teachers have any ill feelings toward you, a grudge?

A: The principal and Karunakaran sir have a grudge against me.

Q: Why does Karunakaran sir have such feelings towards you?

A: Because I let the air out of his [scooter] tires.

After questioning Prabhu about the alleged incident, the teacher draws out the connections between Prabhu and the student political organizations on campus:

Q: After suspension, did you visit the college campus?

A: I came for two days.

Q: For what did you come?

A: The student union people told me I should come.

Q: Do you participate in the party?

A: Yes, SFI.

Q: Teachers from several departments have reported troublesome behavior on your part. What is your opinion about that?

A: There are many teachers here who know me. I am prominent in the union. When trouble happens, I'm there just to find out what happened. Because they know me, they report me. Otherwise, I am simple and humble [*pawam*].

Although Prabhu might assert that his demeanor is *pawam*, it is clear that he was not understood that way. However, he was a prominent member of the SFI unit on campus, so that when his suspension was lifted, many believed that he had gotten off because the administration did not want any more trouble with the party. The problem of discipline is wrapped around the problem of politics in that both are grounded in a form of masculine sociality that is reckless and restless.

As one teacher pointed out to me, the initial problem is often not political trouble but "girl trouble," but even these instances turn into overtly political conflicts. Narratives of such incidents proceed in a fairly structured way: a boy speaks to a girl in a way that is considered inappropriate, another boy gets upset about this (perhaps the girl is his *line*, his cousin, or someone from his village) and fights with or attacks the boy. One of them just happens to be associated with a particular political party, the other with a rival party. This will then escalate as members of these groups will be drawn into further clashes. What is at stake in these narratives is a male struggle over the honor and virtue of a woman. This struggle manages women's sexuality by reinforcing the importance for women of maintaining a demure presence in public.

As these examples attest, politics confronts the public space of the college in the form of everyday problems of (in)discipline that are then understood to be the machinations of "outside forces" (that is, political parties). College administration and civic-minded students attempt to produce a "civic public" within the space of the college, not only by depoliticizing the student union but most notably by fostering student associations that are explicitly antipolitical.

Here, the student-citizen moves from being simply the object of the educational process (and therefore in some senses an object of development) to being an agent of development. This notion of the student-citizen is institutionalized on a national level in the National Service Scheme (NSS). The NSS is a nationwide organization of college students that has a unit in almost every state-affiliated college: they build gardens, dig tube wells, run blood drives, and conduct rural surveys. Sometimes they are census enumerators as well. In short, they do not destroy but build. The organization encourages participation by giving them extra points on year-end examination marks. Students also like to join since it is relatively easy to excuse absences from class by producing certificates saying that one was involved in some NSS activity.

A major project of the NSS unit in the college was the building of a garden in the space between the college building and the campus wall. Full of tall weeds, the area was seen as a place of congregation for "bad elements" in the college, as one teacher put it. Students involved in the conversion of this space stayed after class and came on Saturdays to work. They obtained plants from the homes of teachers and parents, as the limited budget did not permit buying them. The highlight of the garden was an area of well-tended green grass in the shape of territorial India that the students involved in the project were sure was going to win them a university-wide competition. The teacher who was in charge of the college's NSS unit described the intention of the garden:

> Every year the NSS has a theme. For this year, the new theme is "youth for sustainable development." Last year it was "youth for national integration." Given that scheme, we made a garden, that garden that you see over there. Yes, according to that scheme, in every college there should be a garden, for the youth [yuvakal]. A place of youth. An assembly place of youth, for their studies, for their day-to-day activities. For their discussions. That is the kind of garden that we are growing, that we made. It is the main scheme of NSS silver jubilee. Nowadays, the preservation of trees, it has become a concern of youth. Also, in the ancient system, for students to sit under a tree in the shade and study, there was that idea as well. In the Vedic period, the old system, students used to sit under trees and study. Then for their congregation, to play, to read, to sit, for all that a special place. Then you grow trees, plants, for the beautification of the environment, the surroundings.

This "place of youth" became a space for the congregation of student-citizens, a space of associational civil society, freely congregating in a developed land. It enacts the Nehruvian model of development on the part of student-citizens who are patriotic and productive (Deshpande 1993)—but it was also a resistance to the "empty place" of youth that the college had become.

The teacher outlined why he thought the NSS could subsume the politics that had incarcerated the college:

> The college is in the grip of this *rashtriyam*. But in the NSS, we have [members from] all [student] groups, KSU, ABVP, SFI. In the NSS there is no problem of politics. On Sundays when they work together, they work together side by side, hand in hand.

Here, the teacher hopes that working together to plant a garden will overcome political divisions between students. He went on to discuss the ways in which the NSS engaged in a kind of antipolitics:

> When they come to the NSS, they must forget their politics. They have to forget all kinds of political beliefs while remaining in NSS. NSS is over politics. We have a seminar and raise awareness. So we tell them as a main point, "Don't get violent." They then spread the message to others.

This struggle between his notion of a "place of youth" and that of the "empty place" of the college is a literal one. Every year that the NSS has tried to build a garden, someone has destroyed it.

> This year we must maintain this project. We have to deal with violence, agitated students. Several times, our garden has been destroyed, vandalized. Then we gave a case to the police. Even though the case did not go anywhere, the kids again made it OK, worked and made it right again. . . . We will make it all neat, neat from this end to that end. It is a tiresome job.

Some students, highly critical of all the *rashtriyam* in the college, were excited about the garden because they thought it would create the kind of public that they wanted to be a part of, a civic public full of opportunity and growth. Biju was someone who was almost frenetic about extracurricular activities. He belonged to the NSS, the National Cadet Corps, and two other noncollege university youth groups. From a lower-middle-class background, his family had achieved a certain degree of middle-class financial security as a result of the labors of his father, who had worked as a welder in a factory in Abu Dhabi for twelve years. Tragically, his father had died the year before as a result of an industrial accident in the Gulf. Biju, his mother, and his brother, who was twelve years younger than he ("Yes, it was great family planning") lived off the small business investments that his father had made—an oil grinding mill, a small matchstick factory, and a half partnership in a local theater. But Biju wanted nothing to do with the Gulf or his father's business interests. While his mother wanted him to take the Indian Administration Service exams, he was more interested in the Indian Police Service because it afforded more "control, discipline, and adventure."

Biju explained that he did all these activities for "public contact." He said, "When we are young, we fear the public. I do this to face the public, so that that feeling will go away." He continued, "Look at this college. It is like a desert. It should be charming and beautiful, full with plants. The garden will make it look different." The college had few activities, nothing to "direct the youth," but in the activities he engaged in, there was "direction" and "equality." He added that even women participated in the National Cadet Corps, studying first aid and signaling, while male students studied shipbuilding and sailing. Within this Nehruvian model of student-citizenship, the student is not a roaming, wayward young man. He has "direction." His activities are arranged in an orderly manner, directed toward his own future and that of his nation. While this Nehruvian public presents itself as gender-neutral, it links a middle-class masculinity with the idea of a demure femininity that will perform its assigned nurturing role (first aid).

Politics, Privatization, and Education

The contestation between the civic and the political takes on a renewed and transformed set of meanings under conditions of neoliberalism that succeeded Nehruvian nationalism, and the new politics of privatization they have generated. The "civic" is increasingly tied to discourses of consumption and a free market. We see this most clearly when education itself becomes an object of politics.

Since the initiation of economic reforms in the early 1990s, the reform of higher education has centered on its privatization. As Kapur and Mehta note, higher education has been massively privatized since economic reforms were initiated (2004). They also point to its haphazard quality: instead of strong overarching state policy initiatives, there is a more piecemeal process of financial resources being withdrawn from public institutions while greater private investment covers a variety of semiprivate and fully autonomous institutions. For example, the government share of investment in higher education in Kerala declined from 75 percent in 1983 to 48 percent in 1999 (Kapur and Mehta 2004, 6). The international regulatory mechanisms such as the General Agreement on Tariffs and Services (GATS) opened up the educational sector to foreign universities, and privatization has also proceeded through the rapid entry of those institutions into the Indian market. This privatization has also been a hotly contested issue. For example, the Foreign Providers Bill in 2006–2007 was intended to regulate the way foreign universities do business in India, specifically to enforce government-sponsored fee structures and reservation quotas for minority groups in such institutions. It has been stalled by leftist parties that have objected to elements in the bill that might grant some exemption to elite universities from abroad that are attempting to set up their own institutions in India.

Despite the rhetoric of those opposed to privatization, who often argue that privatization is a new phenomenon, public and private have historically been entangled, particularly in Kerala. While questions of supply and demand, access, and quality have dominated privatization efforts in education, one aspect of debate centers on "the political," specifically on how much blame for the crisis in education should be placed on the pervasive presence of student (and teacher) politics, usually tied in varying degrees to the politics of major parties. Generally, the arguments against the "politicization of higher education" are tied to causal explanations that link it to the disruption of a proper academic life and therefore to the lowering of academic standards.[15] For both sides, the distinction between private and public has been central.

The large number of higher educational institutions within the private sector in Kerala is unusual within India; in other states public institutions dominate. One important sector of private education is the very powerful and widespread system of educational institutions controlled by Christian churches. Along with several schools and a college set up by the maharajah of Travancore, western missionaries and Christian churches were among the first to establish schools and colleges in the nineteenth century, catering to both the long-standing Christian community within the region and low-caste Hindu converts. The demand for access to education became a central feature of popular struggles by anticaste social reform movements, in particular the Ezhava-based Sree Narayana movement. The struggle for a putatively egalitarian public—the rights of lower-caste groups to walk on public roads, enter temples, go to school, and get government jobs—was a major object of political mobilization in the 1920s and 1930s. Within the volatile coalition-based politics of the last several decades, granting approval for new schools and colleges in various constituencies has been a primary way to attract votes.

The struggle to control these private institutions has been a major feature of Kerala's politics for most of its history since the state's founding in 1956. The contestations over the Education Bill, which was intended to regulate salaries and admissions processes under the sponsorship of the first communist government of 1957–59, starkly reveal the dynamics of this persistent feature within Kerala politics. The opposition to this bill came primarily from the Christian organizations that decried it as government interference and saw it as a threat to their rights as a religious minority. The mobilization against this bill forced schools to close, and students mobilized. In July 1959, after many deaths and arrests, rule by the central government was imposed and the communist ministry was dismissed. Many of the provisions of the bill were not fully implemented until the early 1970s, when private colleges, through their affiliations with public universities, were brought under more state control largely due to the efforts of teachers' unions. From this brief sketch, it becomes clear that the "private" sector that dominates higher education is both private and public. The private here is understood to be primarily the domain of religious minorities and specific upper- and low-caste communities who have some discretion over a portion of admissions and hiring. However, the degree to which they are strictly private is undermined by the structure and extent of state funding and the affiliated university system that allows the government to control appointments, admissions, curricula, and salaries. This kind of government control allows the state to set quotas for hiring and admission and to implement the reservation system, used to redress discrimination against low-caste groups.

However, the market is another realm of the private that colludes and collides with both the private of communities described above and the public of the state. The private market exists in the educational field in two senses. First, despite the control that the state exerts over private educational institutions, "private donations" for job appointments and "capitation fees" for student admissions are rampant. Another kind of private market for education is the widespread presence of parallel colleges. Completely outside the private sector of education outlined above are the private tutorial centers that Biju and Sissan could count on to get them through exams even though they were not attending class. Housed in a few rooms of a building or in a hut often near the regular colleges to which they are quite literally parallel, these colleges have become a widespread phenomenon in Kerala during the postindependence period, a result of policies intended to address a growing demand for higher education that the existing system could not meet.[16]

Thus, the debates in the 1990s about the privatization of higher education in Kerala occurred within an already existing state-saturated private sector of education and an expansive parallel system of private education. These contestations escalated in 1994–95, when the ruling pro-Congress United Democratic Front (UDF) government attempted to allow the establishment of new colleges that would be entirely self-financing and unsubsidized but under some measure of government regulation. Since then, self-financing colleges have greatly expanded, another development in the entangled public-sector and private-sector relations in education. E. T. Basheer, who was then education minister, argued that although nearly 40 percent of the state budget was being spent on education, it was still insufficient. While some had argued that self-financing colleges were elitist and would exclude the poor, he disagreed, stating that those who could afford to pay should have the opportunity to do so and that this would lead to healthy competition and higher quality. The pro–Left Democratic Front (LDF) student and teacher organizations, led by the SFI, launched a broad and vigorous set of agitations to oppose what they called the "commercialization of higher education," including an "education *bandh*" that kept many colleges closed for months.

This process of privatization was both similar to and different from what had occurred earlier, when the private sphere that opposed the government was primarily the Christian churches. One difference is that a new actor has appeared on the scene: the nonresident Indian (NRI). Technically persons who fall into a banking category of the Indian state (intent on attracting the monies of the Indian diasporic community), NRIs are increasingly making claims themselves on that state.[17] In particular, the children of Gulf migrants are unable to study abroad because family visas are rarely given, and furthermore, citizenship requirements within Gulf countries often restrict access to higher education. NRI parents, therefore, demanded that someone open colleges for their dependents, colleges that they could simply pay to have their children attend, circumventing reservation quotas and other admissions requirements. Additionally, they believe that, given their semiautonomous status, the resulting colleges more fully cater to their global trajectories and aspirations through curricula reform and better discipline. These new institutions would be unburdened by the perceived inadequacies of the current educational climate, including the "politicization of education."

The state general-secretary of the SFI brought a court case against the government that reveals the struggle over NRI monies in education. Originally, the state had decided to allow the establishment of several private engineering colleges that would have a quota system for admissions, similar to the one for caste groups. However, in addition to setting up quotas for groups defined as scheduled caste (SC) and scheduled tribe (ST), 40 percent of all admissions were to be reserved for NRIS. As a result of much protest, this was reduced to 5 percent. The stark contrast between a caste reservation category like SC/ST and the more affluent NRI points to the increasing demand made on the state by social groups defined by their ability to consume. In a very tangible way, the private consumer was making a claim on the public.

In addition to the claim that the state is unable to fund the expansion of higher education, those who support the privatization of higher education and the granting of autonomy to new educational institutions focus on two sets of issues. First, existing colleges are criticized for adhering to an archaic and outmoded curriculum. Looking for greater flexibility to create a new curriculum, some worry that the current system of education is unresponsive to the new global economy and the international labor market, while others are simply looking for more room to be more creative and innovative. Second, colleges are understood to be hyperpoliticized spaces that hinder the education of students. It has been argued that the increased autonomy granted to these new self-financing private colleges would allow them to create a more dynamic curriculum and avoid the pitfalls of hyperpoliticization. An antipolitics that is redefining educational institutions as spaces of civic virtue in place of public politics is increasingly asserted through a language of freedom tied to the market. As with the attempt to ban *bandhs* based on the right to "consume" public places such as roads, the college becomes a space for a contestation between civic and political conceptions of citizenship that are being transformed through discourses of consumption.

The attempt by some students to create a debating society, something the college had never had before, reveals the politics of this antipolitics. On one of those days when a strike had been called and most of the students who had shown up for the day had left, I met Sujit outside the compound wall, where he told me with excitement to come to a meeting later that day. It was to be held at a parallel college located in a one-room shack under a tree at the next junction. When I asked him what the meeting was about, he said they were going to try to start a new student organization, the Association for Open Discussion, to debate the issues of the day. The meeting was attended by about thirty students, five of whom were women. Sujit spoke first. His talk ran through the usual litanies about student politics and how it had corrupted education. Rashtriyam prevented students from learning, from getting jobs, and from "doing service" to the country. Echoing the anti-bandh politics, he argued that rashtriyam was not about serving the people but about personal gain and private careers. The purpose of the debating society was to talk about society but to do so in a way that was "not rashtriyam." He went on to say that the act of debating was explicitly not politics because in a debating society two opponents argue about an issue and one may win or lose a debate but the issue is never decided. What is judged is the language. In a debating society, one did not have rashtriyakar (politicians) but wagamar. Because I had never heard wagamar before, I asked him what it meant and he glossed it as "men of flowing words"; one would just have a continuous stream of language. He went on to say that rashtriyam began when a right and a wrong had been established in the minds of followers. In a debate, there was no right and wrong, there was no conclusion, and therefore it would not be explicitly political.

Here, politics is closure, the end of talk, the stating of conclusions. An antipolitics discourse deploys words and their never-ending flow against this closure. This kind of "free talk" did not happen within the space of the college. In fact, Sujit stated that they must not hold the meeting in one of the empty college classrooms. This must be something outside—in that parallel space, that space of consumption, outside the political public. Sujit's notion of "free talk" is located within a notion of a civic public forged by middle-class norms of talk anchored in a bourgeois form of masculinity struggling to articulate itself against a politics rooted in a more unruly form. It relies upon a kind of proceduralism, focusing on and valorizing the process of the production of talk itself rather than the actions that might derive from a process of talk. The latter is understood to be *rashtriyam*, a logic of means and ends based on firm convictions and conclusions.

The discourse of antipolitics that underlies this student's attempt to create a debating society in the college echoes the discourse of antipolitics about creating a garden in the college. The latter was an attempt to instantiate a Nehruvian conception of a productive citizen in the face of what is seen to be a "hyperpoliticization" of the college. However, this Nehruvian conception of citizenship is now linked with discourses of consumption, in which free talk articulates with the freedom to consume. This is a shift from an understanding of citizenship as building the nation to one in which one ought to be free to consume the nation.

Conclusion

The struggle about what constitutes "politics" among a democratic citizenry happens in part through a struggle over literal places and how they are understood. I have therefore traced the ways in which the understanding of a place—for example, a street or the gardens of a college—as public or private becomes the grounds on which official "politics" is contested. Mapped on to the spatial distinctions between public and private are discourses that pit the "private" as the market—specifically as a space of exchange and consumption—against public politics (*rashtriyam*).

The exclusion of women from a political public is interwoven with the ways that politics in public is tied to masculine modes of mobility and traversal. The freedom to move through public spaces, as in the anti-*bandh* demonstrations, and the freedom to consume public goods, like education—a kind of freedom that I have linked to the freedom of choice in consumption—confront the official political domain at its limits within the discourse of antipolitics that underlies privatization efforts. This freedom to consume public space, grounded in a middle-class masculinity that is respectable, orderly, and disciplined, confronts another masculinity that is equally orderly and disciplined if not quite respectable. The empty college emerges out of struggles over the meanings and functions of the public through practices of democratic citizenship in educational settings.

The juxtaposition of youth as consumers and citizens and their mutual imbrications complicates the ways in which consumer culture is pitted against citizenship in discussions of globalization and youth. The shift from midnight's children—when young people were serving their nation and its Nehruvian development goals through political and civic engagement—to the era of liberalization's children, when young people are portrayed as simply interested in consuming in an intensifying globally oriented commodity culture, is not a straightforward transformation. Rather, it is a complex and contested moment of articulation between the postcolonial and the global that has created a cultural politics of modernity and globalization that young people must and indeed do navigate in a variety of ways. Young people are not simply consumerist harbingers of globalization. They are also emerging citizens and their engagements as such are a key site for understanding how democracy and politics are being struggled over and redefined within liberalizing India.

Education, Caste, and the Secular

Religion is a matter of the mind. . . . Don't think that my religion is true and yours is false. This is the place where people live together as brothers and sisters, irrespective of caste, creed, and religion.—SREE NARAYANA GURU

Painted in Malayalam on a building at the entrance of the Sree Narayana College campus, these words signal the formation and location of this college within the movement for caste upliftment and social reform that began among the formerly untouchable Ezhava caste, spearheaded by the spiritual leader Sree Narayana Guru. Part of a broad and far-reaching set of changes that transformed caste relations in the region over the past century, Narayana Guru's plea for tolerance between religions and castes was founded on an anticaste politics that recast religion as a privatized "matter of the mind." The "place" that is referred to in the quote is a complex space of secularism that the college instantiates—one situated between the caste movement's reworking of Hindu tradition and the spaces of secular modernity in India.

Contemporary engagements with education on the part of low-caste communities reveal two intersecting projects. One, education is a key site for the production of the normative citizen-subject of modern India. Understood as secular and modern, this normative citizen-subject is understood also as upper-caste, upper-class, Hindu, and English-speaking—bringing together caste/class, religion, and language in dominant visions of the citizen. The college where I conducted fieldwork is, in the language of the state, an other backward classes (OBC) college, one that occupies a disadvantaged yet middle position between lower-caste and tribe categories—such as scheduled caste (SC) and scheduled tribe (ST)—and upper-caste groups.[1] While discussions of secular citizenship in contemporary India stem from a political urgency to critique the normative citizen-subject and its majoritarian provenance, it is equally important to pay attention to how the formation of this normative citizen-subject is an important context for the negotiation and production of low-caste identities within postcolonial India. In the college, this negotiation of secular modernity hinges on distinctions between the public and private, tradition and modernity. Dalit and other low-caste configurations of community, politics, and identity tend to oscillate between arguments that emphasize caste as a "traditional" practice that often requires mobilizing alternative traditions for the production of alternative histories, and arguments that celebrate colonial modernity and capitalism as the space of liberation from an oppressive and hierarchical Hindu tradition (Omvedt 1994, 1998; Nigam 2005; Prasad 2004; Menon 2006). Rather than focus on the mobilization of "tradition" or the celebrations of "modernity" in caste politics, I examine the ways both get marked and negotiated in the college. While the emergence and ascendence of Hindu nationalism in the 1990s might be dismissed as an upper-caste subterfuge, the politics of low-caste and tribal identities have clearly been reworked through an engagement with Hindu nationalism. "Tradition," understood as "culture" in the form of celebrating the important Kerala harvest festival of Onam, gets reworked as an exclusive "Hindu tradition" as Hindu nationalism makes its presence felt in the college—one that enacts a caste and gender politics.

Second, education is a crucial part of caste, family, and individual strategies for upward mobility. Given the relative success of the developmental state in Kerala, more people have access to higher education throughout the population, including lower-caste communities. This is a result of the relative strength of lower-caste reform movements, such as the Sree Narayana movement, coupled with colleges and universities more rigorously implementing state policies for the reservation of seats for admission within institutions of higher education.[2] As I have already discussed, this has generated a vast group of young people who are educated and unemployed, turning to migration as an important strategy for obtaining jobs. While I have been exploring various invocations of "modernity" within educational and youth cultural sites, it is also sharply marked in terms of the speaking of English in the college. This generates a complicated language politics that once again turns modernity into a contested notion. While the lower castes might have been enthusiastic about colonial modernity and the English education that went with it, as much historical work on caste movements has shown, modernity nevertheless raises issues of identity, class, and gender that are no less complicated for low-caste communities than for upper-caste ones. The contemporary struggle to gain a foothold in a job market that has an increasingly transnational horizon becomes a new backdrop for ongoing contestations about what it means to speak English, how one defines a Malayalee, and what it means to be an educated man or woman.

Caste in Modern India

Far from being the opposite of the secular and the modern, "caste"—as both politicians and anthropologists have deployed the term—is a complicated and messy product of them. Linking the everyday negotiations of caste and secularism to the languages and repertoires of state policy discourse, I examine caste within the larger horizon of secular, democratic citizenship within India. Rather than posit caste as a "traditional" practice anachronistically persisting within modern India, as much literature has done, I situate caste as a site of contestation at the fault lines between notions of the public and private, tradition and modernity, the religious and the secular.[3] In this sense, a critical ethnography of caste entails attention to caste, understood as a relational identity marker, as it gets produced and contested within one important field of discourse and practice that constitutes it, namely, secularism (see Dhareshwar 1993). A larger normative debate about limits and possibilities of secularism within India begs for an exploration of the everyday cultural politics of secularism in the institutional spaces of Indian modernity, such as that of a college.[4] Educational institutions are key sites for embodying the contradictory dynamics of Indian secularism. The everyday cultural politics of caste, religion, and community within a putatively secular space illuminates the educational processes through which modern, secular citizens are produced in globalizing India.

Debates and transformations in academic theories of caste have been entangled with the contested presence of caste within modern India. Early anthropological studies of caste in India have usually studied it as a form of "tradition" and/or "religion."[5] The privatization of religion and tradition and its expulsion from the secular spaces of the state, democratic politics, and civil society is a cornerstone of definitions of modernity. It is this understanding of the religious and the secular, the modern and the nonmodern, that has underwritten the dominant understanding of the Hindu caste system as decidedly "not modern" within the anthropology of South Asia. As Arjun Appadurai notes, caste was a "gatekeeper" concept that defined the very anthropology of the region (1986a, 1986b). Part of a larger critique of Orientalism within anthropology, subsequent scholarship at the intersection of history and anthropology demonstrated how colonial modernity profoundly transformed local-level identities of *jati* into an objectified caste system, one that became the basis for the vigorous mobilization of caste identities within post-independence democratic politics in India, thereby demonstrating caste as entangled with modern state formation (Appadurai 1986a; Cohn 1984; Dirks 1987).

Given the deconstruction of anthropological theories of caste through a historical anthropology of its formations within colonial modernity, how are we to anthropologically apprehend caste in contemporary, post-colonial India? Should anthropology give up a preoccupation with caste and focus on other things like "class" and "family," which intellectuals, political scientists, economists, and sociologists of the liberal and Marxist persuasions concerned with contemporary India cite as more relevant?[6] Situated between the critique of anthropological preoccupations with caste on the one hand, and either larger social scientific dismissals of caste or its containment within a narrow definition of electoral politics on the other, what would a "post-Orientalist" critical anthropology of caste in contemporary India look like?[7]

The everyday cultural politics of caste and caste identities within the context of secular, democratic citizenship in India is an integral part of the cultural politics of education, religion, and secular modernity that young people negotiate. Apprehending caste in relationship to secular citizenship in India requires an understanding of how caste and secularism are debated in public discourse in modern India, how these debates have shifted with the liberalization of the Indian economy, and the centrality of education to these debates.

In 1990, the government's Mandal report recommended that educational and governmental institutions fully implement "reservations" (quotas) of central government jobs and university admissions for OBC groups.[8] While reservations for SC/ST groups had been relatively uncontroversial, the inclusion of a large and somewhat indeterminate category such as OBC generated much protest. Within a week of the release of the report, anti-Mandal, antireservation violence spread throughout North India. The main participants in the Mandal riots were students; some were of elementary and high school age, though most were college students. They feared the increased competition to get into educational institutions and the loss of job opportunities. They blocked traffic, burned buses, fought police, and forced stores to close. Two forms of protest were particularly striking. First, students in Delhi pretended to sweep streets and sell vegetables at roadside stands—the work marking low-caste traditional occupations—to indicate what would happen to them if crucial government jobs were taken away from them. In the second set of protests, which spread through North India, students set fire first to their academic diplomas and certificates and then to their own bodies. The intensity with which these self-proclaimed middle-class subjects of India's modernity defended their educational access and privilege brought to the foreground both the centrality of education to the politics of caste and the role of caste in the production of the modern, secular citizen-subject in India. The rioters succeeded in bringing down the V. P. Singh government while inaugurating a new chapter in debates about reservations.

Supporters of the policies stressed the history and contemporary legacies of historical discrimination and exclusion, namely, the dominance of upper-caste elites in the public sectors of government and education, the private sectors of industry, and the increasingly private educational institutions. Opponents and the general rhetoric against reservations emphasized issues of merit and efficiency. It is argued that if the quotas were implemented, jobs would not go to those who truly deserved them, that is, college students who had worked hard and were best qualified to do the jobs efficiently. Other arguments asserted that the implementation of the commission's recommendations would lead to a further entrenchment of caste feeling and distinctions and eventually lead to a caste war. Still others argued that economically advantaged groups within caste groups, particularly the OBC category—what is referred to as the "creamy layer"—would be the real beneficiaries, to the greater disadvantage of those who truly deserved them, namely, Dalit groups. Most opponents of reservations argued that it is an opportunistic and populist measure designed to win votes.

The question of reservations and caste reemerged in May 2006 as a highly contested and fractious issue. While the Mandal riots of the early 1990s were dominated by contestations about inequality and meritocracy just as economic reforms were being instituted, fifteen years later, the question of liberalization and the globalization of the Indian economy has added a new layer to these debates. The current Indian National Congress government of Manmohan Singh has sought to require reservations for OBC groups within central government institutions of higher education, importantly including new elite institutions for professional education such as the Indian Institutes of Technology (IITs) and the Indian Institutes of Management (IIMs). These institutions create the technical and managerial cadres of India's global elite, and the attempt to implement reservations in them led to widespread protests. Within this context, the controversy surrounding the National Knowledge Commission is instructive. This commission, created in 2005, is a high-level advisory board to the prime minister, charged with "transforming India into a knowledge society," a mantra of economically inflected globalization discourse. Made up of corporate leaders of India's global information technology industry—for example, Nandan Nilekani of Infosys and eminent sociologists and political scientists such as André Béteille and Pratap Bhanu Mehta—the commission was charged with examining the role of education, research, and technology in making India more globally competitive. Beteille (as before) and Mehta came out strongly against the government's decision to implement a reservation policy, eventually resigning from the commission.[9] In addition to the many arguments that circulate about political expediency, entrenchment of caste distinctions, and contested understandings of merit and efficiency, a new issue about who benefits from liberalization and what is necessary for India to continue on its path to become a global economic powerhouse has added another layer.[10]

The politics of Mandal must also be contextualized within the context of the growing political power of the backward classes and Dalits within the electoral system, particularly in North India during the 1990s. Here, the writings of a new generation of Dalit and low-caste intellectuals such as Chandra Bhan Prasad and Kanchiah Ilaiah have also politicized the question of caste and secular modernity in India in new ways (Prasad 2004; Ilaiah 1996).

Given the difficult and contested struggles about caste within modern India, scholars and intellectuals, in both academic and popular registers, have sought to understand caste as a repressed narrative of secular Indian modernity (see Dhareshwar 1993, Nigam 2005, Deshpande 2003). In all these accounts, the "opacity of caste" for scholarship and politics emerges through the deployment of a public/private distinction (Dhareshwar 1993). At one moment, its substantialization within anthropological discourse renders it as the "essence" of a privatized Indian tradition, overcome in the next moment by a modern Indian public that turns caste into a matter of macrostructural social policy. In discourses and practices of Indian secularism, the dynamic relationship between caste and everyday processes of identity formation and cultural politics disappears from view.

However, understanding caste in relationship to secularism requires not only making it visible in secular spaces but also understanding the changing dynamics of caste and religion within Indian secularism. It must be noted that the discourse of secularism within India is not dominated by the question of caste but rather by "communalism," primarily understood through the lens of Hindu-Muslim conflict.[11] This is linked to another watershed within the postcolonial history of India two years after the Mandal riots: the demolition of the Babri Masjid Mosque on December 6, 1992, by an ascendant Hindu right seeking to claim it as the site of a demolished Hindu temple. The rise of political and militant versions of Hindu nationalism has led to a fraught reckoning about the status of India as a secular nation-state (Needham and Sunder Rajan 2006; Bhargava 1998a). While the Hindu right argues that the Indian state is not universalist and secular enough, because of the ways it recognizes minority rights (particularly Muslim), academics and public intellectuals worry about the ways in which the state's politics of recognition and nonrecognition produce a form of secularism that reinscribes the dominance of the Hindu majority.

The interrogations of secularism within India are both descriptive and normative; they seek to examine the historical unfolding of dominant traditions of secular nationalism within India while arguing either for its overthrow, displacement, or continued viability and regeneration.[12] One strand within this exploration has been an attempt to understand the ways in which dominant forms of nationalism are underwritten by ambiguous and ambivalent deployments of a majoritarian "Hindu" identity —what one might call a "Hindu secular"—something that makes secular nationalism complicit with contemporary Hindu nationalism.[13] The weight of this term in contemporary debates has most often been directed toward the question of communalism: in other words, the ways in which Hindu majoritarianism, both of the liberal/left and the right, excludes and subsumes other religious minorities such as Muslims and Christians. However, the production of a "Hindu secular" requires not only a boundary between religions but the containment of caste politics in the name of a unified Hindu identity (see Menon 2006). In this sense, the often quoted phrase "upper-caste Hindu" as indicative of the normative citizen-subject of Indian modernity needs to be more than a simple listing of identity markers. There is a dynamic relationship between the production of "caste" and the production of "religion" (as Hindu) that requires exploration. During the 1990s in Kerala, the complex negotiations between caste and the boundaries of religious identity were intensified by the rise of Hindu nationalism, which became palpable within the ambiguous secularism the college embodies.

Between Hindu Tradition and Secular Modernity

Just beyond the entrance gate that breaks up the campus wall enclosing the SN College, gaily painted with all manner of advertisements, is a small, round building that houses the "watchers," the guards who monitor the entrance. The outside of the building, which was paid for by the Parent-Teacher Association, is covered with painted Malayalam text, quotes from the writings and sayings of Sree Narayana Guru. At the top is painted his most famous saying: "One Caste, One Religion, One God" (*Oru Jati, Oru Matham, Oru Devam*).

This anticaste movement has been part of an important reworking of caste relations within Kerala under the impact of colonial modernity. As many have noted, Kerala had a particularly repressive caste system, one that involved not only untouchability but unapproachability (Menon 1994; Jeffrey 1976, 1992). For Louis Dumont, the intensity of caste restrictions and their coercive, often violent, imposition made Kerala a puzzle and an exception to his understanding of consensual hierarchy as the basis of the caste system (1980, 82). Forms of dress, bodily gestures, practices of naming, and regulations about the visibility and distance between upper-caste and lower-caste bodies marked a terrain of semiotic practices that regulated caste relations (Kumar 1997). The transformations of caste relations within the last hundred years or so involves both upper-caste and lower-caste social reform and struggle at the intersection of a reworked Hindu tradition and an emergent secular modernity.

As I have discussed, vigorous caste-based social reform is an important part of the narrative of Kerala's modernity. While feminist scholarship has challenged the progressivism of this narrative along the lines of gender (and to some extent caste), the idea that caste has somehow been overcome through the emergence of new forms of secular modernity has yet to be fully and critically explored. One dimension of the complex ways in which secular modernity links up with upper-caste dominance is indicated by the career of the nationalist movement in Kerala, in which identification with the Indian National Congress gets entangled with Nair ascendancy. As Dilip Menon argues, in Kerala nationalism and communalism went hand in hand (1994). Identification with nationalist politics, often led by young Nair men, involved attempts to create a wider "Hindu" identity in order to overcome the divisive issue of caste inequality. This is especially evident during the temple entry agitations of the 1920s, particularly the Vaikom Satyagraha of 1924, which became a national issue with the intervention of Gandhi (Menon 1994; Rao 1979). In chapter 4, I discussed this agitation as a key moment in the inauguration of new forms of political practice (the *jatha*) in Kerala. Here, the issue is its particular caste configurations. As noted earlier, caste restrictions within the region prevented members of the untouchable castes from entering temples or even walking along the roads near a temple. Associates of the Ezhava leader Narayana Guru, under the auspices of the Sree Narayana Dharma Paripalana, or SNDP, pushed for temple entry and took their message to the Indian National Congress, which endorsed their claim as a birthright of all Hindus. In 1924, a group of Nair leaders, along with Nair, Pulaya, and Ezhava volunteers, walked the forbidden roads and were arrested, initiating the *satyagraha*.

The interesting dimensions of this moment are the ways in which Gandhi transforms an untouchable-caste demand for equal treatment and justice into a religious movement for the purification of Hinduism, led by the upper castes. Once many Nair leaders were arrested, George Joseph, a former editor of the nationalist paper *Young India* and a member of the long-standing Syrian Christian community of Kerala, assumed charge of the movement. Gandhi writes to him, telling him that this is a "Hindu" matter and that he should let them do the work of removing untouchability (Menon 1994, 81). Similarly, a group of Akalis of the Sikh community came from Punjab to set up free kitchens for the volunteers (Menon 1994, 82; Rao 1979, 62). Gandhi called for the kitchens to be closed, arguing that the people of Travancore did not require charity. The struggle against untouchability within the larger horizon of secular nationalism becomes essentially a religious issue focused on temple entry, one that folds different caste groups into a unified Hinduism, understood as a religious community set apart from others. In this way, the secular nationalism of the Congress Party begins to articulate with the production of a "Hindu secular."

As the historical importance of the communist left in Kerala indicates, this attempt to overcome the politics of caste inequality on the part of the Congress Party has a checkered history in the region. Menon goes on to argue that the rise of the communist left in Kerala can be tied to its more straightforward anticaste position, one that linked the question of caste inequality directly to a revolutionary struggle against feudalism. This is often rendered as a heroic struggle.

In chapter 4, I discussed the seminal play *You Made Me a Communist*, by Thoppil Bhasi, as indicative of the important link between youth, masculinity, and politics. However, the play also reveals the contours of the dominant narrative about caste on the part of the communist left. Paramu Pillai, the character who is "made a Communist," is an older man of a declining dominant Nair family. The transformation of his caste-ridden consciousness into that of a secular communist, initiated by his communist son, is a central narrative of the play. The sexual exploitation of an untouchable girl is another element of the caste-ridden society that needs to be overcome. In these and other plays, the feudal, caste-ridden past was often represented by a low-caste man in a servile pose before an upper-caste Brahmin landlord and revolutionary consciousness by the same lower-caste man marching to the landlord's house, shouting and shaking his fists (Zarrilli 1996, xii).

Despite this narrative of overcoming and the wide support for the communist left among the Ezhava, the "present absence" of caste within the secular modernity of the left is also evident. It can be seen, for example, in the marginalization of lower-caste members within the organizations of the communist left, particularly the CPI (M) (Osella and Osella 2000, 212–13). Most important, the displacement of the specificity of caste oppression through the language of class becomes an important way in which the supposed overcoming of caste reinscribes caste (Dhareshwar 1993; Nigam 2005). Dilip Menon's discussion of the communist leader E. M. S. Namboodiripad's negotiation of his Brahmin identity through his reworkings of Marxism demonstrates some of the complexity between caste and communism in the region (2006).

Within the context of lower-caste reform and struggle in colonial Kerala, the reworkings of modernity and tradition happened from a position of subordination, one that nevertheless produced a complex terrain of positions that significantly vacillated between the demands and opportunities of secular modernity, particularly colonial education and Christianity, and reimaginings of Hindu tradition in the vein of Sree Narayana Guru. The question of conversion, to Christianity, Buddhism, and sometimes Islam among lower castes, sat alongside powerful new reimaginings of Hindu tradition, as well as assertions of atheism and rationalism (Kumar 1997; Menon 2006; Mohan 2005). For example, Isaac (1985) discusses the case of R. Sugathan, though he frames it with an overarching narrative about the move from "caste consciousness" to "class consciousness." Sugathan began his public life within an organization devoted to rationalism and atheism, shifted to becoming a

Buddhist, then joined various Ezhava caste associations, and finally ended as a union member and important leader in the CPI (M). This is but a small example of the larger context of ferment within the lower-caste politics during this time.[14]

Sree Narayana's philosophy, drawing on the Advaita philosophy of Sankaracharya as well as the Saiva Siddhanta traditions of Tamil Nadu, combined individual perfectibility and community improvement (Kumar 1997; Osella and Osella 2000a; Rao 1979). It was a potent message, taken up at the turn of the century by a rising Ezhava elite, embodied in the SNDP, that was eager to shed its untouchable status through missionary education and the opportunities of a new cash economy.

In some sense, a discussion of Sree Narayana's thought raises the question of whether he is located within the traditions of Hindu philosophical and bodily practice or "modern" thinking. The relationship between the elements and innovations within his thought, particularly with respect to the body, are carefully worked through by Kumar (1997). However, the focus in this chapter is not only Sree Narayana's thought but the larger context of the social movement and its organizations, including educational ones. Therefore, the emphasis here is on that aspect of Sree Narayana's thought that creates the conditions for the elaboration of worldly activity and the ways in which the worldly activity he prescribes fits in the larger contours of colonial modernity (education and jobs). While Kumar demonstrates the links between Sree Narayana's anticaste position and those of the Saiva tradition, the ways in which his message was taken up by organizations such as the SNDP create a dynamic relationship between what is understood to be tradition and the secular ideologies of equality, improvement, and freedom.

In Sree Narayana's philosophy, knowledge (arivu) occupies the structural space of "Brahmin," the only essential reality (Kumar 1997). Individual, bodily perfectibility emerges as a way to achieve knowledge. This focus on bodily perfectibility also allows a link to be made between spiritual and worldly existence. Narayana Guru takes this further by moving from individual perfectibility to community improvement to the well-being of the human race, producing a kind of reformed monotheism that encompasses all, without the pernicious caste distinctions, within a universal community.

In this context, caste as a set of distinctions that differentiate the

human race is understood as a false principle. Fundamentally, Sree Narayana relies on a biological essentialism to argue that those who procreate
are members of one jati. A key component of Sree Narayana's reworking
of Hindu traditions within the context of secular modernity is the way in
which he distinguishes between caste (jati), religion (matham), and community (samudayam). It is this set of distinctions that introduces what
Kumar calls the "moment of the social" (1997, 255). This realm of the
social encompasses religious reform within the community, new forms
of prayer and worship in temples, and what one might render as the
narrow space of the secular modern, characterized by trade, education,
and employment. Here, we see a program for the transformation of what
is understood as "tradition" (religious practices, new forms of worship),
along with an embracing of that which is understood to be "modern"
(trade, education, new forms of employment).

While caste is a false principle, religion is a matter of inner belief and
opinion. In this way, the Ezhava caste becomes the Ezhava community.
Untouchability is erased as "caste" transforms itself into "community"
via the privatization of "religion." It is this prying apart of these terms
that enables Sree Narayana's philosophy to articulate with an egalitarian,
secular space that the college instantiates.

However, the secularized community of the Ezhava intersects with
ambiguous conceptions of other notions of "community." In the first
instance, while "community" refers to a collectivity defined by the term
Ezhava, it also refers to the human community and the human race,
instantiating a kind of universal humanism.[15] Within contemporary discourse, the caste association of the SNDP and its associated organizations are often accused of corruption and narrow self-interest. With
respect to education, the control of admissions through private donations on the part of the college management, though a common practice
within many educational institutions, is often seen as evidence of "caste-
ism." Today the caste association is accused of forgetting Sree Narayana's message of universal humanism in the name of narrowly defined
community self-interest and chauvinism. In these sorts of complaints,
the two senses of community, as "Ezhava" and "human," are pitted
against each other. Rather than see this tension between the particular
and the universal definitions of "community" as a historical development in which Sree Narayana's message is corrupted by a narrow caste

association, it might be more fruitful to understand it as a constitutive ambiguity within a caste movement that is contextualized within secular citizenship.

Further, Sree Narayana's thought and the practices of the SNDP project of social reform existed, however contentiously, within the gambit of a larger Hindu Kerala. The status of "Ezhava community" as "Hindu" is a constitutive ambiguity. The movement, at various moments in its history, entertained the possibility of conversion, to either Christianity or Buddhism, a move that Sree Narayana resisted. As Kumar notes, his redefinition of "religion" as individual belief, and "community" as the site of reform, discourages conversion as a strategy in anticaste politics. Despite at times proclaiming that he did not belong to any caste or religion and insisting that his temples did not belong to the Hindu religion, as Kumar has argued, "the redefinition of community and the practices of reform Sree Narayana initiated . . . show that for him the spiritual self-understanding and practices of Ezhavas as community should be within the horizon of the very tradition which had differentiated them as caste (jati) earlier" (1997, 260). While caste, religion, and community are differentiated within Sree Narayana's thought, the oscillations and slippages between community, understood as Ezhava, Hindu, and human, have created the conditions in which the reconfigurations of Hindu tradition within this lower-caste movement sit uncertainly on the fault lines between the tradition/modernity dialectic that secularism instantiates.

As an aspect of the social movement to eradicate untouchability, modern western-style education straddles the diverse namings and reworkings of community that the movement has engendered. The struggle to gain access to modern educational institutions went hand in hand with the struggle to gain access to temples. Alongside these struggles, efforts were made to found community-based educational institutions, something that paralleled the effort to found community-specific temples. The reformation and contestations around temple worship mirror the ones around education, enacting a reworking of that which is marked as "tradition" and that which is marked as "modern." While upper-caste reformers were willing to support temple entry in an effort to reform Hindu tradition for a modern Indian nation, the Sree Narayana movement linked the reformation of tradition to an entry into modernity through education and jobs.

For the social reform movement, the relationship between the temple and the school as key sites of social and political transformation is not simply a pragmatic one. Many SNDP temples have as their central deity Sarada Devi, depicted as the goddess of wisdom, knowledge, and learning in the Brahminical pantheon. The temple at Sivagiri, which has become the center of the SNDP activities and is the final resting place of Sree Narayana, was dedicated to Sarada Devi in 1912 by the guru. His selection of this Brahminical goddess emphasized self-knowledge and education. In this way, Narayana Guru blurred the distinction between school and temple. In later years he even went so far as to call schools the true temples of his religion. The contemporary legacy of this blurred distinction is the shrine or small temple dedicated to Sarada Devi in most colleges, the idea being that students would pray to the goddess before beginning classes. The temple in this Sree Narayana College in Kerala was little used, jokingly referred to as the place where you went not to pray but to meet your line, or romantic interest.

Situated in a project to redefine caste as a modernizing community in the context of colonialism, for the Sree Narayana movement, education mediates the tradition/modernity dichotomy that structured the movement's reform efforts. Though clearly identified as "modern," modern education was separated from, yet linked to, temples through various strategies that redefined both for the struggle against untouchability. The following discussion tracks the ways in which ideas of tradition and modernity, the religious and the secular, become the terrain for negotiating the space of educated modernity that the college enacts.

Politics of the Secular

The absent presence of caste within the life of the college is palpable. Caste is quite literally unspeakable, something that followed directly from Sree Narayana's teachings. Crucial to this unspeakability are the norms of naming. All students are officially known, within the documents of the college and in the ways they are referred to in everyday talk, by their first names, followed by an initial, for example, "Niju P." or

"Geetha S." While this partakes of a wider set of South Indian naming practices, this way of naming students was explicitly linked to Narayana Guru's teaching, which involved the shedding of all caste markers, including names. One was not supposed to know what caste anyone belonged to, because caste was a false principle of differentiation. In this sense, while upper-caste "repressions of caste" are understood as helping to consolidate the dominance of the upper-caste Hindu, the explicit erasure of caste within this low-caste college emerges out of a critique of caste.

However, this explicit erasure of caste has become entangled with the ways in which the secular represses caste. More informal interactions among students involve a complex structure of knowing and not knowing caste backgrounds, some mixing and transgressing of caste hierarchies within friendship networks and romantic relationships in the spaces in and around the college, and an avoidance of each other's homes where violations of caste regulations or the desire to conform to them might become more explicit and embarrassing.

Making, or not making, the private spaces of one's family and home available to the public world of college life was an important way in which caste was marked without being named. Scholarship on caste within modern India has demonstrated the importance of the public/private distinction for negotiating tradition and modernity. As Nigam (2005) and Hancock (1999) note, discussions of "compartmentalization"—in which caste in the private sphere is separated from a secular identity in the public sphere—are usually ensconced within modernization narratives. Here, I discuss the negotiations of public and private less as a cultural adaptation to modernity and more as a fraught and complex negotiation of a distinction between tradition and modernity that secularism itself instantiates.

When I first started my research, I imagined that it might be possible, some time relatively early in the research, to be able to visit students in their homes. When I asked students about their family backgrounds, answers were deliberately vague and general. It took me some time to realize that this vagueness about one's family was, at least in part, a deflection of caste in the space of the college.[16] While, over time, I was able to maneuver this boundary with some success, the difficulties of navigating home and college are instructive.

Sunita, a bright, articulate, English-speaking student of politics, took me home the first day she met me, to a middle-class house in a middle-class neighborhood on the outskirts of town. Her family came from one of the prominent upper-caste Nair families in and around the town. Her upper-casteness did not seem to necessitate the evasion that seemed to constitute the production of the "casteless" person by someone from the lower castes. Given my gender, she was quite open and hospitable. While she did not know conclusively, on that first day, that I was not an Ezhava, my American English and status as a Ph.D. student produced a sense of novelty, enthusiasm, and affiliation (she was one of the few students at the college who spoke fluent English) that trumped the ambiguity of my background.

Another student, Meena, also readily invited me to spend the weekend at her family home in a small village two hours by bus from the college. She came from a poor fishing community. By asking me where my family was from in Kerala and hearing me mention my cousin's name (Annie), she recognized me as a Christian. Coming, as she did, from a Christian community seemed to create some sense of affiliation that made it relatively easy for her to indulge her curiosity about me by inviting me home.

The politics of caste and religion play into the ways in which the public of the college and the private of the home are negotiated. A formal and official erasure of caste in the college intersects with the more ambiguous sociality through which caste, community, and religion are marked. This separation between public and private expressions of caste is often rendered, within anthropological literature, as evidence of the "persistence" and "reality" of caste, evidence that reveals its essential properties. The desire to avoid caste marking is often seen as a desire to emulate the upper castes, part of the process of "Sanskritization." In an excellent discussion of the ways in which untouchability is negotiated between the public and private realms in a Kerala village, Osella and Osella equate Sanskritization with "passing" (2000a, 220–46). However, it might be useful to examine the ways in which the two are not so similar. While Sanskritization might too easily naturalize the logic of practices among the lower castes within a teleology of community upward mobility, passing focuses our attention on the actual dynamics and politics of traversing caste geographies. In particular, the formulation of passing helps to focus our attention on the secular modern as a space of a highly ambiguous caste erasure that is negotiated differently by upper and lower castes.[17]

The erasure of caste and its intersections with a more ambiguous, informal negotiation of caste and community within the space of the college broke down in an incident during the middle of the academic year. The dynamics of this incident reveal the complex articulations between caste, religion, and secularism within this low-caste college.

The ambiguity of community, in particular the ambiguous association between "Ezhava" and "Hindu" is inserted into a political space that is increasingly besieged by a more exclusivist notion of Hindu nationalism, reflected in the increasing popularity of the Akhil Bharatiya Vidyarthi Parishad (ABVP) student political party. If the long-dominant Student Federation of India (SFI) student party, affiliated with the CPI (M), demonstrates by shouting "Inquilab Zindabad!" (Long live the revolution!) through the corridors of the college, the ABVP will march in the opposite direction, singing the militant nationalist song *Vande Mataram* (Hail to the Motherland). And in the everyday life of the college, it is the ambiguous status of the "Hindu" within the space of the secular that is increasingly tested.

At the insistence of the principal, the student union was asked to organize a celebration of Onam, one of the most important holidays in Kerala that I discussed briefly in chapter 2. It had never been celebrated at the college in living memory. As the principal and teachers stated, the celebration was intended to bring the student community and teachers closer together. This was, of course, a reference to the highly charged and politicized events discussed in chapter 4, which had kept colleges closed for months and polarized the administration and politicized the students. Part of the culture of the college for many years, a few recent and spectacular incidents of "campus politics," including the destruction of college property, had galvanized the principal to initiate some initiatives to improve "campus life." The celebration of Onam was an attempt, among several others, to instill a kind of "civic culture" within the college, one that would contend with the politicization of campus life through the unifying celebration of a cultural program.

The celebration was organized as a series of competitions, two of which prominently featured women, most of whom came dressed that day in Kerala saris. First, every academic department entered its version of a *pukulam*, a round design on the floor made out of flower petals, which was created by the women students. The second competition was for the best rendition of the *thiruvathirakali* regional dance. For this event, a number of female students from each department, dressed in traditional saris and with jasmine flowers in their hair, did a circular dance in the wide-open central area. Under the protection of a "cultural program," this was the most visible that the women had been in the public spaces of the college.

The most popular event was the "fancy dress" competition, made up of half a dozen male students. With its playful rendition of different personas, it was the highlight of the day. First, there was Veerappan, the legendary Tamil bandit who occupied the forests that straddle Kerala and Tamil Nadu. Dressed in tattered khaki clothes, his face painted in camouflage, his head covered with leaves, he entered the makeshift stage, a space in front of the college office where the principal, teachers, and students stood. He pranced around menacingly but seemed to point his toy machine gun only at the principal and teachers, much to the amusement and encouragement of his fellow students. The next competitor elicited the most excitement. Played by a male student, "she" was a poor, low-caste woman dressed in a cheap cotton sari that was half falling off, a begging bowl on her head, a pile of firewood under her arm. Coarse, loud, vulgar, and hypersexualized, he/she seductively sidled up to the principal and each male teacher, licking her lips, making eyes, and swinging her hips. Here, we don't have the hypersexualized "modern girl" but her hypersexualized opposite, the lower-caste girl, who can be allowed to appear only in drag.

The final contestants enacted the role of King Mahabali, whose benevolent, mythic reign is celebrated at Onam. One understanding of Kerala is as the land of Asuras, ruled by the demon king Mahabali, who defeats the Vedic gods, only to be tricked by Vishnu in his avatar as the dwarf Vamana. Within the textual tradition, Mahabali makes a transformation from being an enemy of the gods to becoming a demon devotee who, through charity and religious rectitude, finds liberation at the feet of Vishnu (Hospital 1984). Within the larger context of the Bali tradition, interpretations that stress Mahabali as a Dravidian, lower-caste-affiliated demon who contests the Brahminical pantheon are common (Omvedt 1998). However, as a cultural hero of the Malayalee-speaking region,

Mahabali is most significantly portrayed, through the sponsorship of the state government and the tourism board, as a good and righteous ruler, charitable and generous toward his subjects. The festival celebrates the return of King Mahabali to visit his adoring and appreciative subjects. In this version of the story, after being fed and taken care of, Vamana is offered a boon by the king. Vamana asks for three paces of land and the king readily agrees. Soon, the dwarf begins to expand. With the first step, he covers the sky, blotting out the stars. Next he straddles the nether world. One more step and the earth will be destroyed. Realizing his defeat and being the dedicated king that he is, Mahabali offers his head as the last step. Since the ruler was loved by his people, he is allowed to return once a year on the occasion of Onam.

The celebration of Onam within the college, initiated as it was by the administration, was an attempt to subsume and unify the politicized college within a larger cultural celebration that coheres around a regional Malayalee identity. Understood less as religion and more as culture, Onam nevertheless emerges out of a Hindu secular lexicon that is given new meaning with the rise of Hindu nationalism within the region, as the incident to be discussed reveals.

The dress competition had two Mahabali contestants. First was the "modern" Mahabali, dressed in a pair of shorts, a T-shirt, sneakers, and sunglasses, strutting and carrying a brightly colored umbrella. He pranced around to much amusement and laughter. The second Mahabali was accompanied by a student playing Vamana, both dressed in traditional attire. They enacted the three paces, with Vamana finally stepping on the head of Mahabali.

Within celebrations of Onam, the right to appear as King Mahabali on tiruvonam, the last day of the ten-day festival, historically went to members of the low-caste performing castes such as Malayans, a practice that speaks to the non-Brahminical origins of King Mahabali. As the "return of King Mahabali" is recast within the secular and playful context of a fancy dress competition in a college, one in which the identity of the players should not matter, the complexities of caste and religion within the space of the secular emerge.

Veerappan, the Tamil bandit, won the competition. However, what was more contentious than the contest itself was the staging of the Onam story. While "modern" Mahabali was playful and innocuous, the "traditional" Mahabali and Vamana duo got themselves into trouble. By the end of the day, Saiju, who had played Vishnu's incarnation as the dwarf Vamana (he was thought to be eminently suitable because he was so short) was in the hospital, in need of three stitches. He was beaten after the day's activities had wound down. Rumors floated about, with the consensus being that he had been beaten up by students sympathetic to the ABVP. The consistent explanation was that he had been targeted because he allowed his best friend, a Muslim, to play the role of Mahabali, an ostensibly "Hindu" king. While it was too provocative to attack Hasar, the young man who played Mahabali, attacking Saiju was seen as an acceptable warning.

Within a caste-based community college, the ambiguities of being "Hindu" in public are revealed as the "cultural" nature of a program gets elided by specific bodies understood to belong to specific communities. The seemingly innocuous celebration of Kerala's "culture" in the form of a putatively "Hindu" festival becomes problematic when a "Muslim" body takes on the persona of a Hindu king. So far, we have a situation in which "Hindu" is pitted against "Muslim" within the context of a politics of Hindu nationalism that transforms the "cultural" figure of King Mahabali, understood as Hindu, tolerant and inclusive, into an exclusively "Hindu" one. In this way, the marking of "modernity" within the space of the secular in the form of "modern" Mahabali is a playful gesture that simply elicits laughter. It is the marking of "tradition" within the space of the secular that becomes problematic. The "Hindu secular" of Kerala's Onam celebrations becomes the condition of possibility for asserting the fact that, despite the playful subversions of the fancy dress competition, identities written onto bodies do matter.

However, the contours of the secular at stake here are not simply along the fault lines of Hindu and Muslim. The ways in which the low-caste college contends with its "communalization," as it was characterized by teachers and administrators, point to the articulation of a secular identity with caste. A teacher was appointed to investigate the incident and a meeting was held with Saiju and Hasar. Saiju, standing in front of the teacher's desk, explained his version of what happened. He stated that his attackers, before pummeling him, asked him why he, from a Nambudiri Brahmin family, should be best friends with a Muslim. They told him that he should know better.

What is revealed here is that, for the ABVP students, Saiju was not a problematic choice to play Vamana/Vishnu. Not only were his height and his status as a Hindu appropriate but he was also a high-caste Brahmin whose father incidentally still performed priestly religious rituals. Who could have been more appropriate from the perspective of Hindu nationalism? He became problematic only when he transgressed the boundaries of religious community to fraternize with a Muslim, one who was "allowed" by him to play the role of a "Hindu" king.

The politics of caste initiated by the ABVP students was contested vigorously by the teacher. However, the ways in which the teacher reacted rely upon secularism's own ambivalent politics of caste. On hearing what Saiju had to say, the teacher became irate, shouting, "Tell him this is SN College! No jati, matham, one God! We are all humans first! Remember this is SN!" Furious, he went on to say that in the next meeting he was going to ask Saiju's attacker his last name and then ask him his caste. He derisively snorted that the student must be an SC/ST because they were the ones who were zealous about Hindutva, or Hindu nationalism.

The teacher's narrative reveals the slippages between caste, religion, and community within a putatively secular public. In the first instance, this incident reveals the complex politics of caste that Hindu nationalism represents. Deploying the hierarchy of caste to berate the transgressive Saiju, the ABVP and other organizations within Kerala were also working hard to attract and subsume lower-caste organizations and communities within a larger Hindu identity.[18] The success of the ABVP within this college is testimony to that strategy. However, the secular apprehension of this "communalization" of the college reveals the workings of caste hierarchy within the production of the secular self. The teacher drew on the teachings of Sree Narayana to vigorously contest what he saw as the caste-ism of these Hindu nationalist students. He drew on Narayana Guru's denial of caste as a reality ("no jati")—and the guru's affirmation that above and beyond separate religions (matham) the ultimate community is a universal human one under one God—in order to chastise the reference to caste by the Hindu nationalist students. However, his comment about their possible caste background revealed the ways in which his self-understanding as secular was tied to a politics of his relative caste privilege that was far from erased. From the point of view of this adamantly secular teacher, the ABVP students "must" have been from the lower castes. It is only they who could have been drawn to the irrational, the nonmodern, and the antisecular. Drawing on the anticaste formulations of Narayana Guru, the teacher denied caste as a valid category when reference was made to the Brahmin Nambudiri caste background of the beleaguered Saiju; making reference to the caste name of the student offended this teacher's secular sensibilities. In the next instance, however, he drew on the bureaucratic state language of caste categories (sc/st) in order to express the relatively upper-caste identity that underlay his sense of himself as secular.

The incident began as a Hindu-Muslim conflict and then got displaced onto a caste conflict by the teacher. He had little to say to Hasar, the Muslim student. The teacher was most upset that Saiju's attackers referenced, in fact actually spoke, his caste. In the putatively secular space of this community-based college, no reference to one's caste is allowed, as caste had literally become unspeakable. When the teacher, angry with students for referencing their victim's caste, threatened to publicly ask the offending students to state their last names and reveal their caste, he was transgressing a line in order to embarrass these students. This attempt to embarrass the students was also an attempt to reinscribe his own secular credentials by asserting his caste status as above that of the socially inferior sc/st. This secularism was rooted in his relative caste privilege.

The Education of English

The marking and negotiation of tradition within the college goes hand in hand with a contested marking and negotiation of modernity. The previous section examined the politics of tradition in the college as a way to examine caste and religion within the ambiguous secular space of an educational context in India. And it showed how lower-caste negotiations of tradition take place within the dominant horizon of the upper-caste Hindu as the normative citizen-subject of democratic India. However, this normative citizen-subject is not only "upper caste and Hindu" but also "upper class and English educated."

How does one understand education as a marker of modernity within low-caste communities? The historical importance of and enthusiasm for education on the part of lower-caste communities enacts a politics of language and class that reveals educated modernity to be an ambivalent space of aspiration that is increasingly transnational. The desire for education emerges out of a contestation about the meanings of modernity for lower-caste communities. Within the space of the college, this is most apparent in the ways that the speaking of English is contested.

As a marker of educated modernity, the speaking of English is situated in a class-specific understanding in which modernity is respectable, middle class, and now increasingly transnational. As studies of migration have shown, one of the main investments of upwardly mobile nonresident Kerala families, particularly from among minority and non-elite groups, is education, but more specifically education in English-medium schools (Zachariah, Mathew, and Rajan 2001, 57). Within the context of a Sree Narayana College, the speaking of English as a marker of modernity and the politics of resentment that surrounds it must be situated within the politics of caste and class within the Ezhava community. Here it is helpful to further situate the SNDP and its ancillary organizations, including the trust that runs the college, within the broader context of Kerala politics. As Tharakan and Isaac argue, during the 1930s and 1940s, a split began to occur within the Ezhava community between those who supported a reformist anticaste agenda spearheaded by the SNDP and affiliated with the Congress Party and those who began to support the communist left. As the left began to consolidate itself organizationally, these differences became more marked and articulated. Within the college, the speaking of English is often articulated as a pretension of the wealthier members of the Ezhava community, including many members of the college administration and trust management, who are seen to be more interested in upward mobility, respectability, and securing jobs and marriages abroad for their children than in equality and justice. A member of the SFI might well mark his differences from the college administration and teachers he thought were unsupportive by referring to their perceived political affiliations (Congress Party supporters), invoking their wealth, the fact that their children attended English-medium schools, the children and family they had abroad, and the higher "status" (the English word is often used, sometimes the Malayalam word margam) of the teachers. However, although this mapping of class, language, and political affiliation might provide some context for understanding the contested nature of English within the college, its everyday negotiations were not always so neat.

Technically, all classroom instruction is supposed to be in English at the university level, with the exception of language classes such as Malayalam, Hindi, and Sanskrit. The students write their exams in English as well. But at this college, that rarely happens. In classroom after classroom, teachers will write notes on the blackboard in English, which the students dutifully copy. The teaching itself happens in Malayalam. While there may be some attempt to get a student, here or there, to reply to a question in English, the student will generally either answer in Malayalam or having said a few words of English, lapse into Malayalam.

Students who come to the college having studied at English-medium schools find life difficult when they try to speak English in the college. This became abundantly clear during the celebration of Freshers' Day, when new students are welcomed to their respective departments. This event often involves some form of ridiculing the new students, a mild form of what is called "ragging." Ragging is a college phenomenon that has received much public attention in recent years in India. Incidents of ragging in which students berate, harass, and assault new students have become a matter of discussion and regulation. The more violent and spectacular incidents, usually involving young men, emerge out of an everyday politics of negotiating the boundaries of belonging in the college, often tied to caste and class hierarchies. If women's fashion is one terrain for negotiating that boundary in the college (as discussed in chapter 2), the speaking of English is another.

During one of the Freshers' Day celebrations, the head of one of the departments spoke (in English), describing the facilities that were available at the college, talking about recent rank holders (those who did well on public exams) who had come out of the department, and inviting students to freely approach him if they had any trouble. Next the principal spoke, laying out (in Malayalam) the history of the college's founding, its more recent troubles, and the changes that were going to return it to a more disciplined and orderly institution. It was then the turn of elected members of the student union to speak. Sarita urged students, in Malayalam, to enter politics in addition to studying. Bullas, the head of the ABVP at the college, also spoke in Malayalam. However, his Malayalam was highly Sanskritized and flowery, eschewing the many English words that find their way into everyday Malayalam. For example, instead of using the English word *subject* to describe an academic area, quite common in ordinary discourse, he used the word *visheyam*. Even Dhanya, his SFI-affiliated political opponent, was impressed. She leaned over to me and said that she wished she could speak like that. In the substance of his speech, he drew parallels between the writings of Swami Vivekananda and Sree Narayana Guru, describing their mutual desire for a revitalized Hinduism. He finished to huge applause.

The meeting became more unruly and raucous with the next speaker. Standing on the dais in jeans, a T-shirt, and sneakers, Shinu began with a series of quotes in English: "Opinions are our cheapest commodities." The audience stopped listening and the heckling began. As he continued, students from the audience started shouting, "Speak in Malayalam!" Next to me, Dhanya yelled out: "You need to learn your mother tongue. Go get a nursery school teacher!" Shaken by the response, Shinu quickly finished with a set of platitudes about welcoming new students and sat down. After a poetry recitation by Kavitha in Malayalam, Rajiv got up and tried to speak in English. A chorus of voices shouted back at him: "Speak in Malayalam!" A loud voice from the audience shouted, "We are not *naden sahippus* here!" This phrase is a powerful indictment. As discussed earlier, *naden* is a complex locational marker that in this context can be understood to refer to Malayalees in general. *Sahippu* is a term, related to the Hindi word *sahib*, used to refer to the British. The phrase refers to Malayalees who think and act as though they are white. Flustered and unsure, Rajiv rushed off the stage, his speech unfinished. Finally, Simmi gave a summing up. Because she was known in the college as someone who came from an educated, middle-class Nair family, there was some expectation that she might speak in English. Dhanya muttered that if she did, Simmi would hear it from her. Having understood her audience, Simmi safely gave her speech in Malayalam.

Such contestations about the speaking of English in the college reveal a class politics of language that is increasingly spatialized. While the Freshers' Day example fits easily into colonial-era debates about identity, language, and class centered on acting British and speaking English, contemporary experiences of migration have transformed those debates into a cultural politics of foreignness that marks the struggles of young people as they navigate the impossibilities and possibilities of migration through further study, jobs, and marriage. Here I focus on the relationship between the speaking of English and the increasingly migratory trajectories that young people feel they must undertake.

As a foreign-returned Malayalee who spoke fluent, American-accented English, I was a source of curiosity, novelty, suspicion, and envy. While some applauded my apparent desire to learn something about my motherland and wondered how and where I had learned Malayalam, others wondered why I had chosen to come back to a place that so many were struggling so hard to leave. My "success" as someone who was born in Kerala but who had migrated abroad elicited endless questions about how one went about studying abroad, finding money, applying for a job, and fulfilling visa regulations. While many students had their own family networks for juggling the prospects of going abroad, many did not. The speaking of English was woven into these conversations, with many wondering just how much English one needed to know to get by. For many self-consciously aspiring students, the speaking of English went hand in hand with the possibilities of migration.

This desire to learn English in order to migrate was not something that was easy to openly admit to on campus. The example of Prasad is a good case in point, and it reveals how the speaking of English is tied to a broader desire for education and mobility in a transnational context that is contested in the college. Its most immediate manifestation is a confrontation between respectable and unrespectable masculinities. Prasad's family lived in town, where his father was a clerk in a government office and his mother a housewife. Coming from a somewhat educated Ezhava family with enough income to send him to a convent school, Prasad came to the college able to speak relatively fluent English, something that was rare. Prasad tried to explain why he was so picked upon for speaking English during his first year, drawing on the language of psychology:

> That is a very complex thing. What I mean is: it's like a complex, an ego thing. If someone does well, you don't like that. That is, if I can do something that you can't, how would you feel? They will feel jealous of it. They will try and suppress you, or they will pick on your weak points.

He then went on to outline the ways in which the disciplining of his English was tied to politics:

> Two or three folks caught me and gave me a lashing. I am just standing there talking to my friend in straight English. Here speaking English is thought of as showing your status [*margam*]. But in this case, that is not why I was talking like that. We were just doing it to develop our language. They understood us to be that way. They had political backing. The guy that gave me that lashing—he was a political leader. He has the authority, the power. So, he immediately suppressed me. He called me and warned me. . . . First he asked me, "Where did you study?" I told him that I studied at a local Christian school. He then asked me why it was that I was trying to act so big [*waliya*]. Then he really gave me a lashing, swearing at me. I just listened. If I was in the second year, I would have responded. Given the background of that time, I could not have responded. I just came to the college one and half or two months prior. I didn't even have any friends. In my second year, I would have raised my voice. Who is this guy to say something to me? I would give it back to him. If he says something, I have my classmates, the contemporaries of that year. So there will be a struggle. I will have my folks and he will have his. There will be a mutual fear. If the problem persists, then other political folks [*rashtriyakar*] will come and the problem will be settled.

This narrative reveals Prasad's embattled sense of bravado in the face of a certain amount of ragging in his first year, which was tied to an enforced marginalization at the hands of an intimidating and unruly masculinity that sought to police him within the college. Throughout I have been tracking the workings of a lower-caste, lower-class masculinity that attaches itself to the signifiers of globalization through fashion, commodification, and assertiveness in public. In the last chapter I discussed how this *chethu* masculinity articulates with the assertiveness of masculine political activity. Prasad's desire to "develop his language" by speaking English—something he could have taken for granted in his English-medium convent school—began to mark his middle-class and respectable aspirations as opposed to those that mark the *chethu* style.

However, this set of aspirations was embattled not only because of other students who contested his desire for respectability. Prasad was painfully aware of his marginalization with regard to his location within educational hierarchies. He described the struggle to find some kind of foothold in the job market:

> A student who studies at Delhi School of Economics, or St. Stephen's college. . . . In his life, whatever his ambition is, he will be able to do it, IAS or IIT. At the same time, think about a student from here. We are thinking: OK, I have to somehow pass SSLC. Then I have to pass pre-degree. OK, I'll try the entrance for this, that, or the other, and see what happens. OK then B.Sc., then M.Sc., B.Ed. or then maybe M.Ed. or some clerical thing, or some test. It just goes on and on.

Here, Prasad was expressing the frustrations and fatigue that come with the well-known pattern of having to juggle various courses of study in endless succession at this or that institution in the hopes of gaining some kind of job, a pattern that often extends the category of "youth" and "student" well into the twenties for many young people, especially men. Situated within a chronic crisis of the "educated unemployed," calculations about courses of study become extremely sophisticated and sometimes endless as students struggle to find ways to enter the job market either within Kerala or outside, in metropolitan centers within India or abroad. For example, some students in the college were trying to figure out how and where they might get a master's in social work, because they had heard that there might be opportunities to migrate to Canada and the United States as drug and alcohol rehabilitation officers.

As Prasad envisioned it, students from elite institutions in metropolitan Delhi (St. Stephen's College or the Delhi School of Economics) simply figure out what they want to do and are then able to do it. From his perspective, their ambitions must coincide with elite trajectories such as becoming an officer in the Indian Administrative Service (IAS) or gaining admission to elite institutions such as the Indian Institute of Technology (IIT). While they aspired for the top, here he was, after getting his Secondary School Leaving Certificate (SSLC) and passing his pre-degree courses, perhaps maneuvering from a bachelor's of education (B.Ed.) to maybe a master's in computers (M.Sc.), or perhaps writing an exam to try to get a job as a clerk in a bank or post office. At the same time, if he was offered a job as a clerk, should he take it or look to get another degree that might allow him to migrate abroad?

This juggling act was not something that was spoken about very much at the college. Understood to be part of a whole set of private family strategies that included using connections and money (for gaining admission into various courses of study) to place young people in jobs at home, in other parts of India, and abroad, it was seen to be another marker of who was capable of such strategizing and who was not, another marker of inequality within an increasingly commodified educational marketplace. And of course, these private strategies often sit uncomfortably with the stated public political affiliations and ideologies of students themselves. And, despite his frustrations, Prasad had many ambitions, ones that eloquently spoke to the geography of his imagination of marginalization and aspiration.

One day I ran into him at the train station, going to Thiruvananthapuram, the capital city. I asked him where he was going. Initially, he evaded the question by saying he was just going to wander about (*karenguga*), for "no reason" (*chumma*). Eventually, he sheepishly told me that he was going to the city to take coaching classes for gaining admission to an MBA course that had just opened up. He made me promise not to tell anyone we knew because they would make fun of him. As we took the train together, he then went on to let me in on his real ambition: he desperately wanted to join the United Nations. Surprised by this, I asked him why, and he went on to explain that if one was part of the UN, "One can go anywhere in the world and command respect. I can be a 'world citizen': any country, and they will accept me."

As the train rumbled toward our destination, I was struck by the multiple resonances of Prasad's desire for a cosmopolitan, worldly citizenship. Unable to make his aspiring respectability "command respect" in the college and yet acutely sensitive to his own caste and class marginalization within the hierarchical educational geography of India, he sought transcendence and respect on a world stage, a space he imagined would allow him to be acceptable anywhere. Education as a space of class aspiration and respectability for Prasad was caught between a more radical vision of modernity as class struggle and his marginalization in caste, class, and geographical terms from dominant visions of educated and respectable modernity that underlie the normative citizen-subject, namely, an English-speaking, upper-caste, upper-class student at St. Stephen's College in Delhi. The struggle for middle-class respectability for Prasad was tenuous and difficult, caught as he was between a rejection of middle-class respectability as a normative horizon for lower-caste communities among his "*chethu-fying*," politicized classmates on the one hand and the precariousness of its achievement within the spaces of the dominant secular modern within India on the other. The projection of himself onto a world stage, imagined through the United Nations, allowed him a way to imagine himself beyond the hierarchical structures of caste and class that he feels are so impenetrable within India.

Femininity, Education, and Aspiration

So far I have examined the negotiations of class aspiration and respectability through tracing the contestations over speaking English in the college, a contest grounded in a confrontation between two class-inflected masculinities. However, Prasad's frustrations about his inability to "command respect" were directed not only at the elite spaces of the nation (St. Stephen's College) or *goondas* (hooligans) of his college, as he sometimes called his politicizied classmates; they were also directed at women in public. And it is here that we begin to see the implications for women of this contest between masculinities within the educational sphere, one that will lead us to a fuller discussion of education as a space of modern aspiration and its gendering. Previous chapters have discussed a modern yet demure femininity as a key condition of entry and possibility for women within modern public spaces. So far, the discussion of this feminine modality has been couched in terms of bodily demeanor, for example, in terms of fashion (the *churidar*) and ways of walking (*oudhukam*). However, the idea of education or being educated is an important part of being demure and feminine, and it reveals the feminized trajectory of educational aspiration.

One can begin to see how femininity inserts itself into education as a structure of aspiration by examining Prasad's frustration at the presence of women in the spaces in which he tried to compete and "improve," as he put it. At debating contests, he argued that judges wanted to "uplift" women and therefore discriminated against him. He insisted that he was for "women's education" but that they should not be allowed to "get ahead" of men. His aspirations toward a middle-class masculinity entailed that equally aspiring women should be kept in their place.

Some of this came to a head for Prasad, in the wake of his participation, along with Sunita, and Sophiya, on a local state television program on youth issues to celebrate Republic Day. One of the main reasons they were chosen was because they all, to various degrees, could speak English. When he got back to the college after the taping, I asked him how it had gone. He said the main "problem" was Sophiya, who was full of arrogance (*gema*). He related that the coordinator wanted Sophiya to speak more, so she just went on and on about women's issues. He stated, "She doesn't really know anything. It was as good as it was because of the editing. Well, they said we had to have two girls. What to do?" He criticized Sophiya's performance for including comments that were too down-to-earth, too full of examples. He summed up by saying, "In a forum like that, one must say things a bit more abstractly, then only it sounds good." Prasad's assertion of his aspiring, future, and goal-oriented masculinity, rooted in his desire to "command respect," produces itself in opposition to a presentist, disorderly masculinity and an educated yet demure femininity that must always be kept in place.

What is the place afforded women within the structures of aspiration and opportunity that educated modernity represents? "Companionship" is the placeholder for a demure femininity that is educated but does not "get ahead." The demure and modern female student must remain the companion to the respectable and modern male student. Her horizon is very much that of the companionate wife and mother—educated and able to be a fitting companion to her upwardly mobile, newly respectable husband, fit to educate and raise their children.

When I discussed the taping of the television show with Sunita and Sophiya, they were excited and happy about it. Sophiya said it gave her "exposure" and helped her develop her public speaking skills. She mentioned that Prasad had been annoyed because she had gotten the most attention. She thought this had to do with his not having much to say about youth issues. All he wanted to do was show off what he knew about current events. That was not what the interviewers wanted to know. They wanted some sense of what it was like to be a young person today in India. To that end, she talked about being a young woman and wanting to educate herself.

In chapter 1, I discussed debates about women's education as a key site for understanding the gender, caste, and class dimensions of modernity in Kerala. Early anxieties about the westernization of women and girls were countered by arguments from male reformers that modern women's education would create modern wives and mothers capable of maintaining a balance between tradition and modernity. Key to this project was the assertion of an educated, female companion for new monogamous and conjugal unions tied to the creation of a modern and respectable middle-class sensibility. The idea of the "educated wife" was discussed in chapter 2. Here, I explore the gendering of education in relationship to ideas about the "educated mother," which pervade the structure of aspirations that govern educational strategies for women.

As an instance of a newly consumerist Kerala, J. Devika discusses the continuation and intensification of such modern domesticity through more contemporary regimes of consumption (2007a). She notes the growing importance of what she calls "child-crafting": "a concentration of time, energies and desires on shaping children into products saleable in the global job market" (2007a, 2468). The construction of the educated mother is crucial for this kind of domestic duty, one that has been intensified through trajectories of globalization and migration.

The construction of this figure and its anxious negotiations is illustrated by examining the narrative of a young mother who supervised a section of the college library, someone I called Sumam Chechy. As I have discussed, while younger students would often call me *chechy*, she was one of the few younger women, slightly older than me in the college, not a student and not a teacher, who took me under her wing as a kind of younger sister. When classes were cancelled and I did not have an interview scheduled or another appointment, we spent many hours in the college library, gossiping about students and faculty, discussing movies and television serials, or arguing about life in the United States versus Kerala. The college library became, as it was for many other students, particularly female students, a safe space of sociality imbued with Sumam Chechy's bubbly and funny personality and her always welcoming smile.

Unlike Sophiya or Sunita, who were struggling hard to better their English and do "civic activities" that would build their confidence and help them with further studies hopefully either in Delhi or abroad, Sumam Chechy was not going anywhere. Married with a young son and daughter, she came from a family that was well connected to Sree Narayana institutions. She and most of her family attended SN schools and colleges. She failed her B.A. exams but somehow got the staff position because one of her uncles "hustled" her into it, as she put it. She narrates that she just went to college, minding her own business, not really studying. Laughing, she says she really stopped studying when her family got a television in 1985. All she did was watch television, and there was no one to tell her to study. Her father had died and her mother would simply lie down after dinner. She had a few uncles who tried to tell her to study, but they were rarely around. While all of this was narrated in a laughing and joking way over many conversations, her failure to pass her B.A. exams emerged as a painful mark, one tied not only to failing an exam but to a failure to achieve the status of educated motherhood that is so central to the structuring of aspiration. In many conversations she would relate how she struggled to help her children study, but kept insisting that she herself did not know much since she had failed her B.A. exams. In one of her desk drawers, she kept a copy of a children's encyclopedia, called *Lokam*, which she would peruse for information she thought might help her to help her children, often switching when she got bored to the other drawer, in which she had a secret stash of women's magazines full of the serialized stories she read so avidly.

One day the usually cheerful Sumam Chechy was upset and angry, near tears, a faraway look in her eyes. She started complaining about how difficult it was to control the kids in the library. Nobody returned the books on time. How was she to keep track of everything? I tried to tell her it was not her fault and that she should not worry. It became clear that what was really worrying her was not her inability to control the students in the library but her supposed inability to adequately mother her own children.

She started to tell me about her daughter, in the second standard, who had been sent to a faraway English-medium convent school, incurring much financial hardship for the family. She was an "average student," as her mother put it. She was smart but would not study unless someone made her do it. Sumam Chechy went on to outline what happened every evening after work. By the time Sumam got back from the college, it was 5 o'clock. She had to do housework until 7 or 7:30 p.m. Every night Sumam tried to instill some discipline. She put a mat on the floor and seated her son on one side and her daughter on the other. She went from one to the next. Maybe this started at seven. Very soon after that, her husband walked in and she had to prepare dinner. Asha, the daughter, would procrastinate further by sitting with her dinner for one hour.

The previous day, Asha had missed her third straight day of school, and her teachers insisted that Sumam go to the school and write out all the class notes that Asha had missed. It was difficult for Sumam to go because of her own work schedule. She told them she had a "small job," but that did not matter to them. She left work early and got there at 4 p.m. She sat at her daughter's desk and wrote out all the sums and class notes she would need to help Asha. The teachers also told Sumam that they would not send Asha for any outside tutoring. The mother should teach a child at home. And if she was incapable, then they should send Asha for tutoring at the school, after class. Asha had a test coming up. If she did not pass, Sumam must send her for tutoring, at the school, from 3:30 to 5:30 every day—something that of course brings the teachers additional income. When Sumam protested that her daughter would refuse, they told her that they did not want to hear anything about transportation problems or the complaints of her daughter. As the teacher put it, "When a mother says something, children listen. Shouldn't a child listen to her mother?" While Sumam recognized the racket that tutoring has become ("It must be to make money. They [teachers] say she is bad and that makes her come to them for tutoring"), she was nevertheless rattled by the idea that she was incapable of educating her daughter. She stated, "But I feel so bad, she [the teacher] says it's the mother's fault." Dejectedly, Sumam said that maybe they should take Asha out of the school and bring her closer to home. They just wanted to give her a good education. But this seemed impossible.

Sumam's narrative reveals the dilemmas of a mother who is made to feel inadequate as a mother because of her lack of education. Her own failure to pass her bachelor's exam produces an insecurity about her ability to educate her children, which is reinforced as she is compelled to leave work early to go to her daughter's class, sit at a desk, taking notes to tutor her daughter, by the English-educated, middle-class femininity of her daughter's teachers. Within the logic of longitudinal generational progress, her failure to reach middle-class respectability portends failure for her daughter. The space of education is structured by a set of caste-, class-, and gender-specific aspirations through which educated children should become educated husbands, fathers, wives, and mothers. Sumam does not quite embody the demure, educated femininity necessary to be a companion to her counterpart, someone who can produce well-schooled, obedient children.

While Sumam struggles to produce herself as a fitting mother for the aspirational logic of her family and caste, Prasad's struggles in the college reveal how he must navigate an alternative class-inflected masculinity that challenges his own middle-class ambitions. While low-caste movements have historically demonstrated an enthusiasm for secular modernity, given their subordinate position within "tradition" and the caste structure, it nevertheless inserts them into a cultural politics of Malayalee identity (as the politics of English reveals) that is class inflected. The enthusiasm for secular modernity on the part of low-caste communities also inserts them into the gendered structures that underwrite education as secular and modern. This long-standing interaction between education, caste, and modernity now plays itself out on a horizon of possibility increasingly marked by migration, either to other parts of India or abroad.

Conclusion

The modern transformations of caste relations within Kerala reveal a terrain of reimaginings of caste hierarchy, on the part of both the upper and lower castes, within the horizon of secular modernity. The specific instance of the Ezhava-based, anticaste Sree Narayana movement reveals a reworking of Hindu tradition and an engagement with educated modernity. This low-caste-based college embodies the ambiguous complexities of definitions of community, understood as Ezhava, Hindu, and human within the movement, in the context of a significant reworking of religion and secularism as Hindu nationalism emerges as a cultural and political force during the 1990s.

Education is also a space of upward mobility and aspiration. While the college emerges as a quintessentially "modern" institution, it must nevertheless negotiate the fault lines between marked conceptions of that which is public and private, traditional and modern, religious and secular. The meanings and negotiations of education for young people in this college are tied to a social movement that sought to eradicate untouchability. Education has played a key role in the massive social transformations of caste relations within Kerala, expanding opportunities and transforming the conditions under which young members of this caste community struggle to produce their future lives. In fact, this college and its associated institutions are an important vehicle for these transformations. However, the space of educated modernity is not a straightforward space of upward mobility. Situated within the larger context of producing the normative citizen-subject within India, this low-caste modern college exists at the fault lines that constitute the secular modern in India, revealing modern forms of caste, class, and gender politics that make the space of educated modernity an ambivalent and contested one. The structures of aspiration that underwrite low-caste educational strategies, both for the caste movement and for individuals and families, reveal their caste, class, and gender configurations while simultaneously pointing to the ways in which these trajectories and aspirations intersect with an expanding and increasingly commodified educational marketplace linked to transnational imaginaries and horizons.

Consumer Citizenship
in the Era of Globalization

These chapters have highlighted youth and gender—as subjects, objects, and identities—and globalization in India. I have focused attention on key youth social and cultural practices—fashion, romance, politics, and education—in a small college in a provincial town in Kerala as complex enactments of consumer citizenship at the intersection of gender, caste, and class. These explorations suggest that such an ethnographic focus is a productive lens for understanding larger cultural and political trans-formations in liberalizing India, drawing attention to the variety of ways that young people mediate their lives across the relations between states and markets. Highlighting everyday experiences and negotiations of contemporary global transformations, I have also contextualized these practices within regional and national histories, tracking the ways they are both structured by and transformative of the legacies of colonial and postcolonial modernities. Attention to these practices and their everyday mediations link articulations of youth as consumers to youth as citizens, bringing together consumer practices and discourses associated with globalization with transformations in state-derived understandings of citizenship, politics, and democracy.

The recent award-winning Bollywood blockbuster *Rang De Basanti*, hereafter referred to as *RDB* (dir. Mehra, 2006), and the cultural and political phenomenon that it has become demonstrate the continuing centrality and importance of youth, gender, and consumer citizenship within liberalizing India.[1] A brief discussion of this film and its impact reveals how the gendered stakes of consumer citizenship continue to inform discourses of "India Rising." However, much has also changed since I began this research in the mid-1990s. At that time, economic liberalization was a relatively new phenomenon, its cultural mediations just emerging. I conclude by reflecting on some of the more contemporary resonances of what I have explored so far, while pointing to some new directions.

Glossed as "A Generation Awakens," the blockbuster film *RDB* is a political coming-of-age story of five happy-go-lucky male college students in the nation's capital city, New Delhi. The story begins with narration by a British officer in India who had to oversee the jailing of Bhagat Singh and other iconic heroes of the anticolonial struggle who died in 1931; the events leave him guilt ridden because of his admiration for their patriotic sacrifice.[2] His British granddaughter, a filmmaker, discovers his diaries, which inspire her to travel to India to make a film about those heroes. She enlists a female friend to find actors, settling on a group of five college friends, representing different communities and backgrounds, who initially have no interest in her film. Living hedonistic lives, they have no relationship to heroes they know only through textbooks. They also express deep cynicism about contemporary Indian society, arguing that it is corrupt. The film moves back and forth between sepia-tinted images of patriotic struggle, sacrifice, and valor during the 1920s and 1930s and the contemporary moment, as the young men are enlisted to make the movie, become inspired by the story of the freedom fighters, and are emboldened to act, through violent means and sacrifice, when a friend is killed because of the actions of a corrupt politician.

RDB is one of several recent films to represent Indian youth in the wake of liberalization, one that celebrates globalized Indian youth while revealing anxieties about their allegiances to the nation.[3] The first part of

RDB, which focuses on the carefree lives of five friends, emphasizes an effortless blending of a globalized Indian youth in metropolitan and "local" India. These young men are not simply imitators of the West; they easily blend a global cosmopolitanism and their local contexts. Several characters dress in worn jeans, army jackets, leather jackets, and traditional Indian *kurtas* in ways that are understated and cool without overtly trying to brand them as globalized. They move between spaces indexed as "global" (such as a five-star hotel) and the food stands of a local street. They effortlessly weave English, Hindi, and a very local Hindi-Punjabi slang. The film is particularly adept at depicting an aimless loitering associated with college-age life and its exuberant masculine excesses (biking, drinking). The dominant image of the film, in posters and advertising, of these young bare-chested men as they run through a field of tall grass, one of them whipping his shirt around overhead, led one journalist to describe the film as "Bhagat Singh Topless, Waving in Jeans."[4]

In such mass-mediated figurations of liberalization's children, there is a careful calibration of the global and the local in the production of a youth identity coded as Indian. *RDB* emphasizes the "local" feel of globalized Indian youth, one that nevertheless relies on representations of the social category of youth as metropolitan, middle class, assertive, hip, and confident. In fact, despite its eschewing of overt branding and conspicuous consumption as excessive representations of liberalized Indian youth within the film itself, Aamir Khan, the main star of *RDB*, and the Coca-Cola Company made Bollywood history by launching "Coca-Cola–Rang De Basanti" special edition collectible bottles, marketed only in Mumbai and Delhi; it was the first such venture linking a Bollywood film to a branded product, one that is iconic of globalization.[5] Further, the film depicts liberalization's children as disengaged from contemporary Indian society through its portrayal of masculine hedonism as witty, carefree play—biking, loitering, and drinking—all to a soundtrack that shifts easily from standard Hindi film music to hard rock.

In its second part, the film begins to question this disengagement, wondering whether today's consumerist Indian youth can be inspired by the heroism of the past to engage the problems that plague contemporary Indian society. This anxiety about the status of youth as citizens of the nation partakes of a wide-ranging and globally circulating discourse in which a perceived decline in civic and patriotic values among young people is linked to their rampant consumerism, a discourse that once again positions consumerism against citizenship. However, as I have suggested in these chapters, the anxious harking back to older narratives of patriotism and sacrifice should not obscure the ways in which attempts to reclaim citizenship by liberalization's children reconfigure citizenship differently for the purposes of a newly globalized middle class.

This can be seen by examining the way RDB represents contemporary Indian society. As I have suggested, for midnight's children, India's problems are rooted in the rural masses, which must be modernized and uplifted by the middle class—they are reformers in the service of the nation. Rather than invoke the poverty and suffering of these masses as central to what ails Indian society today—problems that Nehruvian nationalism sought to resolve through state-centric development—RDB constructs an image of Indian society as a corrupt and unscrupulous democratic political establishment. Echoing a wide-ranging discourse, here liberalization's children critique the postcolonial state. The film's "popular patriotism" emerges from a reengagement with citizenship on the part of India's globalized consumerist youth, inspired by the valor of nationalist freedom fighters. However, the invocations of an earlier anticolonial and nationalist language of citizenship rooted in self-sacrifice belie the reworking of citizenship in the contemporary moment. Drawing parallels between a corrupt and illegitimate form of colonialism and the workings of Indian democracy today, the film fashions a globalizing middle class that seeks to lay claim to the Indian state. While the shift from midnight to liberalization might have involved a throwing off of ideological baggage, enabled by the fashioning of new consumer identities through the liberalization of the Indian economy, this perceived shift has also generated another: one that seeks to refashion the Indian state and its languages and repertoires of politics and citizenship for the purposes of the new middle class.

The perceived impact of RDB on middle-class mobilizations on behalf of young middle-class women and against lower-caste claims on the state reveals some of this reworking. The film was understood to have directly inspired opposition to a high-profile verdict involving suspects in the murder of a young upper-middle-class woman named Jessica Lal at a popular night club in Delhi.[6] When the suspects were exonerated through what was understood to be the bribery of judges and witnesses, the youthful patriotism of *RDB*—what was termed the "Rang De Basanti effect"—was explicitly invoked to mobilize a protest that gathered momentum and eventually led to the overturning of the verdict. This mobilization against a corrupt judiciary has led to the reopening—spearheaded by a Delhi college student—of another legal case involving the murder of a young middle-class woman. In addition, *RDB* was again explicitly invoked as an inspiration in recent student protests against a state reservation policy to increase the number of admissions for lower-caste groups in medical colleges, a policy that, it was argued, would make India uncompetitive in the global economy.[7] The mobilizations over the murders of young middle-class Delhi women, along with the upper-caste and middle-class provenance of much antireservation politics, have led some to wonder when invocations of the spirit of *RDB* will extend to protests involving non-middle-class victims, for example against the killings of a Dalit girl or family and the demolitions of urban slums.[8]

While *RDB* constructs a notion of liberalization's children in and through a national, metropolitan location, this book has tracked enactments of these kinds of consumer citizenship and their gendered effects in Kerala, arguing for a flexible articulation between region, nation, and globe. In the years since I began my research, as is often the case with youth cultural forms, fashions and styles have shifted. What was so new and contested then is much more acceptable and widespread now. For example, within the realm of women's fashion, the *churidar* is ubiquitous, even in small villages. The wearing of skirts and jeans by young women is far more common than it used to be. With respect to education, autonomous colleges are now a permanent and widespread feature of the higher education scene in Kerala.

All of this might suggest that Kerala is, indeed, globalizing and that the cultural struggles I have tracked in these pages are over, having been won by those seeking to open up the region to larger global forces and its "liberalizing" effects. However, such a reading of the contemporary context would misread the ways globalization has been framed in this study. Rather than partake of the view that globalization is an external and large-scale force that threatens the "local" culture of Kerala, I have examined globalization as discourse and practice, *within* Kerala. In conventional anthropological terms, it is its own "folk" category, invoked, deployed, and mediated in a variety of ways as part and parcel of ongoing struggles over the public life of citizen-consumers. Globalization structures lifeworlds but also becomes an explicit object of contestation and negotiation within everyday contexts. Paying attention to the cultural politics of globalization carefully contextualized within local and national histories enables a careful and nuanced assessment of claims about globalization as a radical new force in the world, neither dismissing nor exaggerating its impact. In these ways, I hope this book might enable a less teleological and more grounded sense of how large-scale social processes such as globalization are shaped by everyday mediations at the intersection between the postcolonial and the global.

In these pages, I have emphasized the importance and centrality of youth and gender for the kinds of consumer citizenship I have been tracking. Despite what may appear to be the greater ease with which young women and men navigate their public worlds, questions persist about the identities and roles of youth and gender. The successful expansion of new cultural forms, styles, and fashions goes hand-in-hand with the persistence of moral panics about young people as consumers and citizens. In 2005, the then education minister, E. T. Basheer, was struggling to impose bans on cell phones, fashion shows, and student political activity.[9] Violent protests against the celebration of Valentine's Day are an annual event. The persistence of these kinds of moral panics demonstrates that, while new spaces and identities have been formed, their conditions of negotiation entail navigating a contested cultural politics of globalization. The gendered stakes of consumer citizenship I have tracked in these chapters continue to inform the reshaping and transformations of youth, generation, and gender in globalizing India.

However, some new cultural forms have emerged that differently mediate region, nation, and globe. In these chapters, I have explored a fraught and contested process by which young women and men differently mediate their identities through gender embodiments and performances of masculinity and femininity. More recently, regionally specific and transnational forms of youth-oriented mass media, including radio, music, and television, have generated new kinds of Malayalee-specific versions of popular music (rock, hip-hop) and style that simultaneously index regional identity and a global cosmopolitanism in ways that might be far less polarizing. The tensions I have tracked between notions of "Kerala," "India," and the "West" are perhaps being reshaped by new cultural forms that more assertively reconfigure a regional Malayalee identity as commodified and globalized. While I have argued that the young women and men I worked with are liberalization's children in their own right, I have done so largely through contextualizing them at the meeting point of regional trajectories of migration and globalization and national discourses of globalization. What might be more fully emerging now is the regional variant of liberalization's children—young, hip, confident, cool, and Malayalee. How does the politics of gender, caste, and class structure the emergence of this figuration of a regionally inflected globalized youth identity? What is the relationship between this articulation of a Malayalee globalized youth and the "chethu-fying" Gulfan? If the churidar indicates the greater acceptability of clothing styles coded as "Indian" for young women in Kerala, how do they live and experience these new configurations of a globalized regional identity? How does the "production of locality" happen in this instance? These questions demonstrate the continued salience of region, nation, and globe and their dynamic transformations, highlighting the continued importance of processes of re-territorialization to the lived experiences of globalization among young women and men, at the intersection between the postcolonial and the global.

NOTES

1. This is not to suggest that productions of Indian nationalism in relation to a larger transnational context are new. As scholars have argued for India, as they have elsewhere, transnational links forged through colonialism, capitalism, and empire have been an important context for productions of national identity (see Niranjana 2006; Sinha 1995, 2006). However, contemporary processes and discourses of globalization point to highly specific transformations in capital, labor, and commodity flows, resulting in new kinds of state restructuring and global integration.

2. Started in the mid-1980s under the leadership of India's then prime minister Rajiv Gandhi, the liberalization of the Indian economy accelerated with comprehensive reforms in 1991 during Narasimha Rao's term as prime minister. India signed on to World Bank and IMF loans, reduced tariffs and duties on foreign goods, liberalized the private sector, and opened up the public sector to market forces. While *globalization* is also used, the more common term, in popular and some scholarly accounts, for marking the impact of "globalization" within the Indian context is *liberalization*, which

refers more pointedly to concrete economic reforms that rework the relationship between the state and the market through processes of privatization. However, the term *liberalization* is also used in a wider and looser way, for example in "post-liberalization India" or "liberalizing India," to point to global forces and their impact in India in the aftermath of these economic reforms. For discussions of these reforms and their impact see Deshpande 2003; Fernandes 2006; Mazarella 2003; Nigam 2005; Oza 2006; and Corbridge and Harriss 2000.

3. For example, the national newsmagazine *Outlook* devotes its January 12, 2004, issue to the cover story, titled "The World's Youngest Nation," including these statistics (page 41). The business community touts the youth of the Indian labor force, looking favorably on the earnings potential of young workers. A recent JP Morgan Stanley report states that India will be the youngest nation in the world by 2010, a fact that will help generate and sustain an 8 percent growth rate ("India Will Be Youngest Nation by '10," *Business Standard*, May 30, 2006). The "second demographic transition," as some have called it, with exploding youth populations in many countries of Asia, Africa, and Latin America, has also been noted by key Indian business leaders such as Nandan Nilekani, CEO of Infosys, an information technology firm that is one of the success stories of the new economic dispensation in India (interview on *The Charlie Rose Show*, March 1, 2006).

4. *Outlook*, January 12, 2004, 52.

5. Ibid., 41.

6. Ibid.

7. Rushdie's novel, considered a hallmark in postcolonial literature, marked a generation through its invocation of Nehru's famous speech at the midnight hour of India's independence on August 15, 1947 (Rushdie 1981). For an example of how *midnight's children* is invoked against *liberalization's children* in contemporary journalistic usage, see "India's Youth," by Manjeet Kripalani, *BusinessWeek*, October 11, 1999 (http://www.businessweek.com).

8. Source: "India's Youth," *BusinessWeek Online*, October 11, 1999 (http://www.businessweek.com).

9. While she focuses on middle-class formation in the metropolitan center of Mumbai, Leela Fernandes's recent study usefully draws attention to the complexities of middle-class formation in the country at large, arguing that much recent scholarship on the impact of economic reforms in India assumes a monolithic middle-class identity that is metropolitan and urban

(2006, xvii). She reminds us of its highly differentiated character, encompassing urban metropolitan locations and middle-class formation in rural and small towns. In addition to differentiation along the rural-urban continuum, one must also add the intersecting complexities of region, community, and caste.

10. For discussions of Nehruvian nationalism, see Deshpande 2003; Nigam 2005; Kaviraj 1991; and Khilnani 1997. In particular, Fernandes's book on how India's middle class is responding to and being transformed by new economic reforms usefully charts the role of the middle class during earlier periods of anticolonial nationalism, during the aftermath of independence during the era of Nehru, and in the wake of liberalization (2006). Her study examines how her middle-class informants in contemporary metropolitan Mumbai lay claim to public space and engage in forms of politics that generate a new discourse of social exclusion from disadvantaged groups, instead of "speaking for" them, as in an earlier Nehruvian articulation.

11. A burgeoning literature examines the articulations between the consumer and citizen in histories of the modern West (see Cohen 2003; De Grazia 1996; Kroen 2004). Comaroff and Comaroff 2000b have discussed the relevance of earlier articulations of the consumer and citizen within the West for understanding contemporary globalizing projects for fashioning a neoliberal consumer within postcolonial contexts. A few contemporary studies examine the intersections between consumption and citizenship in a variety of contexts. Berdahl 2005 examines citizenship and consumption in post-1989 East Germany during the transition from state socialism to a consumer market economy; West 2006 explores citizenship and consumption through debates about health care in the United States; Schild 2000 examines the notion of a "market citizen" in debates about gender, social welfare, and provision in Chile; and Weinreb 2007 examines the desires and frustrations of citizen-consumers in late socialist Cuba. An interesting and important work is a recent study by Lisa Rofel who examines the rise of consumer subjectivity and identities in contemporary China in the context of state socialism and an expanding capitalist economy (2007).

12. I discuss the articulation of this within the Kerala context in chapter 2.

13. As normative horizon and as an object of analysis, citizenship has become a central topic in political philosophy, political, social, and cultural theory, educational studies, anthropology, and cultural and gender studies. Several scholars have pointed to its highly variable, fragmented, and sometimes

incoherent meanings (Bosniak 2006; Shklar 1991). Anthropological approaches, such as that of Holston and Appadurai (1996, 2000) argue, "Citizenship concerns more than rights to participate in politics. It also includes other kinds of rights in the public sphere, namely civil, socioeconomic, and cultural." Recognition of these other axes of belonging has led to formulations of *cultural citizenship*. The term was first used by Renato Rosaldo to refer to the claims of immigrant minorities for inclusion and recognition of their cultural difference while being able to participate in democratic processes within the United States (1994). Aiwha Ong's reformulation of the term pays attention to the dialectical relationship between state practices of racial, cultural, and ethnic inscription and subjectification of minorities of color within the United States and their own productions of self-making (1996). While also privileging the migrant to first world locations, Toby Miller argues that cultural citizenship points to the increasing ways in which citizenship is tied to more than notions of legal status, soil or blood (2001). Increasingly important is access to the capitalist market and the culture industry through technologies of communication and media. While drawing on the anthropological focus on everyday forms of belonging, this book focuses specific ethnographic attention on *consumer* citizenship as it impacts everyday negotiations of public space and life, as an important axis of belonging through which cultural citizenship is being reworked in the era of globalization. In this way, my approach draws on expanded definitions of cultural citizenship without equating it with overly generalized notions of "participation" in cultural life. As I detail, the idea of a "public" is crucial to my approach to consumer citizenship, one that links mass-mediated public culture to everyday negotiations of public space.

14. In an important and recent argument, Partha Chatterjee (2004) suggests that the framework of citizenship, tied as it is to a liberal western bourgeois worldview, provides a limited way of understanding politics in India and other non-western contexts. He suggests that within the postcolonial development state, one has "populations," and not "citizens," in a vast "political society," a terrain that contests the narrow, elite confines of "civil society" and its language of propriety, legality, and proper associational life in India. Given this, he questions the framework and language of citizenship for understanding the wider terrain of politics in India. However, my conceptualization of citizenship locates it between an overly broad understanding of citizenship equated with everyday life in general and an overly narrow one

that confines it to the workings of an elite, western(izing), middle-class formation. Here, the notion of a "public" is crucial, as it points toward ideas of collective belonging and social membership. This public is not confined to an elite, western, middle-class formation, nor can it simply be categorized as part of a nonelite "political society" in which the politics of public space is outside the languages and repertoires of modern citizenship. While the shaping of the modern public life by elites is an important dimension of citizenship formation, educational institutions and the mass media have integrated young people from across the caste and class spectrum into modern publics in ways that make discourses and practices of citizenship powerful mediators of cultural belonging and social life for a variety of young people.

15. While contemporary scholarship emphasizes the links between consumption and globalization, rendering them almost synonymous, anthropological and historical studies of consumption have drawn attention to longer and more diverse trajectories and histories. For a focus on consumption within the discipline of anthropology that predates its link with globalization, see Appadurai 1988. Numerous ethnographies have drawn attention to commodities and consumption (see Liechty 2003; Burke 1996; Foster 2002; Miller 1994). Stearns 2001 and Mintz 1985 provide social histories of commodities and consumption on a world-historical scale.

16. Emergent literature on modern education and schooling has highlighted the importance of such sites for the constitution of citizens in the public spheres of modern nation-states (Foucault 1977; Hall 2002; Kaplan 2006; Levinson 2001; Levinson et al. 1996; Luykx 1999; Mitchell 1991; Stambach 2000). Ethnographies of education have pointed to the everyday contexts of educational spaces, their determination by larger-level discursive practices of citizenship, and the contradictions they engender (Hall 2002; Levinson 2001; Luykx, 1999; Stambach 2000). Within the Indian context, Srivastava 1998; Chopra and Jeffery 2005; and Benei 2005 have drawn ethnographic attention to the relationship between education, nationalism, and citizenship formation.

17. Here I draw on a wide-ranging literature that explores complex meanings and articulations of the public as they are entangled and disentangled from ideas of the private. Theorizations of the "public sphere" have focused on forms of public behavior, speech, and uses of public places as ways of constituting democratic citizenship and politics. The literature on the public

sphere has received renewed attention through critical engagements with Habermas (1989), in which he lays out the conditions for the constitution of a liberal bourgeois public sphere, a normative ideal that he argues was historically constituted in the seventeenth and eighteenth centuries in Europe. Historians have challenged his emphasis on rational critical debate as the defining quality of discourse in democratic public spheres, suggesting it more as an ideal than a reality (Calhoun 1992; Eley 1992; Ryan 1992). Feminists have explored the issue of participation, examining the conditions of exclusion within liberal public spheres and the politics this has generated (Benhabib 1992; Fraser 1992; Landes 1998; Scott and Keates 2005). Postcolonial scholars have also examined the nature of the public and public space in non-western contexts (Appadurai 1996; Breckenridge 1995; Chakrabarty 2000; Chatterjee 2000; Kaviraj 1997). Extending our understandings of public culture, Mark Liechty has insightfully examined and theorized how public places become new kinds of consumer spaces in an expanding, middle-class-oriented consumer society in the urban spaces of Katmandu, Nepal (2003). Lauren Berlant has examined how mass mediations of citizenship discourse produce new kinds of intimacies that entangle public and private (1997, 1998). Drawing on this work, I examine explicit discourses and practices of publicness to understand reconfigurations of citizenship in the era of globalization, arguing that issues of the nature and quality of public life are linked to questions of inclusion and exclusion.

18. Here, I take seriously the notion of intersectionality across the categories of gender, caste, class, and to a lesser extent community. When I examine how modernity shapes the experience of caste in college student life, I do not frame this study as one of a "caste community." Similarly, while centrally concerned with questions of gender as they pertain to young women's experiences, I do not frame this book primarily in terms of their lives. Rather, I deploy an analytical lens that explores the intersectional dynamics of gender, caste, class, and community in negotiations of public life.

19. For an insightful discussion of this in the Tamil context in South India, see Dhareshwar and Niranjana (1996). Osella and Osella (1999, 2000a, 2000b) also discuss new nonelite forms of consumer identity within the Kerala context.

20. There is, of course, a vast critical social science devoted to the study of globalization which is impossible to exhaustively reference. Some key contributions in the social sciences include Appadurai 1996, 2006; Harvey 1990;

Sassen 2001, 2007. Useful overviews of this literature include Held and McGrew 2007; Roberts and Hite 2000; Lechner and Boli 2004; Anna Tsing (2000) has usefully elaborated the similarities between globalization and modernization, demonstrating the ways in which globalization as a reference to a new era of global interconnection and scale entered scholarly, policy, corporate, and popular culture in the early 1990s. Tsing urges that we view globalization through the same critical lens that social science came to view modernization, a lens that emphasizes its cultural and historical specificity as a project through an examination of its social, institutional, and cultural materializations and negotiations.

21. While this literature is vast and varied, encompassing several disciplinary traditions within sociology and anthropology, Sassen (2001, 2007) and Appadurai (1996, 2006) highlight the changing nature of the nation-state in relationship to citizenship. Ong (1999) has discussed transnationalism and citizenship among Chinese migrants. See Bosniak (2006) for an incisive and comprehensive discussion of citizenship as a framework and how it is being reconfigured and debated in light of globalization.

22. Thus, I eschew a dominant framework within the anthropology of globalization, namely, that of the "local-global." A dominant spaciotemporal imaginary within macrosociological understandings of globalization claims the homogenization of both the world and the production of the "new," either through what is understood to be "Americanization" or through various processes of deterritorialization that lead to a purely global space of experience. The anthropology of globalization has contested this image, emphasizing local mediations of globalization, which has led to formulations of "global-local" connections, or "glocality." My ethnographic perspective that emphasizes everyday mediations of large-scale processes of globalization owes much to this approach. However, such emphases on the "local" can easily lead to simplistic conceptions of place, community, and people. Trapped within a binary between the homogenizing impact of globalization and local diversity and resilience, conceptualizations of the "local" can elide complex processes of place making and subject formation that traverse scale and place. Regional, national, and transnational trajectories of such processes collide with, collude with, and contest each other in a complex production of culture and power within a new global era.

23. I discuss Kerala's development experience and the literature it has generated extensively in chapter 2.

24. See Hall and Jefferson 1976; Hebdige 1979; McRobbie 1991. These early studies, mainly focused on Europe and the United States, have expanded to include cultural studies of youth, spatiality, and globalization in a variety of contexts, including the non-West (Cole 2004, 2005; Cole and Durham 2006; Skelton and Valentine 1998; Maira and Soep 2005; Bhavani, Kent, Twine 1998; Nava 1992; Stearns 2005; Manderson and Liamputtong 2001; Dolby and Rizvi 2007).

25. These crossroads produce highly disjunctive understandings of the life cycle; one that counters standard anthropological approaches in which youth is a transitory stage within a maturational life cycle, often tied to a focus on rites of passage (Van Gennep 1960). Rather than view the life cycle as a pre-ordained movement from one stage to another, recent approaches explore shifting constructions of the life cycle itself (see Johnson-Hanks 2002). Osella and Osella discuss constructions of the life cycle in a Kerala context (1999). Cole (2004) and Cole and Durham (2006) explore shifting ideas about the life cycle in the context of globalization, with a focus on Africa.

26. As much scholarship has shown, definitions of culture, community, and nation are often marked through the play of culture and power as it works through gender differences. Ideas of femininity come to mark notions of tradition in ways that are central to projects seeking to define the boundaries of culture. While this insight is made in a wide variety of works, some notable discussions of these issues are available in Yuval-Davis 1997; Kaplan, Alarcon, Moallem 1999; and Menon and Bhasin 1998. However, Rita Felski points to the necessity for feminist theory to move beyond the "single mythic narrative [in which] . . . man . . . assumes the role of collective subject of history, while woman can exist only as Other" (1995, 7). Rather than view woman as the Other of modernity, Felski instructs us to "unravel the complexities of modernity's relationship to femininity through an analysis of its varied and competing representations" (ibid.).

    Cultural historians of South Asia and imperial formations have pointed to the modern gender regimes that emerged under colonialism and nationalism, regimes that reworked traditional patriarchy in new ways (see Sangari and Vaid 1989; Burton 1999; Sinha 1995). However much Indian nationalism "resolved" the "woman question" by placing women within a newly articulated space of privatized tradition, women have sought to, and have had to, negotiate the public spaces of modernity in ways that have deeply implicated the production of femininities (John 2000). Anthropological approaches that explicitly thematize and highlight modernity have not focused on gender (see Lash and Friedman 1992; Featherstone 1990; Inda 2005; Appadurai 1996). Mitchell (2000) and Knauft (2002) do incorporate gender into their theoretical discussions of anthropology and modernity. Notable ethnographies of gender and modernity include Mills 1999; Rofel 1999, 2007; Ong 1987; and Hodgson 2001.

27. This binary is not deployed in order to demonstrate its universality, as was prominent in the early writings on this distinction in feminist anthropology (Ortner 1974; Rosaldo 1974). Rather than understand it to be a feature of social organization that somehow "explains" the universal subordination of women, I focus on its emergence in the context of colonial modernity. Hancock has demonstrated the centrality of a spatial division between private and public to modernization theory within India through her discussion of Milton Singer's notion of compartmentalization—the idea that for modern (male) subjects, home was the space of tradition, and the world the space of modernity (1999, 114–35). While Singer saw this as an adaptation to the contradictions of modernity, which he did not link to questions of gender and power, Partha Chatterjee has located the public/private distinction and a whole set of homologous oppositions (inner/outer, tradition/modernity, spiritual/material) at the heart of the production of a "modern patriarchy" that anticolonial bourgeois nationalism wrought. Rather than being a self-evident adaptation to modernity, these oppositions and their mutual entanglements come to structure the self-conscious fashioning of colonial elites as they seek hegemony as spokesmen for the nation (Chatterjee 1990; Hancock 1999, 15).

    Within feminist scholarship more generally, two major edited collections bring together many strands within the feminist literature on the public/private distinction. Joan Landes (1998) provides a useful overview of classic and new works. With the exception of the article by Sherry Ortner, which does focus on cross-cultural material, there is no discussion of the colonial and postcolonial histories of this distinction. Joan Scott's and Debra Keates's recent collection (2005) does provide a wider, more comparative range of articles, drawing on some colonial and postcolonial histories.

28. See De Alwis 1995, 1998, 1999; Hancock 1999; Chakravarti 1990; Mani 1987; Visweswaran 1994, 1996.

29. The second largest higher educational system in the world, the structure of the Indian system owes much to its colonial experience. Currently there are

over 300 state-sponsored universities and thousands of colleges that are affiliated to these universities whether they are state-sponsored or not. The apex body that regulates all colleges and universities is the University Grants Commission (UGC). This affiliation system started in England but now only survives in South Asia. It is under enormous pressure to transform in the wake of market pressure and the expanding demand for higher education, as is evidenced by the debate about autonomous colleges, discussed later in the book.

30. These designations refer to the state-sponsored system of reservations and quotas to ameliorate disadvantage due to historical discrimination against low-caste communities in the areas of education and jobs. I discuss this more extensively in chapter 5.

31. Given shifts in policy over the years, the larger landscape of higher education in the state includes students in the "pre-degree" system as well as students in the "plus two" system, in which the eleventh and twelfth years are spent in higher secondary schools instead of colleges.

1

LOCATING KERALA

1. Mazarella 2003; Mankekar 1999; Vedwan 2007; Fernandes 2007; Appadurai 1996, 2002; Nigam 2004; Menon 2005; Sundaram 2004; Rajagopal 2001; Favero 2003; Mirchandani 2004.

2. Amin 1991; Prashad 2001; McKibben 1996. For discussions of the ways the Kerala model circulates, see Jeffrey 1993; Parayil 2000; and Parayil and Sreekumar 2003.

3. It is important to note that Sen does not use the term "model" to describe Kerala, preferring to use the phrase "Kerala's development experience" (George Mathew, "Amartya Sen and the Kerala 'Model,'" Hindu online edition, January 9, 2001, http://www.hinduonnet.com). He argues for historical contextualization and specificity in understanding this experience. However, his highlighting of certain development indicators within this experience, contextualized within a comparative framework, parallels much of the Kerala model literature.

4. R. Krishnakumar, "A Kerala Experience," Frontline 18, issue 1, January 6–19 (http://www.hinduonnet.com).

5. As a way of illustrating this point, Sen and his colleague Jean Dreze compare

Kerala to India and China (1995). They argue that China's centralized planning regime produced better gains in certain development indicators than India's less controlled development programming. However, when it came to the prevention of famines, India was better able to act than China because of a vibrant and vigorous public that forced the state to take action. While Kerala was much smaller than either India or China, its population of 30 million, roughly the size of Canada, is not negligible. And, within this state, Sen and Dreze find the best of both worlds: high development indicators, like China, with a vigorous and active public capable and willing to demand rights. In other words, Kerala demonstrates what is possible in the third world as a result of a vigorous social democracy.

6. The territorial map of the region was reconfigured after independence by the States Reorganization Act of 1956 based on linguistic affinities. Kerala was created as a state, drawing together the Malayalam-speaking "native states" of Tiruvitamkoor (also called Travancore by the British) and Kochi (Cochin under the British), which were formerly ruled by indigenous rulers, and the northern region of Malabar, which was under direct British administration in the Madras Presidency.

7. Some sense of the debate about the Kerala model among those with contending views of its causes can be found in the exchange between Sen (1990) and Chasin and Franke (1991) in the *New York Review of Books*. Chasin and Franke argue that his foregrounding of the state policy of enlightened indigenous rulers and matriliny undervalues the role of the CPI (M), the dominant communist party in the region, and valorizes the experience of women of the dominant caste at the expense of women of other low-caste communities.

8. The matrilineal practices of the Nair caste were highlighted by the anthropologist Kathleen Gough and inserted into wider anthropological debates about the definition of marriage, family, and kinship (Gough 1959; Gough and Schneider 1961). From a historical perspective, Jeffrey (1976) discusses the challenges of colonial modernity and the social movement spearheaded by the Nair Service Society. From an anthropological perspective, Fuller (1976) explores changing understandings of matriliny in the contemporary period, in the process challenging some of Gough's understandings of Nair kinship. Saradamoni (1999) examines matriliny, its construction by anthropologists, and its changing character. Arunima (2003) carefully examines the ways the intersection of colonial legal understandings, changing ideas

of property and personhood, gender and generational relations, and larger transformations of colonial modernity conceptualized and transformed Nair matriliny (cf. Kodoth 2001).

9. Devika (2007a) and Awaya (1996) discuss the gendered dimensions of social reform within the caste. Mencher and Goldberg (1967) have discussed kinship within the caste from an anthropological perspective.

10. This is the network of institutions through which I conducted my research, and I discuss this movement in more detail in chapter 5. Aspects of the thought of Sree Narayana Guru are explored by Samuel 1977; Rao 1979; Jacob 1995; Kumar 1997; Chandramohan 1987; and Heimsath 1978. Anthropological studies of the Ezhava caste include Aiyappan 1965 and Osella and Osella 2000a. Isaac and Tharakan 1986 discusses the politicization of the Ezhava caste community and its relationship to the communist movement. Velayudan 1999 explores the gendered dimensions of Ezhava social reform.

11. Kusuman 1973; Kooimann 1991; Saradamoni 1980; Mohan 2005.

12. The literature on the communist movement in Kerala is wide-ranging. A few notable scholars include Menon (1994), who examines its complex origins in Malabar at the intersection of caste and nationalism, and Nossiter (1983), who examines its entry into electoral politics. Patrick Heller examines labor mobilization within the context of party politics (2000). Social histories of mobilization within this movement have been written by Isaac (1985, 1986) and by Lindberg (2001), who explores gendered dimensions of such mobilizations. Jeffrey (1993) discusses various aspects of the political and social consequences of the movement.

13. My approach draws on an anthropological literature that has reoriented away from a unilinear model of cultural change that assumes a transition from tradition to a western-defined modernity; it examines instead the specificities of multiple and interconnected forms of modernity. The anthropology of modernity and multiple modernities includes a few key edited volumes, including Comaroff and Comaroff 1993; Mitchell 2000; Knauft 2002; and Gaonkar 2001. Other works include Rofel 1999; Donham 1999; Piot 1999; Ferguson 1999; and Appadurai 1996. Some sense of the differences entailed when anthropology moves from a singular notion of modernization to that of multiple modernities is nicely captured by Arjun Appadurai, who identifies four shifts that enable a more complex appreciation of the active production of meanings of modernity in multiple locations (1996, 9). First, an anthropology of modernity is not teleological, in that it does not

presume the triumphalist claims of modernization. Second, the ethnographic locus of an anthropology of modernity is rooted in the "everyday," not in "large-scale projects of social engineering." Third, this anthropology is open ended about what "modernity" might entail in terms of "nationalism, violence, and social justice." It is "deeply ambivalent" about where "modernity" is heading. Finally, it is transnational in scope, disrupting the foundation and horizon of modernization theory, namely, the nation-state.

14. For an exploration of the ambiguous and complex meanings of *sambandham*, see Kodoth 2001.

15. Devika (2007a) notes that the image of the passive and victimized Antarjanam, which comes through in much of the social reform literature, needs to be complicated so as to take account of the complexities of agency available to women within the spaces of the *illam*.

16. Devika notes that there arose the idea that modern education leads to unproductive males and effeminacy but this was not dominant during the early years of social reform (2007a, 86).

17. A wide range of responses to Tharamangalam (1998) can be found in volumes 3 and 4 of *Bulletin of Concerned Asian Scholars*, 30.

18. For an exploration of migration within the South Asian region, see Osella and Gardner 2004; Osella and Osella 2000b discuss the impact of migration within the Kerala context.

19. Jason DeParle, "Jobs Abroad Support 'Model' State in India," *New York Times*, September 7, 2007 (http://www.nytimes.com).

20. Of the 3.75 million migrants (out of a population of 30 million) in 1998, about 1.36 million are international migrants, with the rest comprised of return migrants and migrants to other parts of India (Zachariah, Mathew, Rajan 2001).

21. Migration increased by 120 percent between 1988/1992 and 1993/1997 and a more recent 2004 study indicates similar rates of growth.

22. Vinson Kurian, "God's Own Country Is Truly a Seller's Paradise Too," BusinessLine, October 20, 2004 (http://www.thehindubusinessline.com). See also Vinson Kurian, "Consumerism Peddles Branded Goods as Symbols of the Good Life," February 18, 2004, BusinessLine (http://www.thehindubusinessline.com).

23. This struggle gained international attention as a citizens' group took legal and other action to shut down the plant, whose operations were believed to deplete the water levels in the neighboring areas and threaten the livelihood

of residents. This struggle, on behalf of poor farmers and landless laborers, was linked to a broader, more middle-class national struggle against the consumption of soft drinks such as Coca-Cola and Pepsi, which were accused of having unusually high levels of pesticides, leading the state government of Kerala and many schools and cafeterias to ban these drinks (Aiyer 2007; Vedwan 2007). Supported by leftist student and youth groups in Kerala such as the Democratic Youth Federation of India (DYFI) and the Student Federation of India (SFI), this struggle became a focal point for a politics of antiglobalization linked to other such struggles in India and abroad.

24. http://savekerala.blogspot.com.

25. For discussion of this print culture, see Jeffrey 2000, 2004. The most important forms of mass media in Kerala are films and television. I discuss transformations in cinema in relationship to television in chapter 2. Here it is important to note that while cinema has a longer history in the region, television is a 1990s phenomenon, one that has greatly expanded. Government-sponsored telecasting first began in 1985, with the first private Malayalam-language satellite station (Asianet) beginning in 1993, which now also has two other channels, one that provides news and the other youth-oriented programming. The Asianet channels are broadcast in sixty countries, including the entire Persian Gulf. In addition to Asianet, two other major Malayalam-language satellite channels round out the television market: Surya, which began broadcasting in 1998, and Kairali, soon after. For a discussion of the women-centered programming, particularly in the form of serials, and gender in television advertising in Kerala, see Usha 2004.

26. These widely cited statistics are drawn from the Kerala State Mental Health Authority which compiles its profile of suicide in the state from national and state crime statistics (http://www.ksmha.org).

27. For overviews and articles that discuss suicide in Kerala, see www.maithriko chi.org, an NGO dedicated to suicide prevention in the city of Kochi.

28. "Student's Suicide Sparks Violence in State," *Hindu*, July 24, 2004 (http://www.hinduonnet.com/thehindu).

29. It is interesting to note that the *New York Times* article on the impact of migration on the Kerala model (see note 19) ends with the portrayal of a migrant family in which a daughter of the family has committed suicide. Such narratives weave crisis and the disintegration of the family into assess-

ments of the impact of globalization. For a discussion of "Gulf wives" see Gulati 1993.

30. *Times of India*, August 22, 1994.

31. Malayalam cinema has been characterized by a set of distinctions between "art," "middle," and "commercial" cinema in order to construct the dominant view of its sophistication and superiority. For a critical discussion of these distinctions, see Radhakrishnan (n.d.[a]).

32. A more recent discussion of Malayalam cinema and Gulf migration lays out the intimate connections between the film industry and capital flows, as well as the impact of the Gulf audience on cinematic developments (Radhakrishnan n.d.[b]).

33. This shift is evident through the stars that are used to depict these different roles. Malayalam cinema is dominated by the complex rivalry and links between its two central stars, Mammooty and Mohan Lal. While Mammooty is the quintessential star of "serious" and melodramatic films tied to the middle-class family, Mohan Lal is the funnier, incompetent "everyman" (Osella and Osella, 2004; Rowena 2002). However, as Rowena argues, in comedy films that feature Mohan Lal, his "everyman" persona is a complex mediation of an upper-caste/class social location in which he wins out over lower-caste coded actors such as Sreenivasan and Mukesh. Comedy films also featured lower-caste-coded characters through actors such as Mukesh, Jagadeesh, Sreenivasan, and later Dileep—a trend that reflects a lower-caste/class assertion of masculinity. These assertions increasingly rely on the denigration of characters coded as religious minorities (Christian and Muslim) and the Dalit other, for example the roles played by Kalabhavan Mani (Rowena 2002).

34. Certain films in this genre explicitly highlight a Gulf returnee, for example, *Varanmaare Aavashyamundu* (Hariharan 1983) and *Mambazhakkalam* (Joshi 2004).

35. "Kerala Bans Camera Cellphones in Educational Institutions," June 26, 2005 (http://www.hindu.com).

2

FASHIONING GENDER AND CONSUMPTION

1. For a detailed discussion of the meanings of Onam, see chapter 5.

2. For a discussion of the meanings of reversals of hierarchy within ritual contexts in Kerala, see Osella and Osella 2000a, 241–42.

3. USA Today, May 18, 2000. The beauty pageant industry exploded in India in the 1990s. Almost every school, college, and kindergarten holds a contest. Delhi is estimated to have had twenty-one major pageants in 1999 (ibid.). Beauty pageants are held by cities, suburbs, and housing colonies. As Pradeep Guha, national director of the *Femina* (a major women's magazine) Miss India contest and executive director of the Time of India group, which owns the Miss India franchise, states, "It's a sociological phenomenon" (ibid.). At the more elite levels, a vast structure of beauty experts and technicians groom young Indian women for modeling careers and beauty pageants on the global stage (*Outlook*, May 29, 2000).

4. *Frontline*, December 13, 1996.

5. Ibid.

6. The other host was Richard Steinmetz, a white Australian. Together, Bali and Steinmetz represented the multiculturalism of corporate globalization, incorporating racial difference. Forms of cultural difference and sameness were also on display, representing India to a global audience as a dynamic mix of "tradition" and "modernity." There were dancers like Mallika Sarabhai and the film actresses Juhi Chawla and Shobana performing classical Indian dances such as *bharatnatyam*, *mohiniyattam*, and *manipuri*. The Indian pop star Alisha Chinai sang. A Kathakali dance troupe from Kerala decorated the stage, amid props that recreated the great ruins of Hampi. And Prabhu Deva, the pop music dance sensation of the new Tamil cinema, worked his magic.

7. Modeled on the latter, Channel V, which is headquartered in Hong Kong and Bombay, has a decidedly "Asian" flavor. Its programs focus on Filipino, Japanese, Indian, and sometimes Arab pop music. Many shows marketed for a specifically Indian audience are produced within India, and they include a complex of Hindi film song countdowns, the burgeoning Indian English/Hindi pop not tied to films, and pedagogical shows teaching the history of Euro-American rock and classic Hindi film songs for younger audiences, along with contemporary western pop music videos.

8. While their Indian diasporic identities and first-world accents make these women emblems of global India, Wilson (2004) and Ong (1999) discuss the role of mixed-race Eurasian figures in indexing and marketing a pan-Asian global identity in East and Southeast Asia.

9. For overviews and discussions of the pageant and protests, see Oza 2006 and Ahmed-Ghosh 2003.

10. The fact that "Americanization" is often indexed by cultural forms associated with specifically African American cultural production speaks to the centrality of and saturation of American popular culture by black cultural forms.

11. The journal *Inter-Asia Cultural Studies* has been engaged in a project to explore the "popular" across the many regions that compose "Asia," importantly focusing on youth culture, consumption, and globalization in relationship to highly variable experiences of modernity and nationalism in the region. These have included discussions of football fandom in South Korea (Cho 2004), pop cultural artifacts among Thai youth (Siriyuvasak and Shin 2007) and alternative youth media in Indonesia (Juliastuti 2006).

12. The interdisciplinary field of cultural studies and feminist analysis of consumer culture have both highlighted the role of consumption practices and fashion in producing youth and gender identities. Arguably, it is a focus on youth and consumption that inaugurated British cultural studies. See Hall and Jefferson 1976 and Hebdige 1979. Felski 1995 explores the place of the feminine within modernism through the imagining of the consumer as a feminine Other. Peiss 1986 provides an account of young working women's leisure and consumption practices in turn-of-the-century New York. For the role of consumption in contemporary girls' youth culture, see McRobbie 1991; Nava 1992; Bhavnani et al. 1998; Bettie 2003; Wilson 2004; and Cole 2004.

13. Of course, this shift does not mean that distinctions along class, caste, age, and gender do not pertain. They are now worked out differently in a new "regime of fashion." See Wilson 1985 for a discussion of fashion, modernity, and dress within the Euro-American context. See Tarlo 1996 for an excellent discussion of clothing and dress in the South Asian context.

14. For discussions of this, see Cohn 1996; Hardgrave 1968; Kumar 1997; and Devika 2007a.

15. Osella and Osella briefly mention this term but do not fully examine its gender implications (1999, 997). Though not popular all over Kerala as a form of youth slang, it was prevalent in southern Kerala where this study is located.

16. The expanding literature on masculinity has been helpful in shifting the study of gender beyond that of women and femininity to processes of gender that structure gender relations. Within the South Asian context, the work of Jeganathan (1997, 2000) and Dhareshwar and Niranjana (1996)

focus on non-elite forms and practices of masculinity. For an interdisciplinary focus on masculinities in South Asia, see Chopra, Osella, and Osella (2004) and Srivastava (2004). For a discussion of different styles of masculinity in the context of migration and the cash economy in Kerala, see Osella and Osella 2000b. Radhakrishnan (2005) and Rowena (2002) provide critical discussions of masculinization in Kerala during the 1990s.

17. Toddy (*kallu*) is an alcoholic beverage created from the sap of palm trees such as palmyra and coconut. Toddy tapping is the process by which this sap is extracted and was among the most important traditional occupations of the Ezhava caste in Kerala.

18. These are elite schools of national repute.

19. The film *Roja* has been widely and critically interrogated and debated (see Niranjana, 1991, 1994; Chakravarty and Pandian 1994; Barucha 1994; Dirks 2001).

20. Three hits of this genre that Devan was particularly a fan of include *Kakkakum Poochakkum Kalyanam* (dir. Haridas, 1995), *3 Men Army* (dir. Nizar, 1995), and *Mannar Mathai Speaking* (dir. Kappan, 1995).

21. While in more general usage, the term *churidar* refers to the baggy trousers that bunch up tightly at the calf over which a long *kurta* top is worn, within this context the term was used to refer to a wide variety of styles involving long tops worn over either loose or tight-fitting bottoms.

22. "Sareeyude Charitram," *Vanitha*, March 11, 1995.

23. This was especially true for middle-class Nair and Syrian Christian women. The one-piece sari replaced the *mundum-neryathum* and the *mundum-chatta*, respectively.

24. See De Alwis 1995, 1999; Visweswaran n.d.; Wickremasinghe 2003; and Azim 2002.

25. Shilpa Nair, "Where's the Pavada?" *The Hindu*, November 13, 2003 (http://www.hinduonnet.com/thehindu). See also N. V. Vijayakumar, "A Swan Song for the 'Pavada'?" August 31, 2006 (http://www.hinduonnet.com/thehindu).

26. For complex discussions of the term *nadu* in Tamil, see Daniel (1984) and Mines (2005). They too stress its locational character.

27. *Para* refers to a crowbar, used between pieces of wood to move them apart (2002, 129). While Rowena attributes the everyday naming of these practices as *para* to the comedy films, it is unclear how the circuit of mediation works in this instance.

28. For a fuller discussion of this kind of behavior, see chapter 3. These prac-

tices have become increasingly contested by feminist activism through the framework of sexual harassment, for example through the P. E. Usha case during the 1990s. For a discussion of these contestations and reactions to them within the Kerala context, see Radhakrishnan 2005. For a discussion of how the law has understood these practices, see Baxi 2001.

29. An example of the common ways in which contemporary Malayalam mixes Malayalam words with English constructions, a form of "Malglish."

30. Osella and Osella (2000b) discuss this style of masculinity.

31. Rowena (2002) discusses the ways in which lower-caste consumerist masculinity within youth-oriented films turns on its more marginalized masculine others (Muslim, Christian, and Dalit masculinities).

32. Of course, these contradictions do not mean that styles coded as "traditional" do not get reworked by fashion and modern consumer spaces. The rise of "ethno-chic" traditional styles is a case in point (Tarlo 1996).

33. These are not "youth" films, marked by explicit attention to consumption and fashion, in the way Kaadhalan is and in that sense they do not operate through highly elaborated valorizations of consumer agency and "fun." However, discussions of the films have pointed to the ways they mediate the moment of liberalization and middle-class formation through the figure of the upper-caste, upper-class hero and the conjugal family (Niranjana 1991). In Bombay, we do see a non-upper-caste, non-upper-class feminine character, Shaila Banu, but her identity as a Muslim mediates her low-class status.

3
ROMANCING THE PUBLIC

1. The Hindu, February 13, 2006.

2. Washington Times, February 14, 2005.

3. The fact that minors were possibly involved led to allegations of sexual exploitation that are still pending.

4. Within this larger context of these rather more spectacular cases of rape and sexual exploitation, two legal cases brought sexual harassment into the public sphere in Kerala in a new way. The first of the sexual harassment cases, involving a nonteaching employee of Kerala University, P. E. Usha, centered on her complaint that she was sexually harassed by a male co-worker, after having talked about another incident of sexual harassment and violence that she had endured on a bus after leaving work. The other case involved Nalini Netto, an Indian administrative service employee, who

accused a minister of sexual harassment. These became issues as these women struggled to have a 1997 Supreme Court ruling on sexual harassment applied to their cases.

5. This article in the *Indian Express* newspaper by Sooryamurthy (1997) is cited by Sreekumar (2007, 54).

6. For an excellent overview of this literature, see Orsini 2007. Historical works on romance in the context of colonial modernity include Raychaudhuri 2000 and Kaviraj 2007 for Bengal. Ethnographic works on love within the South Asian context include Trawick 1990; Ahearn 2001; Mody 2002; Gold 2007; Seizer 2004; and Liechty 2002. Further afield, Abu-Lughod 1986 provides a sensitive analysis of love and honor within Bedouin society. A useful collection that reframes the question of emotions with anthropology is Lutz and Abu-Lughod 1990.

7. This view of romantic love has been borne out in several studies focused on young women. Arguing against male bias and the privileging of public performances of self within youth cultural studies, Angela McRobbie laid out the ostensibly private world of teen romance and magazine reading as constitutive of young women's cultural worlds, marked by passivity, coyness, and submissiveness (1991). In the United States, ethnographic and sociological studies examined the impact of a peer-based romantic culture on college-going young women (Eisenhart and Holland 1992). Tracking educational achievement, this study argued that while women enter college in high numbers as high achievers, they leave college with their career aspirations and routes greatly diminished. The study focused on the negative impact of a culture of romance and the sexual marketplace on young women's educational and career trajectories. In the 1980s feminist scholars developed a more nuanced way of understanding romance, one that paid attention to the pleasures and complexities of the romantic narrative (Modleski 1990; Radway 1984; Pearce and Stacie 1995). In particular, Janice Radway moved beyond a textual approach to examine the practices of reading that constitute women's engagement with romance novels, emphasizing the pleasures of romance within the context of patriarchal family demands. She also argued that the desire for and valorization of another love object is often the seeking of nurturance, a desire that could lead to resistance. While some have contested her account, seeing an adaptation to patriarchal culture where she sees resistance, Radway's work opened up romance as a complex site for understanding the negotiations and constructions of gen-

der identity within patriarchy and the structuring of social and emotional desire and life expectations.

8. Here I draw on Robin Jeffrey's discussion of Gowriamma's political career (1992).

9. This brief discussion of Ajitha's biography is taken from an interview with her in the *Times of India*, March 15, 2005.

10. Niranjana (1991) has argued that this and other Mani Ratnam movies of the 1990s situate a new kind of secularism, rooted in the privatized space of romantic love in an attempt to consolidate a secular, humanist, modern conjugality rooted in upper-caste, upper-class privilege.

4

POLITICS AND CITIZENSHIP

1. Studies of politics and youth have undergone a major shift. The postwar period was preoccupied with generations and their implications for social change, while the events of the 1960s, particularly the student uprisings of 1968 around the world, generated much research on student politics and its implications for social conflict and transformation within disciplines like political science and sociology. While this is a vast literature, some key examples for India include Rudolph and Rudolph 1972 and Altbach 1968. Grew 2005 discusses shifts in the ways the scholarship on youth and children have dealt with the question of politics. Later youth cultural studies expanded its focus against a narrow definition of politics to insist on the importance of cultural politics in the realms of consumption and mass-mediation. While more contemporary research on youth, in nonwestern contexts, continues this focus on youth and on mass-mediation and its cultural and political connotations, particularly in Africa, youth research has highlighted the importance of paying attention to youth and official party politics, given the close link between the two in many postcolonial locations (see Diouf 1996; Durham 2004). For north India, see Jeffrey, Jeffery, and Jeffery 2008.

2. Foucault 1977; Hall 2002; Levinson 2001; Levinson et al. 1996; Luykx 1999; Mitchell 1991; Stambach 2000; Kaplan 2006. Within the South Asian context, many historical works have examined the relationship between education and colonialism. See Kopf 1969; Lelyveld 1978; Metcalf 1982; Wood 1985; Crook 1996; Kumar 1991; and Minault 1998. For a revisiting of colonialism and education in India through the lens of postcolonial studies, see

Viswanathan 1989 and Seth 2007. Contemporary ethnographic studies of education include Thapan 1991, Srivastava 1998, Benei 2005, and Chopra and Jeffrey 2005.

3. By denoting the market as "private," I do not mean to suggest that the market does not function within the public realm or that the state does not function within the "private" realm. My intent is to track the discursive construction of the market as "private" that confronts the "public" of the state within privatization discourses.

4. I borrow "antipolitics" from Ferguson (1994) in his study of development discourse and practice in Lesotho. However, the sense in which I use it here is somewhat different. Ferguson argues that development produces antipolitics, by which he means a process of depoliticization in which development discourse and practice masks its own very instrumental operations—namely, the bureaucratization and expansion of state power—by turning poverty into a technical problem in Lesotho. The "politics" that Ferguson marks as being "depoliticized" is an analytically stable entity, rendered most specifically as the workings of political parties. In this way, what constitutes "politics" is naturalized. My analysis uses the language of "politics" and "antipolitics" in order to examine a self-consciously produced political field within Kerala so as to understand its limits and possibilities. Here, rather than assume what "politics" is, I examine discourses about its shifting meanings and registers. This approach to the study of politics draws on the insights of Judith Butler, who argues that the very act of delimiting the boundaries of a political field is a political act and that tracking contestations over what is political and what is not is a revealing moment for examining questions of citizenship and belonging (1992). Appadurai (2002) and Comaroff and Comaroff (2000a) focus attention on the ways in which explicit political discourses of democracy and civil society operate within everyday contexts and in popular discourses.

5. This resonates with what Kaviraj (1997) calls the "plebianization of the public" in Calcutta. He tracks the changing valences of public space in the city, marking the ways in which parks, for example, shift from being understood as middle-class spaces to plebian ones.

6. *Satyagraha*, meaning nonviolent struggle, was a key weapon in the evolving language and practice of Gandhian forms of protest. *Jathas*, *bandhs*, *hartals*, and *satyagrahas* became the language of nationalist politics, with the Vaikom Satyagraha being an important early example.

7. The uniqueness of unapproachability within the caste structure of the region has often been noted (Dumont 1980).

8. This form of protest, with its regimented marching, slogans (usually "Inquilab Zindabad") and the raised, clenched fist, entered the representational repertoire in the narrative of Kerala's modernity and in cultural productions such as plays, songs, and posters, all of which were crucial to the history of politics and social transformation. Especially in plays, the break with the feudal, caste-ridden past and the entry into revolutionary consciousness was usually represented by a low-caste Pulayan or Peruma caste member standing before an upper-caste Nair or Nambutiri Brahmin landlord, ten, twenty, or thirty paces away, one hand over his mouth, the other across his chest, in a pose of servility and supplication. That same man then proceeds to march right up to a landlord's house, shouting slogans, fist clenched in the air (Zarrilli 1995; cf. Jeffrey 1993).

9. Within Kerala, there are also political organizations, such as the Democratic Youth Federation of India (DYFI), that primarily cater to young men in their twenties and early thirties outside the educational system. However, given the educational history of Kerala, the relationship between politicized youth and the educational system is clear and strong.

10. For discussion of the semiotics of *khadi*, see Cohn 1996; Tarlo 1996; and Chakrabarty 2002.

11. This is not to say that civic conceptions of the public were not important and did not exist during the colonial period and after in Kerala. As I discuss extensively in chapter 2, the progressivism of social reform and the left went hand in hand with the rise of a middle-class, reformist outlook that generated many institutions, including colleges and schools, that interacted with and mediated nonelite political demands. Chatterjee (2004) discusses, though does not theorize, the mediations between civil and political society. Given that I am exploring left politics in an institution such as a college, it should be clear that the mediation and tensions between political and civil society are crucial to my analysis.

12. I do not want to imply here that all mobilizations of consumer discourse erase "politics" as such. The mobilization of consumption against official forms of politics is a form of politics. Further, consumer identities have been mobilized in order to insert a language of politics into conceptions of citizenship. For the United States, Cohen (2003) discusses forms of politics generated by the mobilization of consumer identities. More recently, the

antisweatshop movement mobilizes consumer identities in antiglobalization politics. In India, movements against the raising of prices of essential goods have also mobilized consumer identities. Most importantly, the Swadeshi Movement—the economic boycott of foreign goods in favor of domestically produced goods—politicized the consumption of commodities in the name of anticolonial nationalist politics in India. For a discussion of the changed ideological meanings given to consumption in the Swadeshi Movement and contemporary period, see Deshpande 1993. A good example of the mobilization of consumer identities for the purposes of environmental activism in India, see Vedwan 2007.

During the 1990s in Kerala, consumer forums and magazines emerged ostensibly to help consumers navigate the increasing influx of goods into the marketplace. Interestingly, they quickly became spaces to complain about, and seek solutions to, what was perceived to be the difficulties of dealing with state services such as getting telephone service and paying an electricity bill. Increasingly, these organizations began to take on the state, for example in the antibandh movement described above, through joining with civic organizations.

13. The gender-neutral, universalist language of citizenship, politics, democracy, and rights belies its masculinist character whenever the universal is equated with the masculine. For a discussion of the ambiguous deployment of rights discourse within the Kerala context, see Arunima 1995 and 2003.

14. For a discussion of the Emergency and its legacies, see Tarlo 2003.

15. For an assessment of the "crisis in higher education" and the role of politics in institutions of higher education in India, see Beteille 1995.

16. While the state has allowed the number of formal educational institutions to expand dramatically in the last forty years, it has clearly not been enough. Private registrants make up as much as 40 percent of the total student enrollment in regular colleges.

17. While in previous chapters I discussed the NRI as an important construction of consumer lifestyle that is marketed for the purposes of producing a global India, the category and the population it covers is also being more directly addressed by the state. It started out as a banking category to facilitate remittances from abroad. More recent examples include the Indian state's attempt to create graduated categories of citizenship for what it calls "persons of Indian origins," including a qualified form of dual citizenship. Starting in 2003, the government of India inaugurated an annual

event, the Pravasi Bharatiya Divas, to highlight within India the role of the overseas Indian community. The state government of Kerala has also become more active with respect to its migrants, in December 1996 creating the Department of Non-Resident Keralite Affairs (NORKA). This government agency has worked to rehabilitate migrants during times of war in the Gulf; implements rehabilitation, employment, and investment programs for returning migrants; provides insurance and pension schemes; and works against illegal labor recruiting practices.

5
EDUCATION, CASTE, AND THE SECULAR

1. Given its affiliation to the state university system and the control the state has over admissions, the college must follow the reservations policies set by the state. However, the college retains a "management quota" that allows it to cater to its own constituency, and it is understood to be among the more prominent colleges that cater to the Ezhava caste community. While this community is formerly an untouchable caste, it is not classified as Scheduled Caste, understood as the most disadvantaged caste groups, nor is it understood as Dalit, a term usually associated with untouchable castes. Within the terms of Dalit critical analysis, it is what D. R. Nagaraj called a "non-Dalit, ex-untouchable" caste that practiced its own forms of caste discrimination against lower-caste groups such as Pulayas and Pariahs, who are considered SC. Osella and Osella discuss the "structural middle" that the caste occupies (2000a).

2. This is generally true for the southern states of India as opposed to the north, where reservations were not as vigorously implemented and caste reform movements were not nearly as strong.

3. Here, the task is not to simply bring forward the public space of secular citizenship at the expense of private emotions, beliefs, and practices, where some might argue caste somehow "really" lies. One anthropological response to critics who point out that modern discourses and institutional practices have transformed caste has been to argue that, while public discourses of equality emerge with modernity, caste as a hierarchical interpretive framework continues to be relevant, albeit in a less totalizing and holistic way, within realms like marriage, religious practice, and so on (Osella and Osella 2000a). Further, longer-term strategies of mobility and social reproduction demonstrate that caste "persists." While one could not

argue with such conclusions, the analysis here is less interested in demonstrating the somewhat mutated persistence of caste within modern India. Rather, I am interested in exploring how ideas of public and private and tradition and modernity structure understandings and negotiations of caste within the everyday life of the college.

4. For some sense of this larger Indian debate, see Bhargava 1998b. Further afield, for discussions of secularism and secularization within the context of colonial modernities, see Scott 1999. For a broader discussion of the origins of secularism and its transformations, as well as ways of problematizing it as an anthropological object, see Asad 2003.

5. Louis Dumont's canonical theory of the Hindu caste system provided a holistic and totalizing vision of a singular caste system in which the religious values of purity and pollution "encompass" economic and political power (Appadurai 1986a; Dumont 1980). Based on the idea of a singular hierarchical principle rooted in differential "substances" and "essences," this theory rendered India as decidedly nonmodern and overwhelmingly "religious." After Dumont, several other approaches have sought to broaden this vision within anthropology. One set of arguments has focused most specifically on the meanings of caste (Berreman 1979; Raheja 1988). While Dumont emphasized purity and pollution as the central organizing principle of a singular caste system, Raheja, for example, was able to demonstrate the importance of other principles such as auspiciousness and inauspiciousness (1988).

6. For example, Béteille makes the argument that the family is replacing caste as the structuring locus and logic of social life in urban India. The struggle for education, jobs, occupational mobility, and the perpetuation of inequality is primarily the function of family strategy, not caste values. Caste matters only inasmuch as it is manipulated by politicians for electoral votes. As he states, "Nothing is easier than to get Government and Opposition together in Parliament to denounce the caste system and ask for its abolition. Who will denounce the Indian family and ask that that be abolished?" (1991, 26).

7. Reflecting, as I do here, on the post-Dumontian understanding of caste within anthropology, this question was posed by Appadurai (1993).

8. India has one of the most widespread positive action programs, one of the few written into its constitution. However, it has been poorly implemented. The commission presented its report reaffirming the practice of reservations (quotas) for government jobs and university admissions in 1980. The

1989–90 protests were in response to the V. P. Singh government's decision to implement the commission's recommendations, which would have reserved almost 50 percent of jobs and admissions for a highly differentiated set of categories of people based upon social, educational, and economic "backwardness." These include what are called scheduled castes (scs), scheduled tribes (sts), and the other backward classes (obcs). While obc generally refers to lower classes, what "lower class" means and how it overlaps with "lower castes" is an ambiguity that added much to the debate and agitation surrounding Singh's announcement. Of course, the history and scope of the reservation system must be contextualized within the larger history of the politics of caste in the emergence of Indian nationalism, the tensions between B. R. Ambhedkar, the low-caste Dalit leader, and Gandhi on the question of separate electorates for untouchables (which Gandhi opposed), and the ways in which the Indian constitution has defined the right to equality. For an overview, see Galantar 1984. See also Deshpande 2006 for a discussion of how questions of merit and reservations operate in the historical unfolding of access to higher education.

9. The immediate reason for their resignations stemmed from comments made by Home Minister Arjun Singh (who initiated the reservation policy) intimating that they did not have enough knowledge of the Indian constitution (cf. Subhajit Roy, "Preposterous Remarks, He's Obfuscating the Issue, Say Panel Members," May 16, 2006, http://www.indianexpress.com). The texts of their letters of resignation can be found at http://www.indiatogether.org.

10. Béteille and Gupta have made these arguments in a number of different arenas since the time of the first Mandal protests. For a more recent and concise discussion of their views see Beteille 2005 and Gupta 2005. Here, they are discussing the possibility of extending reservations to the private sector, a proposal that happened a year before the agitations of 2006. The sociologist Satish Deshpande and his colleague Yogendra Yadav have intervened publicly in the most recent debates about Mandal, pointing out the failures of Indian sociology to examine issues of caste in modern India from a systematic and empirical point of view. Deshpande notes that sociologists who oppose reservations focus on the potential consequences of quotas without examining underlying questions about caste, discrimination, and segregation within education and occupations (2006). Using empirical research, they propose an alternative that seeks to implement a reservation

policy that takes account of stratification within caste communities and gender differences (Deshpande and Yadav 2006).

11. The term can be used in a variety of ways to refer to the mobilization of community identities understood to be "traditional" and divisive, referring as it does to either caste or a religious community. For example, when the CPI (M), the largest and most important communist party in Kerala, within the complicated calculations that mark coalition politics, aligns itself with the Muslim League or seeks support from caste associations, it is often accused of being "communal." However, the term is most commonly used to refer to the Hindu-Muslim conflict. For a discussion of the term and its transformations, see Pandey 1990. Reflecting on the dominance of the Hindu-Muslim axis for understanding the problem of secularism, Dhareshwar writes, "The term 'secular' has of late got locked into a battle with the term 'communal.' Consequently, its use in that ideological register seems to be submerging its other significations. As a 'keyword' in our political culture as much as in our cultural politics, 'secular,' however, has a more varied and heterogenous career in India" (1993, 115).

12. Several differing views are represented in Bhargava 1998a. Ashis Nandy (1998), T. N. Madan (1998), and Partha Chatterjee (1998), for different reasons, argue that secularism is an exhausted and inadequate concept for the Indian context, while Rajeev Bhargava and Akeel Bilgrami argue for its continued viability and regeneration. Both Madan and Nandy argue that secularism is a culturally inappropriate western import that, in its demand that religion be removed from public life, violates the indigenous cultures of religiosity within India. While Madan emphasizes the Christian origins of secularism, Nandy focuses on the violence of the state that turns "religion as faith," which he understands to be an indigenous tradition that is "non-monolithic" and "plural," into religion as ideology, ossified identities that jostle for political and socioeconomic power. Chatterjee, while in line with Madan and Nandy that secularism is exhausted, comes to his conclusions quite differently. He begins with a much more direct question about how best to combat the Hindu right and argues that the Hindu right is actually quite willing and happy to work through the apparatuses of the modern state, including its secular underpinnings. In fact, one version of Hindu nationalism argues that the state is not secular enough, particularly in the way it treats religious minorities. He goes on to demonstrate that the Indian state has hardly ever been secular, particularly with regard to standards of

religious neutrality and nonpreferentialism. In particular, the state has been very active in the reformation of personal law within religious communities. He goes on to argue that the language of secularism is incapable of protecting the rights of religious minorities and that it is religious tolerance that is needed. Finally, he emphasizes internal democratic reforms within different religious communities as the true source of tolerance and argues that they be given proper institutional recognition by the state.

Finally, Bhargava (1998b) and Bilgrami (1998) argue for the continued viability of secularism, using different arguments. Bilgrami critiques Nandy for his uncritical antinationalism and antimodernism and for his nostalgia for tradition. Rather than fold a critique of secularism into an overarching antimodernism, Bilgrami provides a much more delimited and specific critique of Nehruvian secularism for its hyperproceduralism, one that resisted a genuinely communitarian negotiation and imposed a rigid version of secularism from above. He outlines a secularism from below that might have led to a more substantive secularism with more legitimacy. Finally, Bhargava argues that most critics who reject secularism misrecognize its distinctiveness within India. Rather than see its deviations from a western norm as inadequacy and inappropriateness, Bhargava argues that secularism has had a malleable and highly adaptable career within India and that it should be regenerated and renewed.

13. For a discussion of the complex ways in which Gandhi was received and apprehended by a local peasant group through the idiom of popular Hindu ideas and practices, see Amin (1988). John (2000) discusses the consolidation of a secular Hindu identity through the negotiations about reservations at the intersection of gender, caste, and community. Finally, for Kerala, Menon (1994) discusses the ways in which official nationalism of the Congress Party worked through an upper-caste construction of a unified Hindu identity, as I discuss below.

14. Dilip Menon's discussions of lower-caste Malayalam novels of the nineteenth century demonstrate the tensions between tradition and modernity. Focusing on Tiyya (same caste position as Ezhava) writers of the Malabar region of northern Kerala, he argues that rather than the nation, it was notions of community, caste, and self within the space of colonial modernity that were central to the narrative unfolding of Kerala's modernity for the lower castes (1997; 2004). Accounts of the rise of cultural nationalism in Bengal emphasize the creative deployment of "tradition" in the rise of

modern Indian nationalism, which created divides such as inner/outer and tradition/modernity that could be strategically combined for the specific requirements of an anticolonial nationalism. Pointing out that these accounts focus on upper-caste elites, Menon rightly argues that tradition is not so malleable for the lower castes. As he puts it, "To put the question sharply, what solace can untouchables find within Hindu tradition, if they are buffeted by the winds of colonial change? Can a lower caste speak in the name of Hindu tradition let alone deploy it to his/her own advantage? Conversely, do the blandishments of colonial modernity appeal more to the lower caste than the condescending concessions of tradition?" (1997, 292).

15. Here I do not mean to suggest that the universalizing humanism of Sree Narayana's thought is inherently part of a western secular tradition. Clearly, the traditions out of which this humanism emerges are part of the complicated ways in which he combined the Advaita and Saiva traditions. The point here is to emphasize the ways in which his brand of universal humanism articulated with the organizations and projects of a caste association operating within the spaces of secular modernity during the colonial and postcolonial periods in Kerala.

16. Rowena 2002, in the context of Malayalam cinema, discusses the ways films code lower-caste status by being vague about the family background of lower-caste characters.

17. Here I draw on explorations of the complexity of passing in discussions of racial identities within the United States. For example, see Ginsberg 1996. This literature has pointed to the complexities of desire, transgression, critique, and complicity in passing the black/white divide. While there are significant differences between caste and race, here I am simply pointing to the ways in which passing as a phenomenon is rendered more complex than a simple desire to emulate the dominant community.

18. Jayaprasad 1981 discusses the rise of the Rashtriya Sevak Sangh (RSS) in Kerala. For an excellent exploration of the tensions between RSS workers and CPI (M) workers in northern Kerala, see Chaturvedi 2007.

EPILOGUE

1. "Bollywood" refers to the popular Indian film industry, with its center in Bombay (now called Mumbai); it is dominated by Hindi-language films. *Rang De Basanti*, directed by Rakeysh Omprakash Mehra, starred Aamir

Khan among a host of other well-known and lesser-known actors. The critically acclaimed film won many awards in several categories, including "best popular film providing wholesome entertainment" from the state-run National Film Awards in 2006 and a host of other best movie and other awards from private film award competitions in 2006 and 2007, including the Film Fare Awards, Global Indian Film Awards, Zee Cine Awards, Star Screen Awards, and the International Indian Film Academy (IIFA) awards.

2. Considered an iconic Indian freedom fighter who espoused socialism and a violent and revolutionary stance against British rule, Singh was hanged by the colonial authorities for shooting a police official, in response to the killing of another nationalist hero, Lala Lajpat Rai.

3. The international hit film *Dil Chahta Hai* (dir. Akhtar, 2001) is another. Widely understood to break new ground in representing cosmopolitan youth, it centers on life after graduation for three male friends as they pursue romance in Mumbai and abroad. This film, also featuring Bollywood star Aamir Khan, similarly won a National Film Award for Best Feature Film in Hindi and other Film Fare Awards in 2002. While adhering to some conventions of standard Indian cinema, such as song-and-dance numbers, the film's use of music without dancing, its representations of lavish homes and fashionable clothes, and the hip look of the main characters gave it a novel feel. Depictions of a lifestyle marked by art exhibitions, western opera, and effortless travel between India and Australia presented an image of Indian youth as unapologetically and newly globalized. Understood as a film that was not just made for the Indian market, it was oriented toward a global audience, particularly the Indian diaspora. While both *RDB* and *Dil Chahta Hai* seek to depict what I am calling liberalization's children, they do so in somewhat different registers that reveal convergences and tensions of a perceived shift in generational sensibilities under the impact of globalization. Like *Dil Chahta Hai*, *RDB* focuses on a group of young men, either recently graduated or currently inhabiting a college environment. Both films are located in middle-class, metropolitan, "national" locations, namely, Mumbai and Delhi. However, *Dil Chahta Hai* highlights wealth and high-flying transnational travel in a way that unapologetically asserts a youthful, globalized Indian middle-class identity that is disengaged from Indian society, an orientation that *RDB* raises some questions about. While *Dil Chahta Hai* emphasizes the mediation between the national and the

global and *RDB* emphasizes the mediation between the national and the local, both focused on configuring an Indian youth identity in the wake of liberalization.

4. Shoma Chaudary, "Bhagat Singh Topless, Waving in Jeans," *Tehelka*, February 4, 2006 (http://www.tehelka.com).

5. Khan has been criticized for his association with the Coca-Cola Company, given its controversial presence in India. For an announcement of this venture, see http://www.prdomain.com. See Vedwan 2007 for an analysis of the most recent controversies surrounding Coca-Cola in India.

6. Shoma Chaudhury, "Sleeping Idealists?" *Tehelka*, March 18, 2006 (http://www.tehelka.com). It is interesting to note here that the protests began with an SMS text message from the online newsmagazine *Tehelka* asking those who were outraged by the initial "not guilty" verdict to come to India Gate, in the heart of the capital, to protest. This online newsmagazine has been at the center of several investigations seeking to expose corrupt politicians, among them the former defense minister, George Fernandes.

7. "*Rang De Basanti* Colours Anti-Reservation Protests," *Times of India*, April 8, 2006 (http://timesofindia.indiatimes.com).

8. Shoma Chaudhury, "Is This Only Protest Theatre?" *Tehelka*, January 13, 2007 (http://www.tehelka.com). Chaudhury was the first *Tehelka* reporter to herald the invocation and impact of *Rang De Basanti* for politicizing middle-class youth. Here she wonders about its limits.

9. "Mobile Phone Use on Campus May Be Curbed," *The Hindu*, January 7, 2005 (http://www.hinduonnet.com).

BIBLIOGRAPHY

Abu-Lughod, Lila. 1990. "Can There Be a Feminist Ethnography?" *Women and Performance* 5 (1): 7–27.

Ahmed-Ghosh, Huma. 2003. "Writing the Nation on the Beauty Queen's Body." *Meridians: Feminism, Race, Transnationalism* 4 (1): 205–27.

Aiyappan, A. 1945. *Iravas and Culture Change.* Madras: Bulletin of the Madras Government Museum.

——. 1965. *Social Revolution in a Kerala Village: A Study in Culture Change.* London: Asia Publishing House.

Aiyer, Ananthakrishnan. 2007. "The Allure of the Transnational: Notes on Some Aspects of the Political Economy of Water in India." *Cultural Anthropology* 22: 640–58.

Akhtar, Farhan, dir. 2001. *Dil Chahta Hai.* Produced by Sidwhani, Ritesh and Pravin Talreja. Mumbai: Excel Entertainment. DVD.

Altbach, P. 1966. "The Transformation of the Indian Student Movement." *Asian Survey* 6 (8): 448–60.

——. 1968. *Turmoil and Transition: Higher Education and Student Politics in India.* New York: Basic Books.

Althusser, L. 1971. "Ideology and Ideological State Apparatuses." *Lenin and Philosophy and Other Essays.* New York: Monthly Review Press.

Amin, Samir. 1991. "Four Comments on Kerala." *Monthly Review* 42 (8): 28.

Amin, Shahid. 1988. "Gandhi as Mahatma: Gorakhpur District, Eastern UP, 1921–2." *Selected Subaltern Studies,* ed. Ranajit Guha and Gayatri Chakravorty Spivak, 288–348. London: Oxford University Press.

Amit-Talai, Vered, and Helena Wulff, eds. 1995. *Youth Cultures: A Cross-Cultural Perspective.* London: Routledge.

Amjad, R. 1989. *To the Gulf and Back.* Delhi: ILO-ARTEP.

Anzaldúa, Gloria. 1987. *Borderlands/La Frontera: The New Mestiza.* San Francisco: Aunt Lute Books.

Appadurai, A. 1986a. "Is Homo Hierarchicus?" *American Ethnologist* 13: 745–61.

———. 1986b. "Theory in Anthropology: Center and Periphery." *Comparative Studies in Society and History* 28 (2): 356–61.

———. 1988. Introduction. *Social Life of Things,* edited by Arjun Appadurai, 3–63. Philadelphia: University of Pennsylvania Press.

———. 1990. "Disjuncture and Difference in the Global Cultural Economy." *Theory, Culture, and Society* 7: 295–310.

———. 1993. "Caste Representation and the Representation of Caste." Unpublished manuscript.

———. 1996. *Modernity at Large: The Cultural Dimensions of Globalization.* Minneapolis: University of Minnesota Press.

———. 2002. "Deep Democracy: Urban Governmentality and the Horizon of Politics." *Public Culture* 14 (1): 21–47.

———. 2006. *Fear of Small Numbers.* Durham, N.C.: Duke University Press.

Appadurai, Arjun, and Carol Breckenridge. 1988. "Why Public Culture?" *Public Culture* 1 (1): 5–11.

Arunima, G. 1995. "Matriliny and Its Discontents." *India International—Kerala: Progress and Paradox.* Summer-monsoon issue: 157–67.

———. 1997. "Writing Culture: Of Modernity and the Malayalam Novel." *Studies in History* 13 (2): 271–90.

———. 1998. "A Vindication of the Rights of Woman? Families and Legal Change in 19th Century Malabar." *Changing Concepts of Rights and Justice in South Asia,* edited by Michael Anderson and Sumit Guha, 114–39. Delhi: Oxford University Press.

———. 2003. *There Comes Papa: Colonialism and the Transformations of Matriliny in Kerala, Malabar c. 1850–1940.* New Delhi: Orient Longman.

——. n.d. "Fantasies, Phantoms and Funny Jokes: The 'City' and Colonial Modernity." Unpublished manuscript.

Asad, Talal. 2003. *Formations of the Secular: Christianity, Islam, Modernity*. Palo Alto, Calif.: Stanford University Press.

Awaya, Toshie. 1996. "Women in the Nambutiri 'Caste' Movement." *History and Society in South India*, edited by T. Mizushima and H. Yanagisawa, 47–57. Tokyo: Tokyo University of Foreign Studies.

Azim, Firdous. 2002. "Women and Freedom." *Inter-Asia Cultural Studies* 3 (3): 395–405.

Bailey, Beth. 1989. *From the Front Porch to the Back Seat: Courtship in Twentieth Century America*. Baltimore: Johns Hopkins University Press.

Banerjee, Himani. 1991. "Fashioning a Self: Educational Proposals for and by Women in Popular Magazines in Colonial Bengal." *Economic and Political Weekly*, October 26, ws50–ws62.

——. 1995. "Attired in Virtue: The Discourse of Shame (*lajja*) and Clothing of the *Bhadramahila* in Colonial Bengal." *From the Seams of History: Essays on Indian Women*, edited by Bharati Ray, 67–106. New Delhi: Oxford University Press.

Barucha, R. 1994. "On the Border of Fascism: Manufacture of Consent in *Roja*." *Economic and Political Weekly*, June 4, 1389–95.

Basu, Amrita, Inderpal Grewal, Caren Kaplan, and Liisa Malkki, eds. 2001. "Globalization and Gender." Special issue. *Signs* 26 (4).

Baxi, Pratiksha. 2001. "Sexual Harassment." *Seminar* 505, September, 54–59.

Bayly, Susan. 1989. *Saints, Goddesses, and Kings: Muslims and Christians in South Indian Society, 1700–1900*. Cambridge: Cambridge University Press.

Beauvoir, Simone de. 1973 [1949]. *The Second Sex*. New York: Vintage.

Benei, Veronique, ed. 2005. *Manufacturing Citizenship: Education and Nationalism in Europe, South Asia and China*. London: Routledge.

Benhabib, Seyla. 1992. "Models of Public Space: Hannah Arendt, the Liberal Tradition, and Jurgen Habermas." *Habermas and the Public Sphere*, edited by Craig Calhoun, 73–98. Cambridge: MIT Press.

Berdahl, Daphne. 2005. "The Spirit of Capitalism and the Boundaries of Citizenship in Post-Wall Germany." *Comparative Study of Society and History* 5: 253–51.

Berlant, Lauren. 1997. "Introduction: The Intimate Public Sphere." *The Queen of America Goes to Washington City*. Durham, N.C.: Duke University Press.

——. 1998. "Intimacy." Special issue of *Critical Inquiry* (winter).

Berreman, G. D. 1979. *Caste and Other Inequities: Essays on Inequality.* New Delhi: Manohar.

Béteille, André. 1991. "The Reproduction of Inequality: Occupation, Caste, and Family." *Contributions to Indian Sociology* 25: 3–28.

———. 1995. "Universities as Institutions." *Economic and Political Weekly*, March 18, 563–68.

Bettie, Julie. 2003. *Women without Class: Girls, Race and Identity.* Berkeley: University of California Press.

———. 2005. "Matters of Right and of Policy." *Seminar* 549, May, 17–22. www.india—seminar.com.

Bhargava, Rajeev, ed. 1998a. *Secularism and Its Critics.* New Delhi: Oxford University Press.

———. 1998b. "What Is Secularism For?" In Bhargava, ed., *Secularism and Its Critics*, 468–542.

Bhasi, Thoppil, dir. 1970. *Ningalenne Communistakki.*

Bhavnani, Kum-Kum, Kathryn Kent, and France Winddance Twine, eds. 1998. "Feminisms and Youth Cultures." Special issue. *Signs* 23 (3).

Bijoy, C. R., and K. Ravi Raman. 2003. "Muthanga: The Real Story, Adivasi Movement to Recover Land." *Economic and Political Weekly*, May 17–23, 11975–82.

Bilgrami, Akeel. 1998. "Secularism, Nationalism, and Modernity." *Secularism and Its Critics*, edited by Rajeev Bhargava, 380–417. New Delhi: Oxford University Press.

Bosniak, Linda. 2006. *The Citizen and the Alien: Dilemmas of Contemporary Membership.* Princeton, N.J.: Princeton University Press.

Bourdieu, P. 1977. *Outline of a Theory of Practice.* Cambridge: Cambridge University Press.

———. 1984. *Distinction.* Cambridge: Harvard University Press.

———, and J. C. Passeron. 1977. *Reproduction in Education, Society, and Culture.* Beverley Hills, Calif.: Sage.

Bowles, S., and H. Gintis. 1976. *Schooling in Capitalist America.* New York: Basic Books.

Boyarin, Jonathan. 1994. "Space, Time, and the Politics of Memory." *Remapping Memory: The Politics of TimeSpace*, edited by Jonathan Boyarin, 1–37. Minneapolis: University of Minnesota Press.

Breckenridge, Carol, ed. 1995. *Consuming Modernity: Public Culture in a South Asian World.* Minneapolis: University of Minnesota Press.

Brubaker, Richard. 1985. "Rethinking Classical Theory: The Sociological Vision of Pierre Bourdieu." *Theory and Society* 14: 745–75.

Bucholtz, Mary. 2002. "Youth and Cultural Practice." *Annual Review of Anthropology* 31: 525–52.

Burke, Timothy. 1996. *Lifebouy Men, Lux Women: Commodification, Consumption and Cleanliness in Modern Zimbabwe.* Durham, N.C.: Duke University Press.

Burton, Antoinette, ed. 1999. *Gender, Sexuality and Colonial Modernities.* London: Routledge.

Butler, Judith. 1990. *Gender Trouble.* London: Routledge.

——. 1992. "Contingent Foundations: Feminism and the Question of 'Postmodernism.'" *Feminists Theorize the Political.* London: Routledge.

——. 1993. *Bodies That Matter: On the Discursive Limits of "Sex."* London: Routledge.

Calhoun, Craig, ed. 1992. *Habermas and the Public Sphere.* Cambridge: MIT Press.

CDS (Centre for Development Studies). 1975. *Poverty, Unemployment, and Development Policy: A Case Study of Selected Issues with Reference to Kerala.* New York: United Nations, Department of Economic and Social Affairs.

Chakrabarty, Dipesh. 1992. "The Death of History? Historical Consciousness and the Culture of Late Capitalism." *Public Culture* 4: 47–65.

——. 2000. *Provincializing Europe: Postcolonial Thought and Historical Difference.* Princeton, N.J.: Princeton University Press.

——. 2002. *Habitations of Modernity.* Chicago: University of Chicago Press.

Chakravarti, Uma. 1990. "Whatever Happened to the Vedic Dasi?: Orientalism, Nationalism and a Script for the Past." *Recasting Women: Essays in Colonial History,* edited by K. Sangari and S. Vaid, 27–87. Delhi: Kali for Women.

Chakravarty, V., and M. S. S. Pandian. 1994. "More on Roja." *Economic and Political Weekly,* March 12, 642–44.

Chandramohan, P. 1987. "Popular Culture and Socio-Economic Reform: Narayana Guru and the Ezhavas of Travancore." *Studies in History* 3 (1): 53–78.

Chandumenon, O. 2005 [1889]. *Indulekha.* Translated by Anitha Devasia. New Delhi: Oxford University Press.

Chasin, Barbara, and Richard Franke. 1991. "The Kerala Difference." *New York Review of Books,* October 24, 72.

Chatterjee, P. 1986. *Nationalist Thought and the Colonial World: A Derivative Discourse?* London: Zed.

——. 1990. "Colonialism, Nationalism, and Colonized Women: The Contest in India." *American Ethnologist* 16: 622–33.

——. 1998a. "Community in the East." *Economic and Political Weekly*, February 7–13, 277–82.

——. 1998b. "Secularism and Tolerance." *Secularism and Its Critics*, edited by Rajeev Bhargava, 354–79. New Delhi: Oxford University Press.

——. 2000. "Two Poets and Death: On Civil Society and Political Society in the Non-Christian World." *Questions of Modernity*, edited by Timothy Mitchell, 35–48. Minneapolis: University of Minnesota Press.

——. 2004. *Politics of the Governed: Reflections on Popular Politics in Most of the World.* New York: Columbia University Press.

Chaturvedi, Ruchi. 2007. "Down By Law: Violence and the Work of Politics in Kerala, South India." Ph.D. dissertation, Columbia University.

Cho, Han Hae-joang. 2004. "Beyond the FIFA's World Cup: An Ethnography of the 'Local' in South Korea Around the 2002 World Cup." *Inter-Asia Cultural Studies* 5 (1): 8–25.

Chopra, Radhika, and Patricia Jeffery. 2005. *Educational Regimes in Contemporary India.* New Delhi: Sage.

Chopra, Radhika, Filippo Osella, and Caroline Osella, eds. 2004. *South Asian Masculinities: Context of Change, Sites of Continuity.* New Delhi: Women's Unlimited Press.

Chua, Beng-Huat. 2000. *Consumption in Asia: Lifestyles and Identities.* Routledge.

Cohen, Lizabeth. 2003. *A Consumer's Republic: The Politics of Mass Consumption in Postwar America.* New York: Alfred A. Knopf.

Cohn, B. S. 1984. "The Census, Social Structure and Objectification in South Asia." *Folk* 26: 25–49.

——. 1987. *An Anthropologist among the Historians and Other Essays.* New York: Oxford University Press.

——. 1996. "Cloth, Clothes, and Colonialism: India in the Nineteenth Century." *Colonialism and Its Forms of Knowledge*, 106–62. Princeton, N.J.: Princeton University Press.

Cole, Jennifer. 2004. "Fresh Contact in Tamatave, Madagascar: Sex, Money, and Intergenerational Transformation." *American Ethnologist* 31 (4): 571–86.

——. 2005. "The Jaombilo of Tamatave, 1992–2004: Reflections on Youth and Globalization." *Journal of Social History* 38 (4): 891–914.

Cole, Jennifer, and Deborah Durham. 2006. *Generations and Globalization: Youth, Age and Family in the New World Economy.* Bloomington: Indiana University Press.

Comaroff, J., and J. L. Comaroff. 1990. "The Impact of Mission Education on Black Consciousness in South Africa." Unpublished manuscript.

———. 1991. *Of Revelation and Revolution: Christianity, Colonialism and Consciousness in South Africa*. Chicago: University of Chicago Press.

———. 1992. *Ethnography and the Historical Imagination*. Boulder, Colo.: Westview Press.

———. 1993. Introduction. *Modernity and Its Malcontents*. Chicago: University of Chicago Press.

———. 2000a. *Civil Society and the Political Imagination in Africa: Critical Perspectives*. Chicago: University of Chicago Press.

———. 2000b. "Millennial Capitalism: First Thoughts on a Second Coming." *Public Culture* 12 (2): 291–343.

Corbridge, Stuart, and John Harriss. 2000. *Reinventing India: Liberalization, Hindu Nationalism and Popular Democracy*. Malden, Mass.: Blackwell Publishers.

Crenshaw, Kimberly. 1991. "Mapping the Margins: Intersectionality, Identity Politics, and Violence against Women of Color." *Stanford Law Review* 43 (6): 1241–99.

Crook, Nigel, ed. 1996. The Transmission of Knowledge in South Asia: Essays on Education, Religion, History and Politics. New Delhi: Oxford University Press.

Daniel, V. 1984. *Fluid Signs: Being a Person the Tamil Way*. Berkeley: University of California Press.

De Alwis, Malathi. 1995. "Gender, Politics, and the 'Respectable Lady.'" *Unmaking the Nation: The Politics of Identity and History in Sri Lanka*, edited by P. Jeganathan and Q. Ismail, 137–57. Colombo: Social Scientists Association.

———. 1998. "Maternalist Politics in Sri Lanka: A Historical Anthropology of Its Conditions of Possibility." Ph.D. dissertation, University of Chicago.

———. 1999. "'Respectability,' 'Modernity' and the Policing of 'Culture' in Colonial Ceylon." *Gender, Sexuality and Colonial Modernities*, edited by Antoinette Burton, 179–94. London: Routledge.

de Certeau, Michel. 1984. *The Practice of Everyday Life*. Berkeley: University of California Press.

de Grazia, Victoria, ed. 1996. *The Sex of Things: Gender and Consumption in Historical Perspective*. Berkeley: University of California Press.

Deshpande, Satish. 1993. "Imagined Economies: Styles of Nation-Building in Twentieth Century India." *Journal of Arts and Ideas* 25–26: 5–35.

———. 2003. *Contemporary India: A Sociological View*. New York: Viking.

———. 2006. "Exclusive Inequalities: Merit, Caste and Discrimination in Indian Higher Education Today." *Economic and Political Weekly*, June 17–23, 2438–444.

Deshpande, Satish, and Yogendra Yadav. 2006. "Redesigning Reservations: Castes and Benefits in Higher Education." *Economic and Political Weekly*, June 17–23, 2419–24.

Devika, J. 2005. "The Malayali Sexual Revolution: Sex, 'Liberation' and Family Planning in Kerala." *Contributions to Indian Sociology* 39 (3): 343–74.

———. 2007a. *En-Gendering Individuals: The Language of Re-Forming in Early Twentieth Century Keralam*. New Delhi: Orient Longman.

———. 2007b. "Fears of Contagion? Depoliticisation and Recent Conflicts over Politics in Kerala." *Economic and Political Weekly*, June 23, 2464–70.

Devika, J., and Praveena Kodoth. 2001. "Sexual Violence and the Predicament of Feminist Politics in Kerala." *Economic and Political Weekly*, August 18–24, 3170–77.

Devika, J., and Mini Sukumar. 2006. "Making Space for Feminist Social Critique in Kerala." *Economic and Political Weekly*, October 21–27, 4469–75.

Devika, J., and Binitha Thampi. 2007. "Between 'Empowerment' and 'Liberation': The Kudumbashree Initiative in Kerala." *Indian Journal of Gender Studies* 14 (1): 33–60.

Dhareshwar, Vivek. 1993. "Caste and the Secular Self." *Journal of Arts and Ideas* 25–26: 115–26.

Dhareshwar, Vivek, and Tejaswini Niranjana. 1996. "Kaadalan and the Politics of Resignification: Fashion, Violence and the Body." *Journal of Arts and Ideas* 29: 5–26.

Diouf, Mamadou. 1996. "Urban Youth and Senegales Politics, Dakar 1988–1994." *Public Culture* 8 (2): 225–48.

Dirks, N. 1987. *Hollow Crown: Ethnohistory of an Indian Kingdom*. Cambridge: Cambridge University Press.

Dolby, Nadine, and Fazal Rizvi. 2007. *Youth Moves: Identities and Education in Global Perspective*. New York: Routledge.

Dumont, Louis. 1980 [1970]. *Homo Hierarchicus: The Caste System and Its Implications*. Chicago: University of Chicago Press.

Durham, Deborah. 2000. "Youth and the Social Imagination in Africa: Introduction to Parts One and Two." *Anthropological Quarterly* 73 (3): 113–20.

———. 2004. "Disappearing Youth: Youth as a Social Shifter in Botswana." *American Ethnologist* 31 (4): 589–605.

Durkheim, E. 1979. *Essays on Morals and Education*. Edited by W. S. F. Pickering. London: Routledge and Kegan Paul.

Dwyer, Rachel. 2000. *All You Want Is Money, All You Need Is Love: Sexuality and Romance in Modern India*. London: Cassell.

Dwyer, Rachel, and Christopher Pinney. 2003. *Pleasure and the Nation: The History, Politics and Consumption of Public Culture in India*. London: School of Oriental and African Studies.

———. 2004. "Disappearing Youth: Youth as a Social Shifter in Botswana." *American Ethnologist* 31 (4): 589–605.

Eley, Geoff. 1992. "Nations, Publics, and Political Cultures: Placing Habermas in the Nineteenth Century." *Habermas and the Public Sphere*, edited by Craig Calhoun, 289–339. Cambridge: MIT Press.

Erwer, Monica. 2003. *Challenging the Gender Paradox: Women's Collective Agency in the Transformation of Kerala Politics*. Goteberg: Goteberg University.

Favero, Paolo. 2003. "Phantasms in a 'Starry' Place: Place and Identification in a Central Delhi Market." *Cultural Anthropology* 18 (4): 551–84.

Featherstone, Michael. 1990. *Global Culture: Nationalism, Globalization and Modernity*. London: Sage Publications.

Felski, Rita. 1995. *The Gender of Modernity*. Cambridge: Harvard University Press.

Ferguson, James. 1994. *The Anti-Politics Machine: "Development," Depoliticization, and Bureaucratic Power in Lesotho*. Minneapolis: University of Minnesota Press.

———. 1999. *Expectations of Modernity: Myths and Meanings of Urban Life on the Zambian Copperbelt*. Berkeley: University of California Press.

———. 2005. "Decomposing Modernity: History and Hierarchy after Development." *Postcolonial Studies and Beyond*, edited by Ania Loomba, Suvir Kaul, Matti Bunzl, Antoinette Burton, and Jed Esty, 166–81. Durham, N.C.: Duke University Press.

Fernandes, Leela. 1997. *Producing Workers: The Politics of Gender, Class and Culture in the Calcutta Jute Mills*. Philadelphia: University of Pennsylvania Press.

———. 2006. *India's New Middle Class: Democratic Politics in an Era of Economic Reform*. Minneapolis: University of Minnesota Press.

Firestone, Shulamith. 1970. *The Dialectic of Sex: The Case for Feminist Revolution*. New York: Farrar, Straus and Giroux.

Foley, D. 1990. *Learning Capitalist Culture: Deep in the Heart of Tejas*. Philadelphia: University of Pennsylvania Press.

Fong, Vanessa. 2004. *Only Hope: Coming of Age under China's One Child Policy*. Palo Alto, Calif.: Stanford University Press.

Foster, Robert. 2002. *Materializing the Nation: Commodities, Consumption and Media in Papua New Guinea.* Bloomington: Indiana University Press.

Foucault, M. 1977. *Discipline and Punish: The Birth of the Prison.* New York: Viking.

———. 1980. *Power/Knowledge: Selected Interviews and Other Writings.* Edited by C. Gordon. Brighton: Harvester.

Franke, Richard, and Barbara Chasin. 1992. *Kerala: Development through Radical Reform.* Delhi: Promilla, in collaboration with the Institute for Food and Development Policy, San Francisco.

———. 1998. "Kerala: A Valid Alternative to the New World Order." *Critical Asian Studies* 30 (2): 25–28.

———. 2000. "Is the Kerala Model Sustainable: Lessons from the Past, Prospects for the Future." *Kerala: The Development Experience, Reflections on Sustainability and Replicability,* edited by G. Parayil, 16–39. London: Zed Books.

Fraser, Nancy. 1992. "Rethinking the Public Sphere: A Contribution to the Critique of Actually Existing Democracy." *Habermas and the Public Sphere,* edited by Craig Calhoun, 109–42. Cambridge: MIT Press.

Fuglesang, M. 1994. *Veils and Videos: Female Youth Culture on the Kenyan Coast.* Stockholm: Department of Anthropology.

Fuller, C. J. 1976. *The Nayars Today.* Cambridge: Cambridge University Press.

Galantar, Marc. 1984. *Competing Equalities: Law and the Backward Classes in India.* New Delhi: Oxford University Press.

Gaonkar, Dilip Parameshwar, ed. 2001. *Alternative Modernities.* Durham, N.C.: Duke University Press.

García Canclini, Nestor. 2001. *Consumers and Citizens: Globalization and Multicultural Conflicts.* Translated by George Yúdice. Minneapolis: University of Minnesota Press.

Geetha, J. 1994. "Disciplining the Feminine: Cinema and Ideology." Paper presented at the International Congress on Kerala Studies, Thiruvananthapuram, August 27–29.

George, K. M. 1993. Introduction. *Inner Spaces: New Writing by Women of Kerala.* Delhi: Kali for Women.

Ginsberg, Elaine, ed. 1996. *Passing and the Fictions of Identity.* Durham, N.C.: Duke University Press.

Giroux, H. 1981. "Hegemony, Resistance, and the Paradox of Educational Reform." *Interchange* 12 (2–3): 3–26.

Goffman, Erving. 1959. *The Presentation of Self in Everyday Life.* Garden City, N.J.: Doubleday.

———. 1967. *Interaction Rituals: Essays in Face-to-Face Behavior.* Chicago: Aldine Publishing Company.

Gorsuch, Anne. 2000. *Youth in Revolutionary Russia: Enthusiasts, Bohemians, Delinquents.* Bloomington: Indiana University Press.

Gough, Kathleen. 1959. "The Nayars and the Definition of Marriage." *Journal of the Royal Anthropological Institute* 89: 23–34.

———. 1970. "Palakkara: Social and Religious Change in Central Kerala." *Change and Continuity in India's Villages,* edited by K. Ishwaran, 129–64. New York: Columbia University Press.

Gough, Kathleen, and David Schneider, eds. 1961. *Matrilineal Kinship.* Berkeley: University of California Press.

Greer, Germaine. 1970. *The Female Eunuch.* New York: Farrar, Straus and Giroux.

Grew, Raymond. 2005. "On Seeking Global History's Inner Child." *Journal of Social History* 38 (4): 849–58.

Grewal, Inderpal, and Caren Kaplan. 1994. *Scattered Hegemonies: Postmodernity and Transnational Feminist Practices.* Minneapolis: University of Minnesota Press.

Gulati, Leela. 1993. *In the Absence of Their Men: The Impact of Male Migration on Women.* New Delhi: Sage Publications.

Gupta, Akhil. 1998. *Postcolonial Developments: Agriculture in the Making of Modern India.* Durham, N.C.: Duke University Press.

Gupta, Dipankar. 2005. "Limits of Reservation." *Seminar* 549, May 23–25. www.india—seminar.com.

Habermas, Jürgen. 1989. *The Structural Transformation of the Public Sphere.* Cambridge: MIT Press.

Hall, Kathleen. 2002. *Translated Lives: Sikh Youth as British Citizens.* Philadelphia: University of Pennsylvania Press.

Hall, Stuart, and Tony Jefferson, eds. 1976. *Resistance through Rituals: Youth Subcultures in Post-War Britain.* London: Hutchinson Press.

Hancock, Mary. 1999. *Womanhood in the Making: Domestic Ritual and Public Culture in Urban South India.* Boulder, Colo.: Westview Press.

Hannerz, U. 1992. *Cultural Complexity: The Social Organization of Meaning.* New York: Columbia University Press.

Hardgrave, Robert L. 1968. "The Breast Cloth Controversy: Caste, Consensus, and Social Change in Southern Travancore." *Indian Economic and Social History Review* 5 (2): 171–87.

Hariharan, M. T., dir. 1983. *Varanmaare Aavashyamundu.*

Harvey, David. 1990. *The Condition of Postmodernity.* London: Blackwell Publishers.

———. 2005. *A Brief History of Neoliberalism.* New York: Oxford University Press.

Hebdige, D. 1979. *Subculture: The Meaning of Style.* London: Methuen.

Heimsath, Charles. 1978. "The Function of Hindu Social Reformers—with Special Reference to Kerala." *Indian Economic and Social History Review* 15 (1): 21–39.

Held, D., and Anthony McGrew, eds. 2007. *Globalization Theory: Approaches and Controversies.* Cambridge: Polity Press.

Heller, Patrick. 2000. *The Labor of Development: Workers and the Transformation of Capitalism in Kerala, India.* Ithaca, N.Y.: Cornell University Press.

———. 2001. "Moving the State: The Politics of Democratic Decentralization in Kerala, South Africa, and Porto Alegre." *Politics and Society* 29 (1): 131–63.

Hendrickson, Hildi, ed. 1996. *Clothing and Difference: Embodying Colonial and Post-colonial Identities.* Durham, N.C.: Duke University Press.

Hodgson, Dorothy, ed. 2001. *Gendered Modernities: Ethnographic Perspectives.* New York: Palgrave.

Holland, Dorothy, and Margaret Eisenhart. 1992. *Educated in Romance: Women, Achievement, and College Culture.* Chicago: University of Chicago Press.

Holston, James, and A. Appadurai. 1996. "Cities and Citizenship." *Public Culture* 8: 187–204.

hooks, bell. 1984. *Feminist Theory from Margin to Center.* Boston: South End Press.

Hospital, Clifford. 1984. *The Righteous Demon: A Study of Bali.* Vancouver: University of British Columbia Press.

Ilaiah, Kanchiah. 1996. *Why I Am Not a Hindu: A Sudra Critique of Hindutva Philosophy, Culture and Political Economy.* Calcutta: Samya.

Ilouz, Eva. 1997. *Consuming the Romantic Utopia: Love and the Contradictions of Capitalism.* Berkeley: University of California Press.

Inda, Jonathan Xavier. 2005. *Anthropologies of Modernity: Foucault, Governmentality and Life Politics.* Oxford: Wiley-Blackwell.

Inden, R. 1990. *Imagining India.* London: Oxford University Press.

Isaac, T. M. Thomas. 1985. "From Caste Consciousness to Class Consciousness: Allepey Coir Workers during the Interwar Period." *Economic and Political Weekly,* January 26, PE5–PE18.

Isaac, T. M. Thomas, and Richard Franke. 2002. *Local Democracy and Development: The Kerala People's Campaign for Decentralized Planning.* Lanham, Md.: Rowman and Littlefield.

Isaac, T. M. Thomas and P. K. Michael Tharakan. 1986. *Sree Narayana Movement in Travancore, 1885–1939: Social Basis and Ideological Reproduction.* Working Paper No. 214, Center for Development Studies, Trivandrum.

——. 1995. "Kerala: Towards a New Agenda." *Economic and Political Weekly,* August 5–12, 1993–2004.

Jacob, George. 1995. *Religious Life of the Ilavas of Kerala: Change and Continuity.* Delhi: ISPCK.

Jeffrey, Craig, Patricia Jeffery and Roger Jeffery. 2008. *Degrees without Freedom?: Education, Masculinities and Unemployment in North India.* Palo Alto, Calif.: Stanford University Press.

Jeffrey, Robin. 1976. *Decline of Nayar Dominance: Society and Politics in Travancore, 1847–1908.* Delhi: Vikas.

——. 1993. *Politics, Women and Well Being: How Kerala Became "A Model."* Delhi: Oxford University Press.

Jeganathan, Pradeep. 1997. "After a Riot: Anthropological Locations of Violence in an Urban Sri Lankan Community." Ph.D. dissertation, University of Chicago.

——. 2000. "A Space for Violence: Anthropology, Politics, and the Location of a Sinhala Practice of Masculinity." *Subaltern Studies 11: Writings on South Asian History and Society,* edited by Partha Chatterjee and Pradeep Jeganathan, 37–65. Oxford: Oxford University Press.

John, Mary. 1996. *Discrepant Dislocations: Feminism, Theory, and Postcolonial Histories.* Berkeley: University of California Press.

——. 1998. "Globalisation, Sexuality and the Visual Field: Issues and Non-issues for Cultural Critique." *A Question of Silence? The Sexual Economies of Modern India,* edited by Mary E. John and Janaki Nair, 368–96. New Delhi: Kali for Women.

——. 2000. "Alternate Modernities? Reservations and Women's Movement in 20th Century India." *Economic and Political Weekly,* October 28, 3822–29.

Johnson-Hanks, Jennifer. 2002. "On the Limits of Life Stages in Ethnography: Toward a Theory of Vital Conjunctures." *American Anthropologist* 104 (3): 865–80.

Joshi, M., dir. 2004. *Mambazhakkalam.*

Juliastuti, Nuraini. 2006. "Whatever I Want: Media and Youth in Indonesia Before and after 1998." *Inter-Asia Cultural Studies* 7 (1): 129–43.

Kannan, K. P., and K. S. Hari. 2002. *Kerala's Gulf Connection: Emigration, Remittances and their Macroeconomic Impact, 1972–2000.* Centre for Development Studies, Working Paper No. 328.

Kaplan, Caren, Norma Alarcon, and Minoo Moallem. 1999. *Between Women and Nation: Nationalisms, Transnational Feminisms and the State*. Durham, N.C.: Duke University Press.

Kaplan, Sam. 2006. *The Pedagogical State: Education and the Politics of National Culture in Post-1980 Turkey*. Palo Alto, Calif.: Stanford University Press.

Kapur, Devesh, and Pratap Bhanu Mehta. 2004. "Indian Higher Education Reform: From Half-Baked Socialism to Half-Baked Capitalism." Working Paper No. 108, Harvard University Center for International Development, September.

Kaviraj, Sudipta. 1992. "The Imaginary Institution of India." *Subaltern Studies VII, Writings in South Asian History and Society*, edited by Partha Chatterjee and Gyanendra Pandey, 1–39. New Delhi: Oxford University Press.

——. 1997. "Filth and the Public Sphere: Concepts and Practices about Space in Calcutta." *Public Culture* 10 (1): 83–113.

——. 2007. "Tagore and the Transformations in the Ideals of Love." *Love in South Asia: A Cultural History*, edited by Francesca Orsini, 161–82. Cambridge: Cambridge University Press.

Kemper, S. 1993. "The Nation Consumed: Buying and Believing in Sri Lanka." *Public Culture* 5 (3): 377–93.

Kett, Joseph. 1978. *Rites of Passage: Adolescence in America, 1790 to the Present*. New York: Basic Books.

Khilnani, Sunil. 1999 [1997]. *The Idea of India*. New York: Farrar, Straus and Giroux.

Knauft, Bruce, ed. 2002. *Critically Modern: Alternatives, Alterities, Anthropologies*. Bloomington: Indian University Press.

Kodoth, Praveena. 2001. "Courting Legitimacy or Delegitimizing Custom? Sexuality, Sambandham, and Marriage Reform in Late Nineteenth-Century Malabar." *Modern Asian Studies* 35 (2): 343–84.

Kooiman, Dick. 1989. *Conversion and Social Inequality in India: The London Missionary Society in South Travancore in the Nineteenth Century*. Delhi: Manohar.

——. 1991. "Conversion from Slavery to Plantation Labour." *Social Scientist* 19 (8–9): 57–71.

Kopf, D. 1969. *British Orientalism and the Bengal Renaissance: The Dynamics of Indian Modernization*. Berkeley: University of California Press.

——. 1979. *The Brahmo Samaj and the Shaping of the Modern Indian Mind*. Princeton, N.J.: Princeton University Press.

Krishnamurti, J. 1973. *Education and the Significance of Life*. New Delhi: BI Publications.

Kroen, Sheryl. 2004. "A Political History of the Consumer." *Historical Journal* 47 (3): 709–36.

Kumar, Krishna. 1991. *Political Agenda of Education: A Study of Colonialist and Nationalist Ideas*. New Delhi: Sage Publications.

Kumar, Udaya. 1997. "Self, Body and Inner Sense: Some Reflections on Sree Narayana Guru and Kumaran Asan." *Studies in History* 13 (2): 247–70.

Kurien, John. 2000. "The Kerala Model: Its Central Tendency and the 'Outlier.'" *Kerala: The Development Experience, Reflections on Sustainability and Replicability*, edited by G. Parayil, 178–97. London: Zed Books.

Kusuman, K. K. 1973. *Slavery in Travancore*. Trivandrum: Kerala Historical Society.

Landes, Joan, ed. 1998. *Feminism, the Public and the Private*. London: Routledge.

Lash, Scott, and Jonathan Friedman, eds. 1992. *Modernity and Identity*. Oxford: Wiley-Blackwell.

Lechner, Frank, and John Boli. 2004. *The Globalization Reader*. London: Blackwell Publishing.

Lelyveld, D. 1978. *Aligarh's First Generation: Muslim Solidarity in British India*. Princeton, N.J.: Princeton University Press.

Levi, Giovanni, and Jean-Claude Schmitt. 1999. *A History of Young People in the West*, vol. 2: *Stormy Evolution to Modern Times*. Cambridge: Harvard University Press.

Levinson, Bradley. 2001. *We Are All Equal: Student Culture and Identity at a Mexican Secondary School, 1988–1998*. Durham, N.C.: Duke University Press.

Levinson, Bradley, Douglas Foley, and Dorothy Holland, eds. 1996. *The Cultural Production of the Educated Person: Critical Ethnographies of Schooling and Local Practice*. Albany: State University of New York Press.

Liechty, Mark. 2003. *Suitably Modern: Making Middle-Class Culture in a New Consumer Society*. Princeton, N.J.: Princeton University Press.

Lindberg, Anna. 2001. *Experience and Identity: A Historical Account of Caste, Class and Gender among the Cashew Workers of Kerala, 1930–2000*. Lund: Department of History, University of Lund.

Loomba, Ania, Suvir Kaul, Matti Bunzl, Antoinette Burton, and Jed Esty, eds. 2005. *Postcolonial Studies and Beyond*. Durham, N.C.: Duke University Press.

Ludden, David. 1992. "India's Development Regime." *Colonialism and Culture*, edited by Nicholas Dirks, 247–87. Ann Arbor: University of Michigan Press.

Lukose, Ritty. 2005a. "Empty Citizenship: Reconfiguring Politics in the Era of Globalization." *Cultural Anthropology* 20 (4): 506–33.

———. 2005b. "Consuming Globalization: Youth and Gender in Kerala, India." *Journal of Social History* 38 (4): 915–35.

Lutz, Catherine, and Lila Abu-Lughod, eds. 1990. *Language and the Politics of Emotion*. Cambridge: Cambridge University Press.

Luykx, Aurolyn. 1999. *The Citizen Factory: Schooling and Cultural Production in Bolivia*. Albany: State University of New York Press.

Madan, T. N. 1998. "Secularism in Its Place." *Secularism and Its Critics*, edited by Rajeev Bhargava, 297–320. New Delhi: Oxford University Press.

Maira, Sunaina. 2002. *Desis in the House: Indian American Youth Culture in New York City*. Philadelphia: Temple University Press.

Maira, Sunaina, and Elisabeth Soep. 2005. *Youthscapes: The Popular, the National, the Global*. Philadelphia: University of Pennsylvania Press.

Manderson, L., and P. Liamputtong Rice, eds. 2001. *Coming of Age in South and Southeast Asia: Youth, Courtship and Sexuality*. London: Routledge.

Mani, Lata. 1987. "Contentious Traditions: The Debate on Sati in Colonial India." *Cultural Critique* 7 (fall): 119–56.

Mankekar, Purnima. 1999. *Screening Culture, Viewing Politics: An Ethnography of Television, Womanhood, and Nation in Postcolonial India*. Durham, N.C.: Duke University Press.

Marx, Karl. 1978 [1858]. "The Grundrisse." *The Marx-Engels Reader*, edited by Robert Tucker, 222–94. New York: Norton.

Maskiell, M. 1984. *Women between Cultures: The Lives of Kinnaird College Alumnae in British India*. Syracuse, N.Y.: Syracuse University Press.

Mathew, E. T. 1991. *Financing Higher Education: Sources and Uses of Funds of Private Colleges in Kerala*. New Delhi: Concept Publishing Company.

———. 1997. *Employment and Unemployment in Kerala: Some Neglected Aspects*. New Delhi: Sage Publications.

Mathew, George. 1995. "The Paradox of Women's Development in Kerala." *India International—Kerala: Progress and Paradox*. Summer–Monsoon Issue: 203–14.

Mathews, J. 1986. *Ideology, Protest, and Social Mobility*. New Delhi: Inter-India Publications.

Mazarella, William. 2003. *Shoveling Smoke: Advertising and Globalization in Contemporary India*. Durham, N.C.: Duke University Press.

McCully, Bruce T. 1940. *English Education and the Origins of Indian Nationalism*. New York: Columbia University Press.

McKibben, Bill. 1996. "The Enigma of Kerala: One State in India Is Proving Development Experts Wrong." *Utne Reader*, March–April, 103–12.

McRobbie, Angela. 1978. "Working Class Girls and the Culture of Femininity." *Women Take Issue: Aspects of Women's Subordination*, 96–108. Centre for Contemporary Cultural Studies Working Papers in Cultural Studies. London: Hutchinson.

——. 1980. "Settling Accounts with Subcultures: A Feminist Critique." *Screen Education* 34 (spring): 37–49.

——. 1991. *Feminism and Youth Culture: From Jackie to Just Seventeen*. Boston: Unwin Hyman.

Mead, Margaret. 2001 [1928]. *Coming of Age in Samoa*. New York: HarperCollins.

Mehra, Rakyesh, dir. 2006. *Rang De Basanti*. Produced by Rakyesh Mehra and Ronnie Screwvala. Mumbai: Flicks Motion Pictures and UTV Motion Pictures.

Mencher, Joan. 1976. "Land Reform and Socialism: The Case of Kerala." *Aspects of Changing India: Essays in Honour of Prof. G.S. Ghurye*, edited by S. Devadas Pillai, 163–80. Bombay: Popular Prakashan.

——. 1994. "The Kerala Model of Development: The Excluded Ones." Paper presented at the First International Congress on Kerala Studies, Thiruvanthapuram, August 27–29.

Mencher, Joan, and Helen Goldberg. 1967. "Kinship and Marriage Regulations among the Namboodiri Brahmins of Kerala." *Man* 2 (1): 87–106.

Menon, Dilip. 1994. *Caste, Nationalism and Communism in South India: Malabar 1900–1948*. Cambridge: Cambridge University Press.

——. 1997. "Caste and Colonial Modernity: Reading *Saraswativijayam*." *Studies in History* 13 (2): 291–312.

——. 2002. "No, Not the Nation: Lower Caste Malayalam Novels of the Nineteenth Century." *Early Novels in India*, edited by M. Mukerjhee, 41–72. New Delhi: Sahitya Akademi.

——. 2004. "A Place Elsewhere: Lower-Caste Malayalam Novels of the Nineteenth Century." *India's Literary History: Essays on the Nineteenth Century*, edited by S. Blackburn and V. Dalmia, 483–515. Delhi: Permanent Black.

——. 2006. *The Blindness of Insight: Essays on Caste in Modern India*. Chennai: Navayana Publications.

Menon, Nivedita. 2005. "Between the Burqa and the Beauty Parlor: Globalization, Cultural Nationalism, and Feminist Politics." *Postcolonial Studies and Beyond*, edited by Ania Loomba, Suvir Kaul, Matti Bunzl, Antoinette Burton, and Jed Esty, 206–29. Durham, N.C.: Duke University Press.

Menon, Parvathi. 1996. "Pageant and Protests: A Miss World Show under State Protection." *Frontline*, December 13.

Menon, Ritu, and Kamla Bhasin. 1998. *Borders and Boundaries: Women in India's Partition*. New Delhi: Kali for Women.

Metcalf, B. 1982. *Islamic Revival in British India: Deoband, 1860–1900*. Princeton, N.J.: Princeton University Press.

Miller, Daniel. 1994. *Modernity, An Ethnographic Approach: Dualism and Mass Consumption in Trinidad*. Providence, R.I.: Berg.

Miller, Toby. 2001. "Introducing . . . Cultural Citizenship." *Social Text* 19 (4): 1–5.

Mills, Mary Beth. 1999. *Thai Women in the Global Labor Force: Consuming Desires, Contested Selves*. New Brunswick, N.J.: Rutgers University Press.

Minault, Gail. 1998. *Secluded Scholars: Women's Education and Muslim Social Reform in Colonial India*. New Delhi: Oxford University Press.

Mines, Diane. 2005. *Fierce Gods: Inequality, Ritual and the Politics of Dignity in a South Indian Village*. Bloomington: Indiana University Press.

Mintz, Sydney. 1985. *Sweetness and Power: The Place of Sugar in Modern History*. New York: Penguin Books.

Mirchandani, Kiran. 2004. "Practices of Global Capital: Gaps, Cracks and Ironies in Transnational Call Centres in India." *Global Networks* 4 (4): 355–73.

Mitchell, Timothy. 1991. *Colonizing Egypt*. Berkeley.: University of California Press.

——, ed. 2000. *Questions of Modernity*. Minneapolis: University of Minnesota Press.

Modleski, Tania. 1990 [1982]. *Loving with a Vengeance: Mass Produced Fantasies for Women*. New York: Routledge.

Mody, Perveez. 2007. "Kidnapping, Elopement and Abduction: An Ethnography of Love-Marriage in Delhi." *Love in South Asia: A Cultural History*, edited by Francesca Orsini, 331–44. Cambridge: Cambridge University Press.

Mohan, Sanal P. 2005. "Religion, Social Space and Identity: The Prathyaksha Raksha Daiva Sabha and the Making of Cultural Boundaries in Twentieth Century Kerala." *South Asia: Journal of South Asian Studies* 28 (1): 35–63.

Mohanty, Chandra Talpade. 1988. "Under Western Eyes: Feminist Scholarship and Colonial Discourses." *Feminist Review* 30 (autumn): 61–88.

——. 2003. *Feminism without Borders.* Durham, N.C.: Duke University Press.

Mohanty, Chandra Talpade, and Jacqui Alexander, eds. 1997. *Feminist Genealogies, Colonial Legacies, Democratic Futures.* New York: Routledge.

Morris, M. D. 1979. *Measuring the Conditions of the World's Poor: The Physical Quality of Life Index.* New York: Pergamon Press.

Muraleedharan, T. 2005. "National Interest, Regional Concerns: Historicizing Malayalam Cinema." *Deep Focus,* January-May, 85–95.

Nagaraj, D. R. 1993. *The Flaming Feet: A Study of the Dalit Movement.* Bangalore: South Forum Press.

Nair, P. R. G., and P. M. Pillai. 1994. *Impact of External Transfers on the Regional Economy of Kerala.* Thiruvananthapuram: Centre for Development Studies.

Nandy, Ashis. 1998. "The Politics of Secularism and the Recovery of Religious Toleration." *Secularism and Its Critics,* edited by Rajeev Bhargava, 321–44. New Delhi: Oxford University Press.

——. 2000. "Time Travel to a Possible Self: Searching for the Alternative Cosmopolitanism of Cochin." *Japanese Journal of Political Science* 1(2): 293–327.

Nava, Mica. 1992. *Changing Cultures: Feminism, Youth and Consumerism.* London: Sage.

Nayyar, Deepak. 1994. *Migration, Remittances and Capital Flows: The Indian Experience.* New Delhi: Oxford University Press.

Needham, A. D., and Sunder Rajan, R., eds. 2006. *The Crisis of Secularism in India.* Durham, N.C.: Duke University Press.

Nigam, Aditya. 2005. *The Insurrection of Little Selves: The Crisis of Secular-Nationalism in India.* New York: Oxford University Press.

Niranjana, T. 1991. "Cinema, Femininity, and the Economy of Consumption." *Economic and Political Weekly,* October 26, ws85–ws86.

——. 1994. "Whose Nation?: Tourists and Terrorists in Roja." *Economic and Political Weekly,* January 15, 79–82.

——. 1999. Introduction. Theme Issue. "Gender, Media and the Rhetorics of Liberalization." *Journal of Arts and Ideas* 32–33: 3–8.

——. 2006. *Mobilizing India: Women, Music and Migration between India and Trinidad.* Durham, N.C.: Duke University Press.

Nossiter, T. 1983. *Communism in Kerala: A Study in Political Adaptation.* Berkeley: University of California Press.

Omvedt, Gail. 1994. *Dalits and the Democratic Revolution: Dr. Ambedkar and the Dalit Movement in Colonial India.* New Delhi: Sage.

——. 1998. *Dalit Visions*. New Delhi: Orient Longman.

Ong, Aihwa. 1987. *Spirits of Resistance and Capitalist Discipline: Factory Women in Malaysia*. Albany: State University of New York Press.

——. 1996. "Cultural Citizenship as Subject-Making: Immigrants Negotiate Cultural and Racial Boundaries in the United States." *Current Anthropology* 37 (5): 737–62.

——. 1999. *Flexible Citizenship: The Cultural Logics of Transnationality*. Durham, N.C.: Duke University Press.

Oommen, M. A. 1993. *Essays on Kerala Economy*. Delhi: Oxford and IBH Publishing.

Orsini, Francesca, ed. 2007. *Love in South Asia: A Cultural History*. Cambridge: Cambridge University Press.

Ortner, Sherry. 1974. "Is Female to Male as Nature Is to Culture?" *Woman, Culture, Society*, edited by Michelle Zimbalist Rosaldo and Louise Lamphere, 67–87. Stanford: Stanford University Press.

Osella, Filippo, and Katy Gardner, eds. 2004. *Migration, Modernity and Social Transformation in South Asia*. New Delhi: Sage Publications.

Osella, Filippo, and Caroline Osella. 1999. "From Transience to Immanence: Consumption, Life-Cycle and Social Mobility in Kerala, South India." *Modern Asian Studies* 33(4): 989–1020.

——. 2000a. *Social Mobility in Kerala: Modernity and Identity in Conflict*. London: Pluto Press.

——. 2000b. "Migration, Money, and Masculinity in Kerala." *Journal of the Royal Anthropological Institute* 6 (1): 117–33.

Ouwerkerk, Louise. 1994. *No Elephants for the Maharaja: Social and Political Change in the Princely State of Travancore (1921–1947)*. New Delhi: Manohar.

Oza, Rupal. 2006. *The Making of Neoliberal India: Nationalism, Gender, and the Paradoxes of Globalization*. New York: Routledge.

Pandey, G. 1990. *Construction of Communalism in Colonial North India*. New York: Oxford University Press.

Parayil, Govindan, ed. 2000. *Kerala: The Development Experience, Reflections on Sustainability and Replicability*. London: Zed Books.

Parayil, Govindan, and T. T. Sreekumar. 2003. "Kerala's Experience of Development and Social Change." *Journal of Contemporary Asia* 33 (4): 465–92.

Pearce, Lynn, and Jackie Stacie, eds. 1995. *Romance Revisited*. New York: New York University Press.

Peiss, Kathy. 1987. *Cheap Amusements: Working Women and Leisure in Turn-of-the-Century New York*. Philadelphia: Temple University Press.

Percot, Marie. 2006. "From Opportunity to Life Strategy: Indian Nurses in the Gulf." *Exploring Migrant Women and Work*, edited by Anuja Agarwal, 155–76. New Delhi: Sage Publications.

Pillai, S. Mohanan. 1996. "Social Security for Workers in Unorganized Sector: Experience of Kerala." *Economic and Political Weekly*, August 5, 2098–107.

Piot, Charles. 1999. *Remotely Global: Village Modernity in West Africa*. Chicago: University of Chicago Press.

Prasad, Chandra Bhan. 2004. *Dalit Diary, 1999–2003*. Pondicherry: Navyana Publishing.

Prashad, Vijay. 2001. "The Small Voice of Socialism: Kerala, Once Again." *Critical Asian Studies* 33 (2): 301–19.

Radhakrishnan, Ratheesh. 2005. "PE Usha, Hegemonic Masculinities and the Public Domain in Kerala: On the Historical Legacies of the Contemporary." *Inter-Asia Cultural Studies* 6 (2): 187–208.

———. n.d.(a). "What Is Left of Malayalam Cinema?" Unpublished manuscript.

———. n.d.(b). "The Gulf in the Imagination: Migration, Malayalam Cinema and Regional Identity." Unpublished manuscript.

Radway, Janice. 1984. *Reading the Romance: Women, Patriarchy and Popular Literature*. Chapel Hill, N.C.: University of North Carolina Press.

Raheja, Gloria. 1988. *The Poison in the Gift*. Chicago: University of Chicago Press.

Rajagopal, Arvind. 1999. "Thinking About the New Indian Middle Class: Gender, Advertising and Politics in an Age of Globalisation." *Signposts: Gender Issues in Post-Independence India*, edited by Rajeswari Sunder Rajan, 57–100. Delhi: Kali for Women.

———. 2001. *Politics after Television: Religious Nationalism and the Reshaping of the Public in India*. Cambridge: Cambridge University Press.

Ramachandran, T. K. 1995. "Notes on the Making of Feminine Identity in Contemporary Kerala Society." *Social Scientist* 23 (1–3): 109–23.

Ramamurthy, Priti. 2003. "Material Consumers, Fabricating Subjects: Perplexity, Global Discourses and Transnational Feminist Research Practices." *Cultural Anthropology* 18 (4): 524–50.

Rao, M. S. A. 1979. *Social Movements and Social Transformation: A Study of Two Backward Class Movements in India*. Delhi: The Macmillan Company.

Ratcliffe, J. W. 1978. "Social Justice and the Demographic Transition: Lessons from India's Kerala." *International Journal of Health Services* 8 (1): 123–44.

Roberts, J. Timmons, and Amy Hite. 2000. *From Modernization to Globalization: Perspectives on Development and Social Change.* London: Blackwell Publishers.

Rofel, Lisa. 1999. *Other Modernities: Gendered Yearnings in China After Socialism.* Berkeley: University of California Press.

———. 2007. *Desiring China: Experiments in Neoliberalism, Sexuality and Public Culture.* Durham, N.C.: Duke University Press.

Rosaldo, Michelle Zimbalist. 1974. "Women, Culture, Society: A Theoretical Overview." *Women, Culture, and Society,* edited by M. Z. Rosaldo and L. Lamphere, 67–88. Palo Alto, Calif.: Stanford University Press.

Rosaldo, M., and L. Lamphere, eds. 1974. *Woman, Culture and Society.* Stanford: Stanford University Press.

Rosaldo, Renato. 1994. "Cultural Citizenship and Educational Democracy." *Cultural Anthropology* 9 (3): 402–11.

Rowena, Jenny. 2002. *Reading Laughter: The Popular Malayalam "Comedy-Films" of the Late 80s and Early 90s.* Ph.D. dissertation, Hyderabad Central Institute of English and Foreign Languages.

Rudolph, L., and S. H. Rudolph, eds. 1972. *Education and Politics in India: Studies in Organization, Society, and Policy.* Delhi: Oxford University Press.

Rudolph, L., S. H. Rudolph, and K. Ahmed. 1971. "Student Politics and National Politics in India." *Economic and Political Weekly,* July, 1655–68.

Rushdie, Salman. 1981. *Midnight's Children.* London: Jonathan Cape.

Ryan, Mary. 1992. "Gender and Public Access: Women's Politics in Nineteenth Century America." *Habermas and the Public Sphere,* edited by Craig Calhoun. Cambridge: MIT Press.

Samuel, V. T. 1977. *One Caste, One Religion, One God: A Study of Sree Narayana Guru.* Delhi: Sterling Publishers.

Sangari, Kumkum, and Sudesh Vaid, eds. 1989. *Recasting Women: Essays in Indian Colonial History.* New Delhi: Kali for Women.

Saradamoni, K. 1980. *Emergence of a Slave Caste: Pulayas of Kerala.* New Delhi: People's Publishing House.

———. 1999. *Matriliny Transformed: Family, Law and Ideology in Twentieth Century Tranvancore.* Delhi: Sage Publications.

Sarkar, Tanika. 2001. *Hindu Wife, Hindu Nation: Community, Religion, and Cultural Nationalism.* New Delhi: Permanent Black.

Sassen, Saskia. 2001. *The Global City: New York, London, Tokyo.* 2nd ed. Princeton, N.J.: Princeton University Press.

———. 2007. *A Sociology of Globalization.* New York: W. W. Norton.

Schild, Veronica. 2000. "Neoliberalism's New Gendered Market Citizens: The 'Civilizing' Dimension of Social Programmes in Chile." *Citizenship Studies* 4 (3): 275–305.

Schneider, D., and K. Gough, eds. 1961. *Matrilineal Kinship.* Berkeley: University of California Press.

Scott, David. 1999. *Refashioning Futures: Criticism after Postcoloniality.* Princeton, N.J.: Princeton University Press.

Scott, Joan, and Debra Keates, eds. 2005. *Going Public: Feminism and the Shifting Boundaries of the Private Sphere.* Champaign-Urbana: University of Illinois Press.

Scrase, T. J. 1993. *Image, Ideology, and Inequality: Cultural Domination, Hegemony, and Schooling in India.* New Delhi: Sage.

Sen, Amartya. 1990. "More Than a Hundred Million Women Are Missing." *New York Review of Books,* December 20.

———. 1995. *Economic Development and Social Change: India and China in Comparative Perspectives.* London: London School of Economics.

———. 1997. "Radical Needs and Moderate Reforms." *Indian Development: Selected Regional Perspectives,* edited by J. Dreze and A. Sen, 1–32. Oxford: Oxford University Press.

———. 1999. *Development as Freedom.* New York: Alfred A. Knopf.

Seth, Sanjay. 2007. *Subject Lessons: The Western Education of Colonial India.* Durham, N.C.: Duke University Press.

Shklar, Judith. 1991. *American Citizenship: The Quest for Inclusion.* Cambridge: Harvard University Press.

Singer, Milton. 1972. *When a Great Tradition Modernizes.* Chicago: University of Chicago Press.

Sinha, Mrinalini. 1995. *Colonial Masculinity: The 'Manly Englishman' and the 'Effeminate Bengali' in the Late Nineteenth Century.* Manchester: Manchester University Press.

———. 2006. *Specters of Mother India: The Global Restructuring of an Empire.* Durham, N.C.: Duke University Press.

Siriyuvasak, Ubonrat, and Hyunjoon Shin, 2007. "Asianizing K-Pop: Production, Consumption and Identification Patterns Among Thai Youth." *Inter-Asia Cultural Studies* 8 (1): 109–36.

Skelton, Tracey, and Gill Valentine. 1998. *Cool Places: Geographies of Youth Culture.* London: Routledge.

Smith, Raymond T. 1984. "The Concept of Social Class in Anthropology." *Annual Review of Anthropology* 13: 467–94.

Sooryamurthy, R. 1997. "Strong Consumerism Plus Loose Ties Lead to Suryanellis." *Indian Express* (Kochi), February 3.

Sreekumar, Sharmila. 2007. "The Land of Gender Paradox: Getting Past the Commonsense of Contemporary Kerala." *Inter-Asia Cultural Studies* 8(1): 34–54.

Srivastava, Sanjay. 1998. *Constructing Post-Colonial India: National Character and the Doon School.* London: Routledge.

———, ed. 2004. *Sexual Sites, Seminal Attitudes: Sexualities, Masculinities and Culture.* New Delhi: Sage.

———. 2006. *Passionate Modernity: Sexuality, Class and Consumption in India.* New Delhi: Routledge.

Stacey, Judith. 1988. "Can There Be a Feminist Ethnography?" *Women's Studies International Forum* 11 (1): 21–27.

Stambach, Amy. 2000. *Lessons from Mount Kilimanjaro: Schooling, Community, and Gender in East Africa.* New York: Routledge.

Stearns, Peter. 2001. *Consumerism in World History: The Global Transformation of Desire.* New York: Routledge.

———. 2005. "Preface: Childhood and Globalization." Special issue. *Journal of Social History* 38 (4): 615–16.

Strathern, Marilyn. 1987. "An Awkward Relationship: The Case of Feminism and Anthropology," *Signs* 12 (winter): 276–92.

Sundaram, Ravi. 2004. "Uncanny Networks: Pirate, Urban and the New Globalisation." *Economic and Political Weekly,* January 3, 64–71.

Sunder Rajan, Rajeswari. 1992. *The Lie of the Land: English Literary Studies in India.* Delhi: Oxford University Press.

Tarlo, Emma. 1996. *Clothing Matters: Dress and Identity in India.* Chicago: University of Chicago Press.

———. 2003. *Unsettling Memories: Narratives of the Emergency in Delhi.* Berkeley: University of California Press.

Thapan, M. 1991. *Life at School: An Ethnographic Study.* Delhi: Oxford University Press.

Tharamangalam, Joseph. 1998. "The Perils of Social Development without Economic Growth: The Development Debacle of Kerala, India." *Critical Asian Studies* 30 (1): 23–34.

Tsing, Anna. 2000. "The Global Situation." *Cultural Anthropology* 15 (3): 327–60.

———2004. *Friction: An Ethnography of Global Interconnection*. Princeton, N.J.: Princeton University Press.

Usha, V. T. 2004. *Gender, Value and Signification: Women and Television in Kerala*. Discussion Paper No. 67. Thiruvananthapuram: Kerala Research Programme on Local Level Development, Centre for Development Studies.

Van Gennep, A. 1960 [1909]. *Rites of Passage*. Chicago: University of Chicago Press.

Varier, T. V. Eachara. 2004. *Memories of a Father*. Kerala, India: Asian Human Rights Commission and Jananeethi.

Vedwan, Neeraj. 2007. "Pesticides in Coca-Cola and Pepsi: Consumerism, Brand Image, and Public Interest in a Globalizing India." *Cultural Anthropology* 22 (4): 659–84.

Velayudhan, Meera. 1994. "Changing Roles and Women's Narratives." *Social Scientist* 22 (1–2): 64–79.

———. 1999. "Reform, Law and Gendered Identity." *Rethinking Development: Kerala's Development Experience*, vol. 1, edited by M. A. Oommen, 60–72. New Delhi: Concept Publishers.

Vincent, Joan, ed. 2002. *The Anthropology of Politics: A Reader in Ethnography, Theory and Critique*. Malden, Mass.: Blackwell.

Viswanathan, G. 1989. *Masks of Conquest: Literary Study and British Rule in India*. New York: Columbia University Press.

Visweswaran, Kamala. 1994. *Fictions of Feminist Ethnography*. Minneapolis: University of Minnesota Press.

———. 1996. "Small Speeches, Subaltern Gender: Nationalist Ideology and Its Historiography." *Subaltern Studies* 9, edited by Shahid Amin and Dipesh Chakrabarty, 83–125. Delhi: Oxford University Press.

———. n.d. "The Modesty of the Modern." Unpublished manuscript.

Weber, Eugen. 1976. *Peasants into Frenchmen: The Modernization of Rural France, 1870–1914*. Stanford: Stanford University Press.

Weber, Max. 1946. "Class, Status, Party." *From Max Weber: Essays in Sociology*, edited by H. H. Gerth and C. Wright Mills, 180–95. New York: Oxford University Press.

Weinreb, Amelia Rosenberg. 2007. "Unsatisfied Citizen-Consumers in Late Socialist Cuba." Ph.D. dissertation, University of Pennsylvania.

West, Emily. 2006. "Mediating Citizenship through the Lens of Consumerism: Frames in the American Medicare Reform Debates of 2003–2004." *Social Semiotics* 16 (2): 243–61.

Weston, Kath. 1993. "Do Clothes Make the Woman? Gender, Performance Theory and Lesbian Eroticism." *Genders* 17: 1–21.

White, Merry. 1993. *The Material Child.* New York: Free Press.

Wickremasinghe, Nira. 2003. *Dressing the Colonised Body: Politics, Clothing and Identity in Colonial Ceylon.* Delhi: Orient Longman.

Wilkinson-Weber, Claire. 2006. "The Dressman's Line: Transforming the Work of Costumers in Popular Hindi Film." *Anthropological Quarterly,* 79 (4): 581–608.

Willis, P. 1977. *Learning to Labour: How Working Class Kids Get Working Class Jobs.* New York: Columbia University Press.

Wilson, Ara. 2004. *The Intimate Economies of Bangkok: Tomboys, Tycoons, and Avon Ladies in the Global City.* Berkeley: University of California Press.

Wilson, Elizabeth. 1985. *Adorned in Dreams: Fashion and Modernity.* London: Virago.

Wood, Ananda. 1985. *Knowledge Before Printing and After, The Indian Tradition in Changing Kerala.* New Delhi: Oxford University Press.

Yack, Bernard. 1997. *The Fetishism of Modernities: Epochal Self-Consciousness in Contemporary Social and Political Thought.* South Bend, Ind.: University of Notre Dame Press.

Yuval-Davis, Nira. 1997. *Gender and Nation.* London: Sage Publications.

Zachariah, K. C., E. T. Mathew, and S. Irudaya Rajan. 2001. "Impact of Migration on Kerala's Economy and Society." *International Migration* 39 (1): 63–85.

Zachariah, K. C., B. A. Prakash, and S. Irudaya Rajan. 2000. *Gulf Migration Study: Employment, Wages and Working Conditions of Kerala Migrants in the United Arab Emirates.* Working Paper no. 326. Thiruvananthapuram: Centre for Development Studies.

Zakaria, Fareed. 2006. "India Rising." *Newsweek,* March 6, 34–37.

Zarrilli, Philip. 1995. "Tooppil Bhaasi's Theatre of Social Conscience and the Kerala People's Arts Club." Introduction to *Memories of Hiding,* by Tooppil Bhaasi, vii–xii. Calcutta: Seagull Books.

INDEX

Some of the material in this book has been published previously. Parts of the introduction and chapter 2 appeared in *Youth Moves: Identities in Global Perspective*, edited by Nadine Dolby and Fazal Rizvi (New York: Routledge, 2007). Parts of chapter 2 appeared in the *Journal of Social History* 38, no. 4 (2005): 915–35. Parts of chapter 4 are included in *Cultural Anthropology* 20, no. 4 (2005): 506–33. Parts of chapter 5 appeared in *Social Analysis* 50, no. 3 (2006): 38–60.

RITTY A. LUKOSE IS AN ASSOCIATE PROFESSOR IN THE GALLATIN SCHOOL
OF INDIVIDUALIZED STUDY, NEW YORK UNIVERSITY.

LIBRARY OF CONGRESS CATALOGING-IN-PUBLICATION DATA

LUKOSE, RITTY A.
LIBERALIZATION'S CHILDREN : GENDER, YOUTH, AND
CONSUMER CITIZENSHIP IN GLOBALIZING INDIA / RITTY A. LUKOSE.
P. CM.   INCLUDES BIBLIOGRAPHICAL REFERENCES AND INDEX.
ISBN 978-0-8223-4550-3 (CLOTH : ALK. PAPER)
ISBN 978-0-8223-4567-1 (PBK. : ALK. PAPER)
1. YOUTH—INDIA. 2. CONSUMPTION
(ECONOMICS)—INDIA. 3. INDIA—ECONOMIC
CONDITIONS—21ST CENTURY.
4. GLOBALIZATION—INDIA.
I. TITLE. HQ799.I5.L85 2009
305.2350954—DC22
2009032839